ELVIS

A PERSONAL MEMOIR

BY ONE WHO KNEW HIM

CHRIS HUTCHINS

Neville Ness House

Published in Great Britain in 2015 by

Neville Ness House Ltd

www.nevillenesshouse.com
www.chrishutchins.info
nevillenesshouse@sky.com

Copyright © Chris Hutchins 2015

Chris Hutchins has asserted his right under the Copyright, Designs and Patents Act 1988 to be identified as the author of this work.

All rights reserved. No part of this publication may be reproduced, stored in a retrieval system or transmitted, in any form or by any means, without the publisher's prior permission in writing.

This book is sold subject to the condition that it shall not, by way of trade or otherwise, be lent, resold, hired out or otherwise circulated without the publisher's prior consent in any form of binding or cover other than that in which it is published and without a similar condition, including this condition, being imposed on the subsequent purchaser.

Every reasonable effort has been made to trace copyright holders of material reproduced in this book, but if any have been inadvertently overlooked the publishers would be glad to hear from them.

ISBN: 978-0-9933566-7-4

A CIP catalogue record for this book is available from the British Library.

All rights reserved.

Parts of this book were previously published in Elvis Meets the Beatles by Chris Hutchins and Peter Thompson

ABOUT THE AUTHOR

THE writer and broadcaster **Chris Hutchins** is an established author of highly acclaimed biographies of the rich, the famous and the royals. His first, *Fergie Confidential*, was an intimate biography of the Duchess of York and chronicled her troubled marriage to the Queen's favourite son, Prince Andrew. He followed this with a revelatory biography of the late Princess of Wales, *Diana's Nightmare: The Family*, a book which so established him as an authority on the royals that he was invited to cover Prince Charles' subsequent marriage for American television. Books that followed include *Elvis Meets the Beatles*– a rendezvous he arranged during his close association with all five – *ATHINA: The Last Onassis*, which probed deeply into the world of the Onassis dynasty and *GOLDSMITH: Money, Women and Power*, the biography of the late billionaire entrepreneur, Sir James Goldsmith. More recently Hutchins turned his attention to matters Russian with fearless biographies of the country's leader, *PUTIN*, and best-known oligarch, *ABRAMOVICH: The billionaire from nowhere*. The author returned to the royal stage with a revealing book about Diana's son, *HARRY: The People's Prince*. Then it was back to rock'n'roll with *THE BEATLES: Messages from John, Paul George and Ringo* which featured on its cover one of the postcards John Lennon sent to the author during his travels.

As Prince Charles' former secretary Mark Bolland says of him: 'Chris Hutchins seems to have seen and done it all . . .'

Follow Chris Hutchins on Twitter: ChrisHutchinsFn

CONTENTS

FOREWORD

ONE day in 1969 I was sitting at my desk at the London *Evening Standard* when I got a call from a friend, Chris Hutchins. He had two questions to ask me. Did I want to go with him to Las Vegas to see Elvis Presley make his stage comeback? And did I then want to interview Elvis?

Did I? I'd been dreaming about nothing else since I was fifteen.

At the time there was renewed interest in Elvis following the 1968 *NBC Comeback Special* and the album *Elvis In Memphis,* but, even so, I had to work hard to convince the editor of my newspaper that the opportunity to actually see the rebirth of the man who had invented the very concept of the rock star was worth the cost of the trip.

And, I can now admit, unknown to my editor, even I harboured some doubts about the venture. Yes, I thought, Chris will get me into the show. But a meeting with Elvis? Was that even remotely possible? Apart from a couple of trusted reporters in Memphis and Los Angeles, it was well known that Elvis no longer talked to the Press. Could Chris possibly fix that?

Well, he did, just as four years earlier he'd arranged a meeting between Elvis and the Beatles. When it came to getting to rock stars, and putting people together, Chris had few equals.

I'd first come across him when he'd been a successful fellow journalist, but on the day of the phone call I was aware that he'd moved into public relations, and was representing, among others, Tom Jones. And because of his relationship with Tom Jones, and Tom's friendship with Elvis, Chris met and talked with Elvis on many occasions, at the same time becoming a confidante of Elvis's manager, 'Colonel' Tom Parker.

Not many people got letters from the Colonel explaining his part in the Elvis story, and only one man turned up at Elvis's house in Hollywood with the Beatles in tow – Chris Hutchins. But, from where I stand, the best thing Chris ever did was to make it possible for me to fulfil a boyhood ambition.

Ray Connolly 2015

PROLOGUE: HOW IT CAME ABOUT

THE small room was dimly lit by a single table lamp covered with a heavy shade. Having just stepped in from the brilliance of the mid-day California sunshine, I had difficulty in locating the chair which I was to occupy while awaiting the return of my host Colonel Tom Parker. Many moments passed before I realised I was not alone: seated facing me was another human being.

It was Elvis Presley, the most famous man in the world.

On later pages I describe my memory of this first encounter with the man I was to get to know well in the years ahead, but first let me explain how this most unexpected meeting came about.

It was August 1965 and I was in America with John Lennon, Paul McCartney, George Harrison and Ringo Starr covering the Beatles' second U.S. tour for the *NME* (*New Musical Express*). Three years earlier, in the grimy surroundings of the Star Club in Hamburg, I listened to the four of them lauding the man who had inspired their entry into the music business. They knew that I had established a telephone connection with Elvis's highly-protective manager, Colonel Parker.

'Do you think you could ever fix it for us to meet Elvis?' John asked way back then.

3

'I'll try – but I have to meet him first,' was my reply.

The chances of four then-unknown musicians and a 21-year-old reporter barely out of his apprenticeship with a small Devon weekly newspaper, ever getting together with the world's biggest superstar, seemed remote to say the least.

Like me, the four Liverpudlians had dodged school to spend afternoons listening to his records, and watching back-to-back showings of Elvis's movies *Love Me Tender, Loving You, Jailhouse Rock* and *King Creole*. We belonged to a generation whose male members spent what seemed like hours in front of mirrors practising the curled-lip grimace and trying out the slurred vowels of an accent that originated thousands of miles away in America's Deep South. Every boy wanted to be Elvis.

The Beatles and I were just a few years younger than our hero who was born in 1936. Two of them were older than me (John and Ringo were born in 1940 and two younger – Paul 1942, George 1943). But we had all managed to decipher the words of *All Shook Up, Hound Dog* and *Teddy Bear, well, most of them.*

I was in Hamburg as Little Richard's temporary tour manager having suffered a setback in my *NME* career (more of that later) and Lennon and co were serving their own apprenticeship eking out a living playing five sets a night at the Star Club (John, married and with a son on the way, accompanied strippers on his guitar at another club in the red-light district so he could send a few pounds home.

Much of what followed is relayed in my earlier book *THE BEATLES: Messages from John, Paul, George and Ringo.* I will get back to Elvis in a page or two but first let me relay a telephone conversation I had with Tom Parker on the night of February 9, 1964. I was calling from a phone in the Beatles' suite on the 12th floor of the Plaza hotel in New York just a couple of hours after they had made their first U.S. TV appearance on Ed Sullivan's massively popular show.

The conversation went something like this:

'Colonel Tom, I'm with the Beatles in New York and they've asked me to call and thank you and Elvis for the Good Luck cable you sent them.'

'Yeah, I just saw 'em on the Sullivan show. How much did [their manager] Brian Epstein get for them for doing that show?'

'Ten thousand dollars.'

'Though so. I got 50,000 for Elvis nearly eight years ago.'

'Colonel, I'm sure you've thought of it already, but what about fixing a meeting between the Beatles and Elvis?'

'You know these guys pretty well, huh?'

'Sure, if you watched the TV closely you might have noticed the cuff links John Lennon was wearing. They're mine.'

'A meeting, huh? It did cross my mind. Sure, why not? Tell 'em they can visit us any time.'

Such a meeting would have to wait, however. The Beatles were on the East Coast, nearly 3,000 miles from Elvis in Los Angeles.

But the seed was sewn. The Beatles were going to meet their idol. And I was destined to get to know a wonderful, complex man who just happened to be the greatest star on Planet Earth, the man who was now sitting opposite me in this darkened room.

Since their careers became so intertwined, I make no excuses for chronicling here what was going on with the Beatles during the last years of Elvis's life. After all, I was partly responsible for it.

1

THE MAN WHO MADE ELVIS KING

That's all right

'DO YOU miss Elvis?' I asked. It was not a question anyone had ever been able to pose to Colonel Parker before, let alone get an answer to. Looking away, he spent several moments considering his reply. Finally, returning his gaze to meet mine, he answered 'Frankly, no. There's no point missing what you haven't got. Elvis is dead and buried, but there's still his business to take care of, and if I waste time mourning what has passed, there's plenty of people ready to come in and cut the ground from under our feet.'

This was typical Parker business-speak and having known him for several years, I believed I deserved to hear something personal from the old man's lips. 'Was Elvis the son you never had?' This time he leaned forward and, speaking in hushed tones, brought his face close to mine before answering: 'Chris, I have to be honest and tell you, I can't say yes to that one either. I never looked upon him as a son, but he was the *success* I always wanted. You know, although we were together a lot of years, we never got too close. That's the easiest way to bust up a good partnership. He had his friends and I had mine. I looked after my money and he took care of his – I never tried to advise him on what to do with it, I just made sure we got paid every dime we were entitled to. I couldn't have done that if I'd been out there worrying what he was up to and what time he was getting home at night.

'Managers who operate that way and party with their artists don't stay managers for too long. On the other hand, Elvis knew if he had a problem he could call me any hour of the day or night. There would be times when he'd be home in Memphis, perhaps at two in the morning, and he'd go into a room where he could be in private and call me to talk something over. I had promised him I'd always be there for him, and I was.'

We were speaking in the parlour of the house he had moved to in Las Vegas. It was our first face to face meeting since Elvis had died and I had flown there determined to get a deeper understanding of what these two men – both incredible in their own ways – meant to each other.

He had described their working relationship to those charged with investigating Elvis's death, thus: 'We had a respect for each other, but we were never close socially. I was around as often as I could be. In the early days, I spent about 50 per cent of my time with him. And when he moved into motion pictures, I was spending all my time with him.'

But that was legal speak. Or was it? I remembered being in a car with him when we were searching for Elvis's Los Angeles house prior to the Beatles meeting I had got him to agree to. He wouldn't admit it, but he had never been there, never set foot in the home he had helped his 'star son' to buy with hi share of the fortunes they had made for each other.

It was in a bid to nail the truth that I had travelled 6,000 miles for what turned out to be my final encounter with 'Colonel' Thomas Andrew Parker. This, after all, was the man with one of the richest show business stories of all time who told me that he intended calling his memoirs not 'Elvis Presley and Me' or anything like that, but 'How much does it cost if it's free?'.

Inconspicuous among the Lincolns, Cadillacs and stretch limousines, at the start of that memorable day, a small, plum-coloured Buick had pulled neatly into the outside lane of the glass *porte-cochere* at the Las Vegas Hilton. Behind the wheel was the vivacious 50-something former Miss Loanne Miller, once assistant to the hotel's publicity chief, Nick Naff. At her side was Parker, her husband of two years, now in his 85th year. It was exactly noon on Columbus Day, Monday, 11 October 1993, and the Parkers were right on time for our appointment at the famous Elvis Presley landmark.

'You be seated on the valet-parking boys' bench opposite the hotel entrance,' the Colonel had instructed me. 'Tell 'em you're expecting your uncle, the Colonel. Don't tell anyone where you're going, Chris, and on no account give anyone my address or telephone number.'

In the telephone call to my room at the Hilton three hours earlier, he had been as curt as he was specific. He knew better than anyone that no thorough investigation of the Elvis story would be complete without a close inspection of his own role in it.

Killing time before we met, I had gone up to the 30th floor, where the Imperial Suite was being torn apart to make way for three 'sky villas' suited to the more modern tastes of high rollers. A plaque commemorating the Elvis years at the Hilton had already been torn down and the place was as musty as a mausoleum.

I walked down the three curved steps into the sunken living room, which had been the great party room when Elvis was in residence. The floor was bare and my footsteps echoed. The fireplace was still intact, flanked by bookshelves, which included at least one Elvis-owned titled: a paperback edition of *The Autobiography of a Yogi*. There was a Steinway grand piano awaiting removal, an unstocked bar and some old newspapers. The four bedrooms, six bathrooms, sauna, dining room, kitchen and pantry had also been abandoned. Elvis's bed on its raised dais resembled a pharaoh's sarcophagus that had been well and truly plundered. This was where he had acted out his fantasies until 'medication' had ended the performance some time before he died.

The suite had the faded feel of an old movie set on a redundant backlot. The symbol had lost its substance, and an inconvenient piece of history was being swept on to the scrap heap.

From the patio, there was a view of the Las Vegas Country Club golf course, the greens neat and well-watered. It was a hot, clear day, and the mountain rim showed up on the cratered lunar horizon. Elvis might be long gone, but the Colonel was very much alive and we were to have lunch together.

The lift that took me down to the ground floor was packed with casino types eager for action. It had been nineteen years since my own first visit to Las Vegas with the Beatles. Five years later, in this same hotel, the Colonel had taught me how to shoot craps. I remembered that night as I walked across the pink-and gold flowered carpet of the casino lounge, bigger now and brighter since chandeliers of the finest Austrian Strauss crystal had been installed. Carly Simon was singing 'You're So Vain' above the crash of coins. Row upon row of slot machines made an almost melodic, pipe organ sound as they spun. Cocktail waitresses in black tutus and Keno girls peddling $100,000 promises were continuously on the move.

Bells rang, change clanged and an avalanche of coins clattered out of the chrome mouth and into the plastic bucket of a mute punter. Arms moved automatically up and down, brain and limbs programmed as if by a form of hypnosis. It was depressing just watching the 'grinds', as the low rollers are called.

In a fenced-off area stood the $25-a-spin Double Diamond slots that the Colonel still liked to play. The supervisor, guarding the entrance to exclude the idly curious, was tight lipped about him, but one regular told me: 'He sometimes feeds four machines at a time.' The Colonel's presence still created a buzz.

In the centre of the lounge, a scoreboard announced that the jackpot for the Fabulous Fifties was $1,180,935 and rising. Gambling machines using the latest state-of-the-art technology had names like Megabucks, Quartermania and Motherlode. At the craps table, the action was a little quieter.

It was here that the Colonel had once painstakingly directed my gambling and enabled me to make a modest $300 profit in one two-hour session. Convinced that the sum would have been much larger if he had not forbidden me to raise the small stakes, I waited until he had gone to bed before gambling at my own pace. In twenty minutes, I had lost $3000 but a subsequent deal with the hotel to publicise Elvis's opening more than made up for it.

'I met the Colonel the first day I arrived in Las Vegas in 1971,' recalled Henri Lewin, the Hilton hotels boss. 'He arrived at 8.00 pm sharp, as he had promised, to discuss some points about Elvis's contract with me and my colleagues. We shook hands with the Colonel and took over the contract. The Colonel is a very good man: a handshake is all you need because he never goes back on his word. He knew what he wanted, he knew his product and he had things which other managers never thought about.

'For instance, he was interested in the prices we charged for dinner in the Showroom. He told me that the people who came to see Elvis couldn't afford to spend twenty-five or thirty dollars on a dinner. Make it twelve, he said, and we did.'

The Showroom was now billing *Starlight Express*, but right on cue, as I crossed the lobby at 11.45 and approached the bronze Elvis statue in the lobby, the King's voice could be heard singing 'Burning Love'. I moved through the brass revolving doors and out on to the concourse.

Shimmering above me, the Hilton rose like the three-feathered flight of a silver arrow embedded in the desert sand. Below the rooftop

HILTON sign, the ghosts in the Imperial Suite played to an empty house. Elvis was gone, but the Colonel was about to make his entrance.

Mrs Parker II pulled the Buick away from the hotel, heading down Paradise Road. The Colonel sat next to her in the front passenger seat, safety belt buckled over his paunch. He neither cast a glance back at the hotel that had been the scene of his greatest managerial triumph, nor did he turn to take a closer look at me, yet he was able to venture: 'You haven't changed much.'

That was the Colonel, always pretending to have eyes in the back of his head when he had really stolen a glance in the rear view mirror. I had known him for close to thirty years and had long since learned to respect the ritual dance that accompanied each and every one of our numerous encounters.

A half-hearted attempt to return the compliment was greeted by the response: 'For a man going on 85, I'm in reasonable shape. I'm up at five every morning to do my bendovers – managed twenty this morning, so this is a good day for me physically.'

The restaurant he had selected for lunch specialized in turkey dishes, and he paused to point with his stick to one of the huge birds roasting juicily on a spit in a large mock fireplace. He recalled 'the desert rat' he had told me I was eating midway during the first meal we had ever shared in his office at Paramount.

I couldn't tell you what it was before you ate it or you would not have enjoyed it,' he said, savouring the moment. 'As a matter of fact, you liked it so much I was sorry I told you it was desert rat because you didn't like the sound of that at all. But you know what it really was, don't you?'

'No. I've always assumed it was desert rat, like you said.'

The Colonel laughed heartily. 'It was quail, one of the finest delicacies. They just happen to look like desert rats without the long tail.'

He always had to have his little joke, and to his way of thinking it was rarely funny unless it shocked the victim. Elvis had once warned me: 'Beware of that ol' man – he can be mean.'

It was in retaliation for such humour that Presley occasionally changed the lyrics of 'Are You Lonesome Tonight?' and, instead of 'Do you gaze at your doorstep and picture me there?', sang: 'Do you gaze at your bald head and wish you had hair?' Elvis convulsed in laughter each time he did it. It was one joke the Colonel never seemed to enjoy.

Leaning heavily on the arm of his second bride, the Colonel made his way to the round table she had reserved for our uncertain reunion. 'That woman is more a nursemaid to him than a wife,' had commented one who regularly observed the Parkers on their Vegas outings. My mind slipped back to my meeting with his first wife at the apartment the Parkers occupied in the Westwood suburb of Los Angeles.

Like the Colonel's maternal grandmother, she was named Marie, although he called her 'MizRee' – so that it sounded like 'misery'. The dark-haired daughter of a Spanish-American war hero, Marie Mott had already been married twice and was the mother of a 10-year-old son by the time she encountered Thomas Andrew Parker. They met early in 1935 at the South Florida State Fair, where she worked on the

Havatampa cigar stand. Elvis had been so fond of Marie that he called his daughter Lisa Marie partly after her. It was because of Marie Parker that the famous Elvis scarf tradition had begun.

'Early in his career, the Colonel took a scarf from his wife's neck and put it around Elvis, saying, "Now you're ready. Go on stage and sing your heart out,"' Henri Lewin told me. 'During the performance, Elvis used the scarf to wipe his face and then he threw it into the audience. The scarf ritual started from there.'

For the last years of her life, Marie was stricken with cancer and was virtually comatose. The Colonel funded round-the-clock nursing for her at their house in Palm Springs until she died from a heart attack in November 1986. His gratitude to her clearly matched his love.

I studied the Colonel across the table as Mrs Parker II fussed over him. As always, he was dressed for comfort rather than effect. He wore navy blue serge slacks and an open-neck blue shirt with a fine white stripe in it. Just in case any newcomer to town might fail to recognize his famous figure, 'THE COLONEL' was embroidered on the breast pocket, clipped to which was his ever-ready pen. He was still very much a player.

In appearance, though, time and tide had actually corroded much of that familiar, well-paunched, heavy-jowled physique. Disfiguring liver spots had aged his skin even beyond his eighty-four summers – the backs of his hands were almost black with them – and the flesh hung in folds at his throat. His shoulder, broken years earlier when it was crushed by a revolving door in Los Angeles, was still giving him trouble.

'Here's a tip for you,' he said. 'If you're ever injured in an accident, don't move until the ambulance arrives. Lie still. I made the mistake of getting up and dragging myself off to see a doctor, and that allowed the building's insurers to maintain that I'd injured my arm someplace else.'

When he removed his off-white Stetson hat – 'a present from George Strait, the country singer, it would have cost me $100 to buy' – it was to reveal a bald head made unsightly by wisps of white hair.

'Let's get this straight,' he told me following a cursory glance at the menu. 'I don't intend giving you any information about Elvis or about me that you haven't already come by through knowing us over the years. But I will guide you. I've already been offered a $2 million advance for my story against $4 for each copy they sell of the book plus the rights to a major motion picture based on it.' The expression of disbelief that must have registered on my face did not escape his attention: 'And if I were to expire before completing it, Mrs Parker here has all the information to finish it,' he added.

Knowing the Colonel as I did and the games he played, I doubted that even Marie (his book-keeper as well as his wife) had known many of the secrets of his highly confidential relationship with Elvis.

The arrival of a waitress other than the one who usually served him disconcerted him for a moment, but he rattled off his order. He liked everything to be familiar – people, places, things.

I asked him about the Elvis display in the Hilton lobby, which included a poem he had written in honour of his star. 'Those people over there know nothing,' he stormed. 'I don't know why you're bothering talking to them. They can't even get the display right. You see that fancy white suit in the glass case next to Elvis's statue? The inscription says he wore it on the first night of his first engagement there. That's nonsense – he never wore anything that decorative until two or three years into his contract at the Hilton. I wrote to the president of the hotel about that.'

He paused.

'By the way, I also called him to tell him you were arriving. Are they looking after you?'

His tone gave me reason to interpret 'looking after you' as 'keeping a close eye on you'.

The Colonel plunged an inquisitorial spoon into the bowl of turkey soup that the unfamiliar waitress had placed before him. 'Where's the turkey?' he demanded. 'I usually get more meat in my soup than this.'

The girl smiled sweetly and began to walk away, but the Colonel was not letting her off that lightly. 'You won't get much of a tip,' he called after her, ignoring the looks of disdain from other diners.

This was his less acceptable side. But that was the nature of the real Colonel Parker, the man who counted the pieces of turkey meat in his soup to make sure he wasn't short-changed. I realized that I had been as guilty as anyone of taking him at face value. Up to this point the real man had successfully eluded me as well.

Mrs Parker II did her best to lighten the mood with small talk as she wiped drops of greasy soup from her husband's shirt. Then, from a phial she carried in her handbag, she produced three capsules. 'Time for your vitamins, Colonel,' she said. Even his wife did not call him Tom.

At this point, I knew that the truth I wanted to establish to my own satisfaction was a simple one. Had the Colonel ever loved Elvis? I had watched the two men fall into each other's arms after Elvis's comeback performance in 1969, and I had seen the Colonel's eyes glisten. But were they tears of love?

The first promise the Colonel ever made to Elvis was that he would take his million dollars' worth of talent and turn it into a million dollars. In fact, he had turned it into $1.5 billion. Now it was the Memphis Mafia who were coining it and the Colonel did not like that one little bit.

'I don't approve of those guys who worked for Elvis making money out of their stories about him,' he said, conveniently forgetting his own $2 million offer. 'One of his boys came to me and told me he'd been offered $100,000 for his story. I said, "Be sure to write about Elvis bailing you out when they were going to take your house away. And be sure to tell 'em it was Elvis who paid the doctor's bills when your wife was sick." But they never write that stuff. That's not what they think people want to read about him, right?'

His sole client had been dead for more than sixteen years, and yet he worked day and night to preserve the image of 'Elvis & the Colonel'. Most of the dollars that the Elvis industry still generated now went direct to the Presley estate after some highly public litigation instigated by his widow, Priscilla, had prised it free of the Colonel's experienced and, some said, voracious grasp. One lawsuit claimed that he had defrauded the Presley estate out of $5 million. Rebutting the charges, he had counter-sued. He had informed me at the time: 'I'm no cheat. These charges are unfair to me and Elvis. I highly respected Elvis Presley, and I have made every effort to honour his name and preserve his memory with dignity. These unjust charges not only attack my name and reputation, they are an insult to the memory of Elvis and his father, Vernon. 'Just as I did with Elvis and Vernon when they were alive, I have always dealt fairly and openly with the executors.

'But in the twilight of his life, the Colonel was keen to talk about money. I jotted down on a paper place mat the stream of figures that came pouring out from his cerebral computer. There was the $50,000 he boasted about getting Ed Sullivan to part with for Elvis's appearances on his TV show. 'The standard fee then was just $750. He offered $1500 for Elvis, but I held out for five weeks until he came up with the $50,000. I told Brian Epstein he should have got me to negotiate the money for the Beatles' appearances on *Sullivan* – I'd have got them a lot more.'

While the waitress, still under threat of an abysmal tip, served his turkey fillet and side salad, the Colonel continued in full cry about the deals he had squeezed and the sums he had handed over to charity. 'I've kept a list of every dime I have given away. For example, every year I paid $125 to one cause so they could send a kid to summer camp. Well, on my 80th birthday, I gave 'em $10,000 so they could send eighty boys.

'I've been offered $50,000 to do a lecture tour of Australia, but I'm not ready to go yet,' added the frail, elderly man who had taken several minutes to negotiate the few steps from his car to the restaurant table.

'Right now, sitting talking to you, I could be getting $12,500 for giving a talk somewhere in this country. 'The offers keep coming in, but I'm too busy working for Barron Hilton. I fix the hotel's radio spots just like I used to when Elvis was singing there.

'I've been loyal to the people I've done business with. RCA gave me a plaque to commemorate our fifty-seven years together, I've been with Hill & Range and the William Morris Agency for fifty years as well. People these days are just too fickle – look at the way they're trying to destroy Michael Jackson. He's a good boy. He came over to see me and have some pictures taken just the other week when he was in Vegas. I feel sorry about what has been happening to the kid – it would never have happened if I'd been managing him. You never saw Elvis in a mess like that.'

The food came and went, and Loanne Parker paid for the meal, conveniently forgetting to undertip the waitress who had dared to serve the Colonel a bowl of soup light on turkey meat. As we left the restaurant, Nevada's most famous yet reclusive resident announced: 'Now I'm going to take you back to the house and show you a few things nobody gets to see.'

I wasn't sure who was more surprised – me or Mrs Parker II. I had repeatedly been reminded during lunch that he would do nothing to enlighten me on the subject of Elvis or the secrets of his own life. Loanne, however, was truly astonished. Raising one eyebrow, she declared: 'You *are* honoured – the Colonel hardly ever takes anyone inside our home. We're very private. It's our refuge. The last one he let in was Bill Clinton's mother, Mrs Virginia Kelley, and he thought twice about that!'

We drove in silence past the forest of neon hotel signs, which glared brighter than the afternoon sun. Marquees proclaimed *Starlight Express* at the Hilton, Engelbert Humperdinck at Bally's and the imminent opening of such new palaces as the Luxor, an enormous black-glass pyramid of Egyptian splendour, Kirk Kerkorian's MGM Grand Hotel (which Barbra Streisand would open, twenty-two years after she had opened the International for the same tycoon) and the Treasure Island hotel/theme park complex. The city was gambling billions on its future.

They were made for each other, Las Vegas and the Colonel. 'You're having lunch with *the* Colonel?' or 'You know the *Colonel?*' were common reactions among Las Vegans when I mentioned my plans. The subject of how well the Colonel looked after his own money was a matter of some debate. An inveterate gambler, he was said by many to have handed much of his personal fortune over to the casino operators as fast as Elvis could earn it. One who knew him well, Liberace's former manager Seymour Heller, says he believes the Colonel lost a million a year on the tables.

'Every time he wanted a rack of chips, he got $25,000 worth at a time,' said Heller. 'He always played roulette. They had to set up a private table for him, and you dared not talk to him – no matter how much he liked you – while he was gambling. You cannot win at roulette if you play all the numbers and he played all the numbers. He put down a big stack on some and just a few chips on others. If he hit the big stack, then he made a lot of money. He had to get something back, but he lost an average of a million dollars a year there.'

As we drove on, I asked the Colonel what keepsakes of Elvis he treasured most. Neatly anticipating that he might yet again break his self-imposed code of silence, Loanne interjected: 'Oh, I think your memories are the most precious, don't you, Colonel?' Ignoring his wife's remark, Parker replied: 'His personal letters. He wrote me a lot of letters, you know, warm and understanding letters. All handwritten. I keep 'em at the house with the rest of my memorabilia. I sold a lot of the stuff to Graceland for their exhibition, but I hung on to the letters and a few other things. You'll see.'

It was a curious statement. I had heard the tape on which the Colonel had given evidence to the district attorney's investigators into Elvis's death which told a different story. 'While he was in the service, there was very little contact with him,' he had said. 'He called three or four times, long distance. I never got any letters. Elvis was not in the habit of writing letters. I got a thank-you note from him one time, but that was all he ever wrote in twenty years.' I never did get to remind him of this.

Our conversation turned to Elvis's early TV appearances. I asked him how he felt about the time that Ed Sullivan had filmed him from the waist up.

'Naw, that was a publicity stunt Sullivan himself dreamed up, 'came the surprising answer, the first indication that the old man was beginning to let his guard down. 'I can tell you now that nobody really wanted to censor Elvis, but those stories in the papers got the show bigger ratings than it had ever had. Sullivan used Elvis, but it didn't do us no harm.'

Having given another man credit for what was one of the most successful publicity stunts in the crucial early stages of Elvis's career, I wondered aloud if the Colonel had suggested that Elvis dress in a tuxedo for the Frank Sinatra show in 1960.

'No, that was the Sinatra people's idea,' he replied. 'They came to me and said, "How do you feel about Elvis wearing a tux?" and I said, "Well, that'll cost you an extra hundred bucks for each one of us." They asked why and I told 'em, " 'Cos we don't have tuxedos and that's how much they cost." They went for it – still got mine at the house, and the shiny black shoes they paid for to go with it.'

The one idea he did take credit for was the very one Elvis was known to have hated: singing 'Hound Dog' to a real canine on the *Steve Allen Show*. 'And they paid for the top hat and tails,' he said.

As Loanne swung the Buick into a small private estate, a guard in the gatehouse raised the barrier and saluted 'the Colonel' as though he were a five-star general. The impressive entrance to the compound was deceptive: a local realtor said later that the larger homes ranged in value between $350,000 and $450,000, a far cry from Beverly Hills' prices, and the Parkers did not have one of the larger houses. Mrs Parker pressed a button to open an electronic door and nosed the Buick inside. The Colonel was anything but abashed by his unpretentious abode.

'You ever see a garage as clean as this?' he demanded. It was carpeted, too. 'It's nice here, isn't it? Private. But cold in the wintertime.'

We stepped on to a modest porch and through the front door into a hallway that was lined with framed pictures, many of which I had first seen on the walls of his office at Paramount. There were pictures of Elvis and of the Colonel with famous friends including one of Elvis's manager with Frank Sinatra and Spencer Tracy. One by one, he read out the glowing testimonials. Both of his favourite female singers, Dolly Parton and Barbra Streisand, had paid pen-and-ink homage to this man, who now stood waving his walking stick at their likenesses as if it were a baton pointing out the areas to be taken on a battlefield plan.

'Somewhere here, I've got a letter from Maurice Chevalier in his own handwriting, saying, "If there were more colonels like you, Colonel, we wouldn't need no wars."' He found one from Elvis. 'Here, read this one out,' he commanded. It was a cable humbly extolling Elvis's thanks to his manager for 'the loyalty you have shown to me and my family', expressing his implicit trust and promising to stay with him 'through thick and through thin'. Yet another pledged Elvis's services to Colonel Thomas Parker 'in all matters'. This one was signed by Vernon and Gladys Presley.

The Colonel had explained his early dealings with Elvis on the investigators' tape: 'As a manager and promoter, I tried to get him in motion pictures, record contracts, tours and personal appearances. For a while, we had a contract when he was underage. Then for a while we went without a contract – we went on a handshake. And then, when I had to sign for Elvis and so on, we made a new contract.

'My percentage fluctuated. It started out at 25 per cent, some deals I created were 50 per cent – some deals were separate. They varied between those two figures. We did our own promotion, the tours and so on. Back in 1955, I was booking shows, and Elvis had a manager who called me to see if I could use Elvis on some dates. We played Memphis and I met Elvis backstage. Then his father called me up and said they wanted to make a new record contract for Elvis. At the time, he was with Sam Phillips at Sun Records. From 1955 to 1960, I was in a contractual agreement to promote Elvis in all fields.'

We had paused briefly in the Parkers' wholesome parlour when the Colonel announced: 'And now you are going where precious few have been allowed to tread.' The look of astonishment returned to Loanne's face, and she made herself scarce while I was led into a den: the Colonel's secret shrine (though he subsequently made it clear he was annoyed with me for calling it that).

The room resembled an Aladdin's cave crammed from wall to wall and stacked from ceiling to floor with bright, gaudy artefacts. There were numerous clocks loudly keeping time, a myriad souvenirs from the Colonel's circus days and at least a score of brass and ceramic elephants mutely contemplating me. Everything had been carefully dusted and neatly positioned.

This was why the Colonel was obsessed about security. He had gathered the most treasured possessions of his entire career into one irreplaceable collection. From a hand-carved swivel armchair, he could focus on any object of his choosing and quietly reminisce about the past glory it symbolized. To lose this to a thief would break his great sentimental heart. Instantly the showman, the Colonel pointed to two huge glass spheres on his desk.

'Biggest crystal balls in the world,' he growled. 'I've been offered $20,000 for 'em.' Another presentation piece – a china circus montage – would, he said, have fetched $100,000 if he had accepted the offer. Many more framed pictures were carefully grouped to make identification easier. In one area, he kept autographed pictures of the US Presidents he had known: Lyndon B. Johnson, Jimmy Carter, Ronald Reagan, George Bush and Bill Clinton, although surprising, in view of the part he had played in Elvis's drug-busting activities, there was no sign of Richard Nixon.

'Have you ever seen so many pictures of presidents?' the Colonel demanded, impressed by his own trophies. Pride of place in the group was occupied by a black and white photograph of the Colonel and Eddy Arnold with President Harry S. Truman.

'I flew with Mr Truman in a helicopter to Mr Johnson's ranch when he was entertaining the President of Mexico to dinner,' he explained. 'Eddy Arnold had been invited, and he asked me if I would go with him. The guy in charge of the helicopter in Austin said, "Colonel Parker, your bus will be here in an hour." I said, "I don't have a bus. I understood I was going in the helicopter." Eddy Arnold was to entertain there, so I remained seated on the couch until the guy came back and said, "I was mistaken – you're going on the helicopter with President Truman." I'd been a friend of Mr Johnson ever since he ran for Congress because we went out in Texas to entertain for his campaign.'

Speaking of political winners, the Colonel drew my attention to a signed photograph of Margaret Thatcher. 'Somebody came here from Mrs Thatcher's office to see me and I gave him a signed picture of myself to take back to the Prime Minister,' he said. 'She returned the compliment to me. But I never use Mrs Thatcher in any of my stories because it's private and it wouldn't be fair. There's a certain protocol involved.'

There was a picture of the Colonel with Andy Gibb, the tragic Bee Gee brother killed by drugs, and another with Frank Sinatra. While I examined an exquisite model snowman carved in gold, he produced from the drawer of his desk a boxed cigar bearing his name and handed it to me.

'Here, have this,' he barked. 'It's my last one, but I shan't be needing it. Woke up one morning and saw an ad in the paper. It said if you sent this guy $98 he would stop you smoking. I thought, "Here's a good way to stop smoking," so I gave it up there and then and saved myself $98 into the bargain.'

Seated in his swivel chair, he pointed his stick again – this time at the cupboard behind me. 'Open it up and take a look inside,' he said. A massive file detailed every dollar that he had ever donated to charity: a round-up in the preface showed a total of $447,000 with a further figure detailing 'expenses absorbed'. Then he pointed to a large tin box. It was crammed with copies of telegrams sent by 'Elvis and the Colonel'.

'There's nearly 4000 in there. That's how I kept Elvis's name alive while he was in Germany,' he said. 'I sent famous people wires on their birthdays, their wedding days, their tour openings. When Elvis got home, he would keep coming to me with a big grin on his face saying that people were thanking him for the cables he had sent them. "Gee,

Colonel," he'd say, "I don't remember wiring those people." That's when I showed him that box you're holding.'

And that's when I asked him the questions that I hoped would open Pandora's Box and reveal just how deep their relationship had been. In conversations with Elvis I had learned he feared rather than loved 'that 'ol man', but was totally dependent on him. As Henry Lewin had put it: 'The Colonel is a strong, very capable man and he never took advantage of anything. If Elvis hadn't had the Colonel, Elvis would have given away 100 per cent before he even received it, he was such a soft-hearted fellow. He needed a man like Tom Parker.'

I asked the Colonel about one of the most controversial areas of his partnership with Elvis. Did he sweet-talk Vernon and Gladys Presley into signing that first contract? The reply was louder: 'Of course Vernon signed the contract for him because Elvis was under-age, but, you know, I never handled Elvis's money. A lot of people who don't know about our arrangements have looked at me in a critical light and asked, "Whatever happened to Elvis's money?" Vernon was his business manager and *he* made his investments.'

Remembering Vernon's early conviction for forgery, I asked as delicately as I could: 'Was he qualified to do so?'

'Well, I guess he knew enough to back off when something didn't look too good. But Elvis trusted Vernon, and Vernon trusted me – he said some very nice things about me on TV and radio. Then as soon as Elvis died, he wrote me a letter asking me to stay on and handle everything.

When Vernon himself died a year later, Priscilla wrote me a similar letter, so I stayed on.'

'What was Gladys really like?'

The Colonel paused and gazed at a picture of Elvis on his desk before replying. 'His mother was a very worried woman, she worried a lot,' he said not unkindly. 'She was very anxious for her boy, and she didn't really want to know about "Elvis the star". He was her son, and when he was on the road, even though he was bringing a lot of money home, she worried about him. She couldn't handle his fame. If she spotted a reporter approaching the house, she would run inside and lock the door.

'I have to say that Gladys Presley was not a well woman, and I suppose I was never comfortable around her. But I was managing Elvis, not his parents.'

On the DA's tapes, the Colonel had answered questions about Elvis's health. 'The first time I noticed any change in him was when Elvis went home one time from Vegas in 1974, and he was home about a month,' he had said. 'He came to my house and he looked terrible. I told him he didn't look well. That's when Elvis told me to stay out of his personal life. He said "No disrespect, Colonel, but I know what I'm doing. Stay out of my personal life."

'I'd say that I first noticed his drugs in the late Sixties, not that it 'specially concerned me. When we were making the movies, he was always good, he was on time, learned his lines and completed the job. Then he went home. What he did when he got there, I don't know because I did not go down to Memphis that often. When I really got concerned was that time in 1974 when he came to my house: he'd gained too much weight. Now, I spoke out, but I couldn't get involved. There were a couple of complaints sometimes when he didn't do a show too good. I was aware he was treated by physicians in Las Vegas and Palm Springs, but I had no personal experience of his visits.

'Sonny West told me one time that he was getting prescriptions in other people's names, but I didn't know about that. Dr Nick was often in the dressing room before a performance. There were always people around [Elvis]. He'd be hyped up and anxious about the show. I never saw Elvis being given drugs, though I know that Dr Nick has said he prepared medications for Elvis before he went on stage and when he came off.

'Let's face it, Dr Nick was there for some reason or he wouldn't have been there. I don't know how you'd judge the overall reaction. You know every performer has good days and bad. He had some bad days, other times he was outstanding. The only time I ever saw him sick while he was on stage was in Vegas one night, when he went off stage for about a minute, then came back and finished his show. He only ever cancelled once – in 1974 in Louisiana when he couldn't go on. A local doctor was called and pronounced him sick and he was flown back to Memphis and admitted to hospital. I was already in the next town and had to cancel the rest of the tour. That was the only time.

'I never heard of him being admitted to hospital for an overdose of drugs. True enough, I was concerned some times, but I couldn't talk to him about it. I never saw drugs. I never saw any member of the entourage in a bad way. I never saw them stumbling or falling about. They may have when they were not working. If they were stumbling, I'd have noticed it. They were all concerned, I'm sure. It's a sad situation. I had no control over him. That was Elvis's choice.'

In 1977, I had asked the Colonel why he refused to express his grief to a sorrowing world. 'If I shed a tear after Elvis died, nobody saw it,' he told me. 'If some people had as much as seen my eyes glaze, they'd have been busy trying to get their hands into our pockets. And I couldn't have had that. No, sir! My partners – Elvis and Vernon – wouldn't have liked that one little bit. Elvis is still with us in spirit, and I won't let up for a minute while he's still around. Elvis would turn over in his grave if I retired.'

His views altered somewhat in the intervening years, especially after writers and film-makers began taking a critical look at his relationship with Elvis. In 1991, he said, 'Everyone seems to think I was a tyrant to Elvis. I don't know why – maybe he painted that picture himself. He was difficult from the start. He always thought of himself as a superman and I had a helluva job controlling him.' This sounded much more like the real story as I understood it.

When the plum-coloured Buick deposited me back at the Hilton, the Colonel was still calling the shots. 'What you gotta do is go to Memphis and talk to the people who really loved Elvis,' he directed. 'Go there in January for the birthday celebrations. Find out where the fans are staying near Graceland, and put a sign on the hotel notice board saying that you're holding a soda pop-and-cookies party for them. They're the ones who know the real Elvis.'

Soda pop and cookies. Nickel mugshots sold for a dime. And, from his circus days, fake canaries, phoney hotdogs and toothless lions. Perhaps he was, after all, just a hustler who had got lucky, but I seriously doubted it. However much he might deny it, the Colonel had really loved Elvis Presley, but not always for the right reasons. His last words made me recall a promise made on the doorstep of 565 Perugia Way, Bel Air, the night Elvis had met the Beatles thirty years ago.

'You know, I never did get that Shetland pony Brian Epstein promised me,' he said. With a wave in the direction of the phantoms lining the ramparts, the old magician was gone, and the Snowmen's League was once again in recess.

After Lisa Presley (she had dropped the 'Marie') married Michael Jackson in the Dominican Republic in May 1994, I rang the Colonel for his reaction. He replied curtly: 'Some lady stopped me and said, "What do you think about the marriage?" I said, "Somebody got married in your family?" She said, "Aw, you know what I'm talking about." So I said, "No, I don't. Goodbye."

'That isn't my affair – that belongs to the Presley family. Sure, Michael has been to see me because I've known him a long time. But I don't get involved in other people's business. I'm like the bull, you know – I don't know nothing. I only know about Elvis and the Colonel.'

2

IN THE BEGINNING

Poor boy

INTERSTATE 55 follows the curve of the Mississippi through bare winter woods, thickets of billboards and acres of fuel storage tanks. It connects with US Highway 51 (now Elvis Presley Boulevard) near a drainage canal not far from Hernando's Hideaway, where a much younger Elvis had met the obliging blonde who had taken his virginity.

This is Memphis, Tennessee, the place Elvis called home. When he came back from his Army stint in Germany, somebody asked him what he had missed about Memphis and he had replied with one word: '*Everything!*' Memphis was his kind of town. 'He was one of us,' Memphian Mimi Phillips explained proudly. 'He never got too grand for his home town.'

Named after the ancient Egyptian city, the Memphis of the American Nile had survived fever, famine and floodtide. Originally built as a fort on the Fourth Chickasaw Bluff overlooking a grand sweep of the Mississippi, the fledgling outpost had been fought over by the Indians, the Spanish, the French and the English until, properly named by

General James Winchester in 1819 and dignified by a town plan, it had dusted itself down, placed a shingle above the porch and declared itself open for business.

The Memphis of the Old South had the 'War between the States' and the Klan, a few heroes like Rhett Butler and even fewer heroines like Scarlett O'Hara. It had a flourishing Cotton Row, unspeakable Jim Crow laws and inevitable race riots. It had the corrupt 'Boss' Crump for mayor, Davy Crockett as its one-time Congressman and an unenviable reputation as the murder capital of America.

Most important of all, especially as far as Elvis Presley was concerned, Memphis had Beale Street and the blues – the genuine, original W. C. Handy *Memphis* blues. 'Mr Crump don't 'low no easy-riders here,' the Father of the Blues had trumpeted in Pee-Wee's saloon. Easy-riders apart, Mr Crump allowed just about everything else in the way of pool halls, pawn shops, bordellos, honky-tonks and jive joints. Jazz and blues in one form or another – rhythm and blues – flowed into Memphis from St Louis in the north, New Orleans in the south and all points on the harmonic compass in between. R&B, the black sound waiting for a white voice to take it out of the ghetto, gave birth to rock 'n' roll and Elvis had been its liberator.

He had travelled a long, hard road from his birthplace, a two room shotgun shack set in woodland on the dusty Old Saltillo Road on the east side of Tupelo, Mississippi. The rags-to-riches script was by Tennessee Williams out of Marvel Comics: Orpheus ascending like Captain Marvel Jr in a flash of lightning from the southern poverty trap. 'I identified with the hero in every comic book I ever read,' Elvis recalled. Captain Marvel Jr was his favourite. 'I could say we lived on the wrong side of the tracks, but in those days in Tupelo, there wasn't really a right side of the tracks. No one was eating too good. We never starved, but we were close to it at times.'

Elvis's mother had been born Gladys Love Smith on 25 April 1912, into a poor family in neighbouring Pontotoc County. Of the five surviving Smith sisters, Gladys was the most striking, a dark, slender beauty who loved flirting and dancing. Her father, Robert Lee Smith, made the best moonshine in the county, a talent that attracted the disapproval of the authorities. They ran him out of Pontotoc and he moved his family to a house in Lee County, four miles from Tupelo, where Gladys fell madly in love with a tall, fair-haired farm worker called Vernon Elvis Presley. It is an ironic truth that, if it hadn't been for 'white lightning', the couple would never have met when they did and Elvis Presley would never have existed.

When Gladys was 21 and Vernon had just turned 17, the couple eloped. They went to Pontotoc County to get a marriage licence because the groom was too young to marry legally in Lee County. Gladys claimed on the licence that she was only 19, the start of a deception about her real age that she maintained all her life. Vernon's age shot up to 22 for the sake of appearances, but no one seemed to care. The young lovers were married on 17 June 1933, at Verona, a few miles south of Tupelo. It was a very physical union.

Elvis was born at 4.35 am on 8 January 1935, half an hour after his twin brother, who had been delivered still-born. Elvis Aron (he later changed it to the biblical Aaron) was to say of Jesse Garon: 'They say that, when one twin dies, the other grows up with all the qualities of the other. If I did, I'm lucky.'

However, the main thing Elvis owed to his brother was not luck but fear about his own mortality and a deep sense of guilt that he had lived while the first-born had been chosen to die. To justify his own existence, Elvis knew from a very early age that he had to be the perfect child. Jesse might lie buried in a shoebox in an unmarked grave at Priceville cemetery, but Elvis and Gladys talked to him constantly. Jesse was always with them in spirit.

The early bonding of grieving mother, anguished son and celestial twin produced a form of co-dependence that crippled Elvis all his emotional life. As soon as he could speak, he started calling his mother 'Sattnin' and both his parents were 'My babies'.

Janelle McComb, a poet and neighbour who nursed the infant Elvis, remembers first encountering him during a visit to a Tupelo beauty parlour.

'Gladys was getting a perm under the hair-drier and Vernon was sitting on the steps holding Elvis,' she told me at her home in East Tupelo, which had since been elevated to 'Presley Heights'. 'Vernon's hair was really light and somebody came in and said, "There is some old white-haired man sitting outside holding a baby that's screaming his head off." Gladys jumped up and said, "That's Elvis!"

'I followed her out to take a look at the baby and that was my first introduction to Elvis Presley. The first time I met him he was looking up at me and crying, and the last time I saw him I was looking down at him and I was crying. It was forty-two years later, on the day of his funeral. All Elvis ever wanted was for somebody to love him.'

When Elvis was an impressionable 3-year-old, the relationship between mother and son became even more intense after Vernon was sentenced to three years' imprisonment at Parchman prison farm on the Mississippi Delta for altering the amount on a cheque from $4 to $40 to buy food.

'I used to go with Gladys and Elvis to see Vernon, and there were other people from here that went, too.' said Janelle McComb. 'We used to get on a yellow school bus and ride down to Parchman – it was a big outing. Let me tell you, we had a way of turning adversity into a fun thing in those days.'

As prisoners were granted conjugal rights, the physical side of the Presleys' marriage continued in the grim setting of a prison hut while Elvis played with the children of other inmates. Pleading family hardship, Vernon was paroled after serving only nine months, but the shame of his incarceration haunted the family. For the rest of their lives, Vernon, Gladys and Elvis feared that this terrible secret would become public and ruin his career. It never did. Tupelo kept its mouth loyally shut. Desperately poor, the Presleys found that the only reliable solution to life's problems was to be found in the Gospels, both written down and sung out loud.

Elvis had inherited a good singing voice from both his parents, a sense of rhythm from Gladys and his blond good looks from Vernon. He learned to play the guitar that his parents had given him for his tenth birthday and sing songs like 'Old Shep'.

'I remember Elvis crossing the levee carrying his lunch in an old molasses bucket,' said Janelle McComb. 'He was going to the Lyric Theatre, where Mr John Glower had a talent show every Saturday morning. Anybody could go and do their act: play the comb, sing, dance or whatever. That particular Saturday, Mr Johnny looked at Elvis and said, "Elvis, what are you going to sing?" And Elvis said, "I'm going to play 'There's a Hole in the Bucket'." And Mr Johnny said, "Do you know it?" And Elvis said, ' "Sure I do – and there really is a hole in my bucket." He was around 10 at the time.'

The Presleys' first home, which Vernon had built with his own sweat on a $180 loan, had been repossessed while he was in prison, and the family now lived near the black Shakerag district of Tupelo. It was here that Elvis first heard the blues. Steaming up from the bayous, distilled in the cotton fields and scented with a whiff of honeysuckle, the bitter-sweet sounds flowed out of the ghetto in the sweltering hush of evening.

Black blues, white country and multi-racial gospel were the sounds of Elvis's childhood and he drew upon them all in his music. He loved the country numbers he heard on WELO, the local radio station, which featured the brother of one of his classmates, an itinerant singer called Mississippi Slim. Elvis followed his hero around Tupelo like any other kid and picked up some new chords. On Sundays, he joined Vernon and Gladys singing hymns at the First Assembly of God church on Adams Street.

'Since I was 2 years old, all I knew was gospel music. That was music to me,' Elvis recalled. 'We borrowed the style of our psalm singing from the early Negroes. We used to go to these religious singings all the time. The preachers cut up all over the place, jumping on the piano, moving every which way. The audience liked them, and I guess I learned from them.'

At the age of 3, Elvis had climbed on to his first stage, the choir platform of the church, where he clapped his hands in time to the music. 'He was too young to know the words, but he could keep the tune,' said Gladys.

Elvis was a true believer from childhood, said Janelle McComb, who kept his memory alive at his birthplace on Elvis Presley Drive. 'He placed his talent in the hands of God, God touched it and that talent became so magnified that the entire world knew him by his first name,' she said.

According to Vernon Presley, he had passed out at the moment of Elvis's conception, and he told of how a mystical blue light had appeared in the sky above his home on the night of the birth. The infant had seemed to be bathed in light as he struggled for life in the makeshift crib. 'Could it have been for me?' Elvis was to ask. He came to believe that it was, uttering the mystifying words at his last concert: 'I was – and I am.'

Elvis not only became a great singer, a great entertainer and a great personality but also great icon, virtually a religion in his own right, he was, said his musical mentor Sam Phillips, an avatar, or messenger from

God signalling the Second Coming. 'We've lost the most popular man who ever walked on this planet since Christ was here himself,' Carl Perkins said in homage.

Janelle McComb observed: 'The Elvis I knew was as gentle as the wind that blows across your cheeks, as compassionate as a benevolent priest, but he could be tempered with steel if somebody stepped on his blue suede shoes. Underneath it all he had a heart that conquered the entire world.

'Everybody asks, "Why do you think the legend still lives?" 'And the answer is that, when Elvis Presley walked on that stage, that little clerk in the audience instantly became the office manager. He gave hope and inspiration to all of those who dream the impossible dream.

'I never knew the superstar in the rhinestone cape. I knew the young boy from Tupelo in the denim jeans who looked at his daddy and said, "Someday I'm going to buy you and Mama the biggest house you can buy." '

When the Presleys did eventually leave Tupelo, it was very much a matter of necessity. Like his father-in-law Bob Smith, Vernon had become involved in the moonshine racket, although his role was that of delivery man for another bootlegger. He was caught by the sheriff, put in the cells and told he could either get out of town or face the consequences. Vernon didn't need any further prompting. After one stretch in prison, the last thing he wanted was any more trouble with the law. Hastily, he gathered up his terrified wife and shy 13-year-old son and headed across the Tallahatchie River on US Highway 78 bound for Memphis, 104 miles to the north.

'We were broke, man, broke, and we left Tupelo overnight,' Elvis said later to explain how he became a Memphian. 'Dad packed all our belongings in boxes and put them on the top and in the trunk of a 1939 Plymouth. We just headed to Memphis. Things had to be better.'

Leaving the hill country behind, Highway 78 cut through the Holly Springs national forest, where great growths of kudzu vine snaked up the trees, the road emerging into green pasture as it neared the Mississippi in Shelby County, Tennessee.

In the autumn of 1948 when the Presleys arrived, the 'Bluff City' was a tough metropolis of 300,000 people. The family encountered more hard times, but at least they were travelling in the right direction. In the Old South, there was hunger, hardship and wounded pride. In the North, there was money, glamour and the promise of a new beginning. Memphis was halfway between the two.

The Presleys lived in a variety of homes, the most wretched of which was a one-room, rat-infested slum at 572 Poplar Avenue, and the most famous a red brick, two-bedroom, ground-floor apartment at 185 Winchester Avenue on a Federal housing project called Lauderdale Courts. Elvis attended the L. C. Humes High School on Manassas Street in North Memphis, Gladys escorting him the few blocks there every day until he was 15. A head-down swagger disguised the fact that he was self-conscious about an outbreak of adolescent pimples, and his face and back were to be badly marked by acne scars. Gladys told him to hold his head up. 'You might come from poor country people,' she told him, 'but you're as good as anybody.'

Bullied for being a mother's boy, Elvis affected the appearance of a screen hoodlum by adopting a Tony Curtis hairstyle and wearing flashy punk clothes. This enraged his crewcut classmates. According to Elvis, they would chase him down the street, shouting: 'Hot dang, let's get him – he's a squirrel, he's a squirrel, get him, he just come down outta the trees!' But he could play the guitar, he could sing and he could dream. 'In those days, he was lost in dreams,' said his friend Marty Lacker.

After three-and-a-half years, the family had to move once more because the combined earnings of Gladys, who worked as a nurse's aide at the nearby St Joseph Hospital, and Vernon, who packed tins of paint into boxes at the United Paint Company, exceeded the maximum $3000 a year allowed to those living on the housing project.

They were evicted in early 1953, the year Eisenhower was sworn into the White House and Marilyn Monroe was elected America's favourite pin-up. The middle-class certainties of the Ike era, which included the flourishing new suburbs of Memphis, did not extend to the Presleys. Gladys could only rave about the first pink Cadillac she had ever seen while walking home from the hospital. 'I'll buy you one of those one day,' her son promised, and he meant it.

The Presleys' next abode was a dilapidated, two-room apartment at 398 Cypress Street in the centre of town. But before Elvis graduated from Humes High later that year, they had found a slightly nicer, though still down-at-heel, place at 462 Alabama Avenue, just across the street from Lauderdale Courts.

'When I met Elvis, he was living on Alabama Avenue in a rough apartment-type house,' the Memphis-born singer/guitarist Johnny Burnette told me in 1962, two years before his death. 'You looked in the front door and saw straight out through the back. I must have seen it a million times, but he wouldn't ever let me go inside. No, sir, me and Elvis were pretty good friends, but he never let me go inside that house – only look.

'He used to wear the wildest clothes. He always seemed to be wearing those purple pants with black stripes down the side, white buck shoes and a white sports jacket. He'd always have his shirt collar turned up and wear his hair real long.

'There was never anything false about him. He didn't talk much, but he knew what he was capable of doing. Wherever he went, he'd have his guitar slung across his back – never did he bother with a case like the rest of us boys. He used to go down to the fire station and sing to the boys there – they were the only ones round Memphis who seemed to have a lot of listening time.

'Every now and then he'd go into one of the cafes or bars and slouch across a chair. He never sat up straight, he'd just sort of lie there with that mean look on his face. Then some folk would say, "Let's hear you sing, boy," and old El would stroll up to the most convenient spot, looking at the ground all the time. Then all of a sudden he'd slide that guitar round to his front and he'd near raise the roof with that real rockin' sound of his.'

Some of the dives Elvis frequented were on Beale Street, which had smartened itself up since its notorious heyday. Encouraged by bribes, Boss Crump had turned a blind eye to its iniquities for thirty years until he shut it down overnight in 1940 as a wartime measure.

After the war, Memphis became a recording centre for musicians heading for Chicago or Nashville, and Beale Street was back in business as the natural habitat of all species of the blues. By this time, Elvis was sure that music was the key to his salvation.

He had always had part-time jobs to bring in extra money, including employment as an usher at Loew's State Theatre, but there was rarely ever enough. After graduating, he drove a truck for Crown Electric for $35 a week, but his prospects were no better than those of any other young man with sideburns, an engaging smile and a headful of dreams. There had to be another way.

'When I was 18, I saw my dad sitting on the edge of the bed with his head in his hands,' Elvis recalled. 'Things were going so bad he couldn't see his way out. I prayed for a miracle and my prayer was answered.'

Even at 18 as Elvis flashed his new pink and black threads from Lansky Brothers, he was really going for it on Beale. Once he got behind a guitar, sex was his talisman and he wore it like a mantle in the dives where he played with the bluesmen. 'Sex is part of nature,' Marilyn Monroe had sighed. 'I go along with nature.' Elvis seemed to concur. He might have been unsure of his natural, God-given talent, but he knew where to go to express it, and, like Marilyn, he was a fast learner.

The sexual vibes came through when Elvis sang. He experimented with his range from deep primitive to high pitched falsetto, scaling octaves like an opera singer. The physical exertion of moving while he played and sang produced the breathy quality that would make him famous.

The Mississippi Delta, so the locals say, begins in the baroque lobby of the Peabody Hotel on Union Avenue. A dozen blocks away at No. 706, Sam Phillips opened the Memphis Recording Service in January 1950 in time to greet the new decade. Half of the population of Memphis was black, and three of his early recording artists were B. B. King, Howlin' Wolf and Little Junior Parker.

Sun Records, Sam's own label, was only two years old when he recorded Elvis for the first time in July 1954 with two country musicians, Scotty Moore on guitar and Bill Black on bass. They cut four songs, but it was 'That's All Right (Mama)', the Arthur 'Big Boy' Crudup number enhanced by a haunting slapback echo, that launched Elvis on his singing career. Crudup was black, and Elvis, for one, had no illusions about the origins of his music. 'The coloured folk been singin' and playin' just the way I'm doin' now for more years than I know,' he said in 1957. 'Nobody paid it no mind till I goosed it up.'

When Elvis laid down the up-tempo ballad 'Blue Moon of Kentucky' as the flip side of 'That's All Right', Sam Phillips let him know that he had finally discovered his unique talent. 'Fine, *fine*, man, hell, that's different!' enthused the studio boss. 'That's a pop song now, little guy. That's good.

'Elvis was to tell me some years later that those were the sweetest words he had ever heard.

The money started coming in. His first royalty cheque from Sam Phillips amounted to $200, and he spent it on a dress and some shoes for Gladys. Her feet were too swollen from years of neglect to wear the fashionable footwear, so she kept them in a plastic bag under her bed.

Elvis was determined to give his parents everything money could buy: a new four-room rented home, made of brick, on Lamar Avenue, a better car and more food than they could eat. Old-time religion and the new-fangled music, which DJ Alan Freed had renamed 'rock 'n' roll', brought earthly rewards that the Presleys had previously only studied in catalogues or shop windows. Material things that could take away the misery assumed a religious significance in Elvis's mind.

In mid-1955, he moved the family to a three-storey house at 1414 Getwell Street with a lawn in the front and back. Luxuries that were to follow, such as air-conditioning and a swimming pool, were gifts from God and they were within reach. Keep praying and He might give your mother a pink Cad.

When Elvis started to find work out of town as a singer, Gladys fretted so much that he might come to harm driving down the dark country roads that she turned to alcohol to calm her fears. Vernon took her to bars, where she drank beer and tried to socialize, but the fear always came back in the morning. It remained until Elvis walked safely in through the front door.

'She wasn't used to the music or entertainment business and she was worried about her boy,' said Todd Morgan, the resident Elvisologist at Graceland. 'It was bewildering, traumatic and overwhelming for her. I'm sure that this was happening so fast it was frightening.'

Gladys put on a great deal of weight and deep, dark circles formed around her panda-like eyes. Her doctor prescribed diet pills and sleeping medication.

'Gladys had a tremendous influence in turning Elvis into a very polite and courteous southern gentleman, but she was very concerned that something might happen to him,' said the Memphis disc jockey George Klein, who had met Elvis in high school. 'She said to me, "George, Elvis has this habit of sleepwalking. If it happens, you just talk to him softly. You say, "Come back to bed, Elvis, everything is going to be OK." And if he talks in his sleep, you answer him and carry on a conversation with him." It happened a couple of times when we were on the road in the early Fifties. I did exactly as she had said, and it worked. He went back to bed.

'The other thing Gladys said was, "When you get in the hotel, Elvis has this tendency to leave his money in his pockets, maybe two or three hundred dollars. When you send his clothes down to the cleaners, be sure you go through his pockets and get the money out." I thought that was kinda cute.'

Everything changed for Elvis when he met the flamboyant Colonel Tom Parker, a virtual Barnum & Bailey rolled into one. In a flash of inspiration, the Colonel decided that he had been born for the sole purpose of running Elvis's career. To be on the safe side, he took chance out of the equation. From the beginning, the Colonel marketed his eager young charge in the manner of a carnival attraction.

'You stay talented and sexy and I'll make us both rich as rajahs,' he promised. He seemed to see Elvis as an exponent of writhing male burlesque set to strangled guitars and thumping bass, more a curiosity than a musician. But what his methods might have lacked in finesse, they made up for in results.

'I met Elvis backstage and became his manager in the fall of 1955,' said the Colonel, whose previous musical experience had been with the country singers Eddy Arnold and Hank Snow. 'In those days, he was on the *Louisiana Hayride*. He was being booked into small towns where he went in and got $200 a time, and that went on for a while until I got him on to television and it all blew up nationwide.'

Actually, the Colonel's first master stroke had been to buy out Elvis's Sun contract and sell the recording rights to RCA Victor for $25,000 and the music publishing rights to Hill & Range for $15,000. With a $5000 royalty settlement from Sam Phillips in his back pocket, Elvis got to work with producer Steve Sholes at the RCA studio in Nashville, a converted church, where he warmed up by singing hymns. Then he went out and spent the money on a pink Cadillac for his mother, even though she couldn't drive.

Two days after his twenty-first birthday, he recorded 'Heartbreak Hotel' with Scotty and Bill plus Chet Atkins on rhythm guitar, D. J. Fontana on drums and Floyd Cramer on piano. Sholes laid on so much echo that the song sounded as though it had been recorded in a catacomb.

Elvis made his first television appearance on *Stage Show,* the TV showcase of the ailing jazz brothers Tommy and Jimmy Dorsey, on 28 January 1956. His first number was a medley of 'Shake, Rattle and Roll' and 'Flip, Flop and Fly'. He gave the two Big Joe Turner million-sellers such a wallop that it seemed as if the truck driver from Crown Electric had been plugged into the main circuit. For sheer audacity, that first performance was not so much a debut for Elvis as an initiation of the incredulous TV millions into what was to come. His face was podgy, his brownish-blond hair was dishevelled and his teeth, later capped, were in need of attention, but the screaming had started the moment he began to shake his left leg. Elvis was invited back five more times, although it wasn't until the third show that he let rip with 'Heartbreak Hotel'.

The reaction was phenomenal. 'Heartbreak Hotel' became his first No. 1 hit and went on to become the biggest-selling single of the year. Other TV moguls could no longer ignore the pulling power of 'Elvis the Pelvis', a title that Elvis hated from the moment he heard it. In March, he left New York and drove to Los Angeles to play the Coliseum and then went down to San Diego in early April to appear on the *Milton Berle Show,* which was being transmitted from the aircraft carrier *Hancock.* He also played two concerts at the San Diego Arena, where 'the effect on bobbysoxers was like that of Frank Sinatra's old black magic days,' according to the *Memphis Press-Scimitar* 'The arena manager had to call out police and a platoon of Shore Patrol to handle the mob which pursued Elvis to a barricaded dressing room.'

In the audience on one of those two nights was a young girl destined to become the sex symbol of another decade: Raquel Welch. She has never forgotten the impact that seeing Elvis perform 'Heartbreak Hotel' made on her.

'The first time I saw Elvis was at a show he gave in San Diego when I was only about 14 and still a virgin,' she told me. 'The only thing I knew about sex was girl talk, but when I saw this raw sensual package called Elvis up there on stage, I felt something stir within me, and I said, "My God, this is it! This must be what sex is all about." He was *that* exciting.'

On his second outing for Berle, Elvis gave a performance of 'Hound Dog' that caused a national scandal. Shoulders hunched in a drape jacket, he seemed to pivot on tiptoe and hang there, gyrating, as though suspended at the end of invisible wires. It was his sexiness on this show that damned him to everlasting fame.

For his next TV appearance, Steve Allen tried to calm things down by dressing Elvis in white tie and tails and getting him to sing 'Hound Dog' to a woeful basset called Sherlock. Elvis hated the gimmick, later calling it 'the most ridiculous performance of my entire career', but even standing still, he pushed the show's ratings past those of Allen's arch rival, Ed Sullivan. The latter had stated publicly that he would never book Elvis on the grounds that his act was obscene. Ratings, however, spoke louder than morality, and Sullivan signed him for three shows.

The only setback that Elvis suffered in his first year of living famously was an ill-advised booking that the Colonel had made for him to play the New Frontier Hotel in Las Vegas. 'He was the opening act for a

Mickey Mouse band called Freddie Martin in the Venus Room,' Liberace's manager Seymour Heller told me. 'He was bombing because the older customers didn't know him and the kids couldn't get in because they were under 21. Lee [Liberace] had heard him on the radio a lot and he said to me, "This kid Elvis Presley is great. I'd like to meet him." We went over to the Frontier that afternoon and I introduced them. An agency photographer was called in to snap some pictures, and Lee said to Elvis, "Let's swap jackets, you play piano and I'll play guitar." That picture went around the world three times. Lee was gentle, generous and goodhearted, but he was also clever. He never let anyone go without an autograph unless he was running for a plane.'

However, Liberace's generosity failed to rescue Elvis in Las Vegas. He was dropped down the billing and the Colonel finally tore up the contract so that Elvis could leave the desert and head for greener pastures. Seymour Heller recalls: 'I met Elvis many times after that and he'd always say, "Nice to see you, Mr Heller." I'd tell him to call me Seymour, and he'd say, "Sure thing, Mr Heller, OK, Mr Heller." He was polite, sometimes over-polite, but he was one of the nicest gentlemen I ever met.'

Elvis dyed his hair black, and *Variety* gave him the title 'King of Rock 'n' Roll', to which he replied: 'There is only one King and that is Jesus.' Even in second place, Elvis had no complaints about his sudden popularity. Hal Wallis, the film producer of *Casablanca* fame, had signed him to a seven-year deal with Paramount Pictures, saying that, in his screen test, Elvis had reminded him of a young Errol Flynn.

However, the year's hectic schedule of recording, touring and making his first film, *Love Me Tender*, with Debra Paget and Richard Egan, had made Elvis ill. He had been taking Benzedrine to keep him going, and sleep became more of a problem than sleepwalking. 'I'm six feet tall and weigh 195 pounds – I've gained about twenty pounds in the last year,' he said at the time. 'I can't understand that because my appetite isn't as good as it used to be. I can't seem to relax ever and I have a terrible time falling to sleep. At the most, I usually get two or three hours of broken sleep.' Sleeping pills were prescribed to knock him out. The Marilyn Monroe/Judy Garland syndrome had begun.

When John Lennon was just climbing out of short pants, Elvis knew that the miracle he had prayed for was coming true. He said: 'My daddy and I were laughing about it the other day. He looked at me and said, "What happened, El? The last thing I can remember is I was working in a can factory and you were driving a truck." It just caught us up.'

Elvis had recorded 'Hound Dog', his first Jerry Leiber and Mike Stoller rocker, during a session at the RCA studio at 155 East 24th Street in New York City. He put down thirty takes and was pleading to do it one more time when the engineers turned out the lights and went home. Steve Sholes was satisfied that he had a massive hit in the can, but Elvis the perfectionist still wanted to make it better.

'My first meeting with Elvis was in summer 1956 when he came to the office of Hill & Range in New York with Colonel Parker,' said Freddie Bienstock, the manager of Elvis's music publishing company. 'It was at the time he was recording "Hound Dog" and doing the *Steve Allen Show*. He was staying at the Warwick Hotel and I chauffeured him around

Manhattan. I also remember walking with him down the street and he had a kind of white sports coat and there were lipstick marks on it from girls who had obviously tried to kiss him.

'I got to know him better when I went down to Memphis just before Christmas when he was planning his second picture, *Loving You*. He picked me up from the airport with some of his gang and brought me to the house in Audubon Drive.'

Elvis had paid $40,000 for the new green ranch-style house with a tiled grey roof and black shutters at 1034 Audubon Drive. There were two Cadillacs (one pink) in the carport. This was the Presleys' first Christmas in a home they could truly call their own, and they were in a mood to celebrate. Elvis and Gladys had bought the biggest tree they could fit into the living-room.

'The first thing I remember is that Elvis asked me to sit down in a particular chair,' said Freddie Bienstock. 'Unbeknownst to me, he pulled a switch and the chair started to vibrate wildly. The sensation was such that I was scared, but he said, "It's very relaxing, Freddie, I'm very proud of this chair. I want you to enjoy it."

'That night Hal Kanter, who was directing *Loving You* for Paramount, came to the house for dinner,' Freddie related. 'Elvis had a maid at the time called Petunia who was very nervous about cooking for a Hollywood director. The food was southern deep fried, but there was nothing to drink on the table, not even water. Kanter asked Elvis politely if he could have some water. Elvis was embarrassed and screamed, "Petunia! Water!" The maid was so nervous she brought in a pitcher of water with ice but no glasses.

'So Kanter kept looking at this and didn't know what he should do. When Elvis realized what the problem was, he screamed, "Petunia, you forgot the glasses!" Kanter said, "It's all right – a straw will do."'

Elvis was due to appear on the *Louisiana Hayride* at Shreveport. Hal Kanter was anxious to accompany him on the trip, to get to know him better and to observe him in action on stage.

'Elvis wanted me to come along, too,' said Bienstock. 'He said to me, "Listen, Freddie, you've got to come because I'm not getting on with this Kanter too well. You heard the remark about the f***ing straw. This guy is supposed to be my director, but he turns out to be a comedian!"'

Kanter was a southern boy himself, from Savannah, Georgia. Elvis fascinated him so much that he included many of the details of the singer's rise to fame in the screenplay of *Loving You*, in which Elvis played a rising rock star called Deke Rivers. Shrewdly, Kanter described Elvis as 'the young man with the ancient eyes and the mouth of a child', an apt early description of the Elvis enigma.

Lizabeth Scott, who co-starred with Elvis in *Loving You*, was also mesmerized by his blue eyes. After describing him as 'the most remarkable young man I had ever, ever encountered', she said: 'He was very young and very adolescent, but he had the most mature eyes. I shall never forget his eyes, so beautiful, so exquisite. And he was so talented. I had great fun making that film.

'Elvis had an entourage of young men around him and he was untouchable. He was one of the most polite young men I have ever met in my life. "Ma'am" this and "Ma'am" that, "Yes, sir", "No, sir" and whatnot. For what he was doing, he was absolutely excellent. He came in prepared, he had a photographic memory, he was on time, he was a gentleman to the very core of him. He was a simple man, a simple little boy. But I feel that he could have been so much more than he was because he had the potential.'

His much hyped first film, *Love Me Tender* ('Mr Rock 'n' Roll in the story he was born to play'), had its world premiere at the Paramount Theatre on Broadway on 16 November 1956. It shared the box-office honours for the year with *Giant*, the dynastic Texan epic starring James Dean, Elizabeth Taylor and Rock Hudson. The critics panned Elvis as an actor, but he was as big as those three Hollywood stars put together.

George Klein, the Memphis DJ, was witness to the impact that Elvis and the Colonel made on the movie capital. As he was planning a career in television himself, George was fascinated to watch the Colonel in action, but he was also baffled.

'Why do you need the William Morris Agency when you're his manager – and why give them another 10 per cent?' he asked the Colonel one night.

'George, I know everything about recording contracts and personal appearances, but I know nothing about movie contracts,' the Colonel answered. 'The sharpest guys in the world are in Hollywood and they will eat you up and spit you out. They know how to manipulate things.

Abe Lastfogel is president of the William Morris Agency and he handles the biggest stars in the industry. If Mr Lastfogel and I both walk into a producer's office, there is no way in the world they are going to cheat us. Mr Lastfogel knows how to handle the movie people and I know how to handle Elvis.'

'It ended up with Elvis getting a $1 million advance and 50 per cent of the picture,' says Klein. 'You know, Elvis was making more money at that time than Brando and Taylor.'

Elvis had declared at the outset: 'New York and Hollywood aren't going to change me none.' But in the same way that 'Heartbreak Hotel' had altered John Lennon and Raquel Welch, there was a fair chance that Elvis just might change Hollywood.

On Merseyside, John Lennon licked back his hair and practised his guitar on the front porch. In his head, he was composing the first stanza of 'The Ballad of John and Elvis'. It was destined to run and run.

3

ELVIS GOES TO THE MOVIES

It's now or never

BY HALLOWEEN 1957, Elvis had achieved the impossible and he knew it. The shimmering iridescence that was the King of Rock 'n' Roll glowed in every corner of the globe. Even in silhouette, his image was unmissable. At 22, he was already the star of two successful movies, *Love Me Tender* and *Loving You*, while *Jailhouse Rock* had just been given its world premiere in Memphis.

That night, Paul McCartney and John Lennon made music together for the first time. John had met Paul at the Woolton village fete on 6 July. 'There's a photo of me with a checked shirt on, holding a little acoustic guitar and I am singing "Be- Bop-a-Lula",' John recalled. 'The day I met Paul I was singing that song for the first time on stage.' The cocky leader of a high school skiffle band called the Quarry Men, John had consumed several pints of the local beer and was quite tipsy. 'He kept putting his arm around my shoulders,' said Paul. 'His breath smelled, but I showed him a few chords he didn't know. I left feeling I'd created an impression.' He was right. John had been greatly impressed by Paul's white sports coat, black drainpipe trousers and Tony Curtis haircut. 'He looked like Elvis,' said John. 'I dug him.'

He invited Paul to join the Quarry Men for a performance at the New Clubmoor Hall in Liverpool. Anxious to show what he could do, Paul played lead guitar, but it was to be for the first and last time. As he didn't know how to restring a guitar for a left-handed player, he played the instrument backwards, making a hash of his solo on 'Guitar Boogie'.

'The Quarry Men started at the time of the skiffle boom, and the first big influence on the group was Lonnie Donegan,' said Bill Harry, the founder of Mersey Beat, a newspaper that avidly charted the Beatles' rise. 'But John had got into Elvis at Quarry Bank High School and he began singing Elvis Presley numbers in the act.'

The group, minus Paul, had already made its debut at the Cavern, where they were upbraided for doing 'Hound Dog' and 'Blue Suede Shoes'. 'You weren't allowed to play rock 'n' roll – it was jazz or skiffle,' said Bill Harry. 'When John sang an Elvis number, the manager sent him a note saying, "No bloody rock!" But John was really into the Elvis thing and he wouldn't give it up. He loved Elvis.'

Although the Beatles later appeared to come from nowhere, they did, in fact, serve a very tough apprenticeship. They played gigs wherever they could find them, including the Jacaranda, a humble coffee bar that charged fourpence for buttered toast and another penny for jam. They played from the back of a flatbed truck on one occasion, fought with their rivals and often dodged hostile fans. Their experiences in the North of England were not unlike

Elvis's own baptism of fire in the Deep South, where he hadn't been too proud to play from the back of a flatbed truck either.

For Elvis, fame had provoked notoriety and jealousy even in his home town. When he returned to Memphis to see Gladys and Vernon after finishing *Loving You,* he was confronted with danger the moment he stepped out into the real world.

'Elvis and I were dragging Main Street, just cruising around looking for some girls our own age to come to a party at Audubon Drive,' recalls George Klein. 'We found some who recognized him, so Elvis pulled up. I went to tell the girls we were having a party and to follow us. I got back to Elvis and there were ten Marines surrounding him. Without realizing it, we had pulled up right in front of a recreation hall for the military. They'd seen Elvis in the car and had come out. They were angry about something and I said to this great big Marine, "What's going on?" Lil ole me, five feet eight inches tall. "Presley has been going out with my wife," he said, "and I'm gonna beat him up."

'I said, "Man, you must be crazy – Elvis just got back in town from making a movie two days ago." They said, "Is that right? "Oh, man, we're going to find out what a movie star is made of!" They had us backed up against the car like a scene from a gangster movie. Elvis reached in his coat and took out this gun and put it right up between the guy's eyes and said, "Now what did you say there?" The guy put his hands up and all the uniforms started backing away, and Elvis said, "Now back up and get out of the way."

'And they started saying, "Mr Presley, don't shoot! Don't shoot! We were just kidding around. Don't shoot!" We eased into the car, Elvis keeping the gun on the Marines, and we drove off. I said, "God, Elvis, where did you get that gun?" He laughed and said: "It's not real – it's a Hollywood prop gun." He had brought it home as a souvenir. It only shot blanks, but it got us away from there.'

The incident shows that Elvis had become a target for anyone with a grudge, and before long he was toting real guns for his own protection. Red West, an old school friend who had once saved him from a beating because of his long hair, became his bodyguard.

The chance for Elvis to sing live again came a few weeks later when the Colonel organized a concert tour starting in Chicago and working its way through St Louis, Philadelphia and Buffalo to Toronto, Montreal and Ottawa. Squeezed in between the end of filming *Loving You* in March and the start of *Jailhouse Rock* in May, the tour proved so successful that Elvis was back on the road in late August, covering the Pacific North-west centres of Spokane, Tacoma, Seattle and Portland. In Vancouver, he flapped his wings so freely that he was accused of inciting a full-scale rock 'n' roll riot among fans. Elvis revelled in it.

But there was serious trouble waiting in Los Angeles, where Elvis ached to give the best show of his life at the Pan-Pacific Auditorium in the heart of Hollywood. More by accident than design, the first performance ended in a bizarre climax, which even Elvis found hard to explain after the damage had been done.

Bathed in white light and clad in a tuxedo woven of golden thread, its lapels and cuffs sparkling with rhinestones ($10,000 from Nudie's of Hollywood), Elvis was at the height of his powers. Even before he opened that first night, 28 October, with 'Heartbreak Hotel', a mounting crescendo of ear-splitting squeals told him he had died and gone to teenage heaven. The vast majority of the audience were impressionable girls of junior high school age: white, affluent and sexually alive. Some were as old as 15, others as young as 10.

Decked out from top to toe in Elvis fashions and waving his publicity picture over their heads like sails in a high wind, they let him know that they were here for some action. He was only too happy to oblige. This was the Teddy Bear Army, its battle colours of Hound Dog Orange, Heartbreak Pink, Love Ya Fuchsia and Cruel Red shining brightly on moist young lips. His own likeness smiled boldly back at him from a multitude of scarves, dresses, dungarees, blouses, sneakers and charm bracelets. He knew he was among the faithful.

Instantly, he was Presley the Performer, a master illusionist who created magical shapes with his flowing torso and liquid limbs. These combined with nerve-tingling sound bites from those curling, bee-stung lips to summon up the libido even in those too young to know they had one. The black pompadour slicked back into the classic ducktail, the kiss curl hanging over the high, noble forehead and the long sideburns now stamped him as arrogant, delinquent and dangerous. Cosmetic artistry had firmed up the classical features and eliminated even the merest hint of any blemish. Some said that he had had a nose job and that skin had been grafted from his backside to cover up the acne scars. Even if such darkly handsome good looks, surrounding a pair of improbable pale blue eyes, owed not a little to trickery, the girls saw only what they wanted: the epitome of white male sexuality.

As he cast his spell, the dynamic that came into play made anything, anything at all, seem possible for a few fleeting moments: the most improbable sexual fantasy might just become reality for the truly devout believer. And these were truly devout believers.

As the vision Elvis created became momentarily real, yet more squeals, tearful cries and ecstatic screams ripped the night air, only to rise even higher the instant the pivotal, pump-action pelvis stopped moving. Once the radioactive particles ceased to vibrate, the illusion faded and the sudden withdrawal was unendurable. All too aware of what he had done, Elvis looked curiously contrite. Standing motionless beneath the spotlights, he was human again and noticeably vulnerable. But still they begged for more and, once again, he obliged.

Maurice Kinn reported that night in the *New Musical Express:*

> 'Throughout the fifty minutes of Presley's shattering antics, the entire auditorium was a seething, contorting mass of wriggling humanity, reacting with shrill screams and convulsive jerks to every breath of the Presley voice, every twitch of the Presley hips. This was not just audience reaction, but sheer mass hypnotism. Fans fainted in dozens, falling like ninepins in the aisles and across the rows of seats. He deliberately sets out with an almost sadistic intent to arouse the fans to fever pitch. They

say that Elvis is the only singer who wears out his trousers from the inside – and now I know just what they mean.'

In a final burst of high spirits, Elvis concluded the show by rolling over and over on the stage with his arms and legs wrapped around a stuffed version of Nipper, the dog normally seen cocking an attentive ear to a wind-up phonograph on the RCA Victor logo. Elvis had ended each performance on the tour by serenading the mascot with a fast and furious rendition of 'Hound Dog'. In Los Angeles, when he suddenly seized Nipper in this undignified and unscripted embrace, the foreplay had been so great that some outraged members of the press thought he was simulating sex with it. Exciting young girls to orgasm was bad enough, but having sexual intercourse with a dog was going too far. The final taboo had been broken.

The LA deputy police chief ordered the Vice Squad to instruct Elvis to eliminate any 'sexy overtones' from his next performance. To underscore the caution, the Colonel was also warned that obscenity charges would be brought against his star if the Nipper act were repeated at the second concert.

Three 16mm movie cameras were hastily dispatched to the Pan-Pacific Auditorium to shoot Elvis from different angles. In the event of a further infringement, the film would be produced in court as evidence.

Bunkered down in the Presidential Suite of the Beverly Wilshire Hotel, Elvis stuck to his usual rejoinder: 'They all think I'm a sex maniac, but I come from a respectable family and I wouldn't do anything to embarrass them. I just act natural.' He rang his mother to reassure her that everything was all right. Gladys worried just the same.

So it was that Dixie's prodigal son came before the West Coast philistines on the most critical night of his life. The powerful overhead lights had already dimmed when an armed escort directed two ticket holders, Ricky (later Rick) Nelson and his girlfriend Marianne Gaba, to their front-row seats. For a few moments, the excited hubbub subsided into a hush. Everyone waited tensely for the King to make his most eagerly awaited appearance.

Slipping unseen into their seats alongside Ricky and Marianne were some of the biggest box-office names on the Hollywood scene: Russ Tamblyn, Carol Channing, Sammy Davis Jr, Nick Adams, Tony Franciosa, Rita Moreno, Vince Edwards and Tommy Sands. Elvis was the hottest ticket in Tinseltown. Edgy officers of the LAPD had insisted that they arrive after lights out to prevent an outbreak of hysteria even before the spotlight picked out Elvis's gold-laméd figure on the blue velour-draped stage.

'I remember we all had to come in late because the crowd was so excited,' recalls Marianne, then a beauty queen of 17. 'It was dark inside and we had police to get us in so everyone would stay quiet.'

No Presley concert had ever been staged in front of such a dedicated turnout of his peers or in such a high-voltage atmosphere of official disdain. He came on with the eyes and ears of the world upon him, with the Vice Squad waiting in the wings and the *crème de la crème* of Hollywood's young talent watching in rapt anticipation from their ringside seats. It was a big moment. Elvis stood briefly speechless as he caught sight of the famous faces. Some he knew well, like Nick Adams and Sammy Davis, but he had never met Ricky Nelson or the entrancing girl seated beside him. Ricky shifted uncomfortably when he realized Elvis was looking at them.

Addressing the crowd, Elvis said: 'I'm sorry this came up, but we're not gonna let it stop us from putting on the best show we can for you people. If they think it's obscene, that's their problem, not mine.'

Before going into his act, he winked at one of the spy cameras, inscribed a halo around his head with a circular motion of his hand and said: 'I'm gonna be an angel tonight.' Pandemonium.

Whatever the city fathers might have thought, the roar of endorsement from the crowd showed that, in their eyes at least, Elvis could do no wrong. After the show, a spokesman for the Vice Squad said that, as Elvis had 'reduced the orbit of his gyrations and gone through no bumps and grinds', he would not be charged with any offence.

'Elvis recognized Ricky in the audience and we were invited to a big party he was holding at the Beverly Wilshire,' Marianne told me years later, reliving that night.

Even by the epic standards of Los Angeles, the Wilshire was special. Host to European royalty and Hollywood celebrities, it had never seen anything quite like Elvis Presley. By the time he moved in, the brown Tuscan stone facade had already survived at least one major earthquake. However, the new rock-age hysteria that followed Elvis wherever he went sent tremors of a very different kind coursing through the tree-lined streets of Beverly Hills. As Ricky and Marianne were swept past the massed ranks of police and security guards, it seemed that the fever of the concert had invaded the hotel. They moved past the arches containing chic Parisian boutiques into the lobby, where they gazed at Corinthian columns that stretched up to glass mosaic skylights. Marianne was dazzled.

'The whole of the Memphis Mafia were there and a lot of the celebrities I had seen at the concert,' she recounted. 'I was only 17 at that time and very star-struck. As soon as we walked into his suite, Elvis spotted Ricky and came dashing over. He shook my hand politely and then grabbed Ricky in a bear hug and lifted him up.

'Ricky had just had a hit record of his own and become a huge idol, but he was completely in awe of Elvis. We both were.'

To Elvis, however, Ricky was an important figure not because of his budding rock career, but because he starred with his parents in the *Ozzie and Harriet Show*, one of his favourite TV series. Far from taking offence that Ricky had mimicked him in a recent episode, he was flattered that the Nelsons should regard him as important enough to include in their show. He kept pumping Ricky with questions about his family that Ricky had difficulty in answering. He was so nervous and excited that his throat had seized up and he could barely speak.

'As we left the party, I said to Ricky, "I'm never going to wash my right hand again," and Ricky said, "Nor me" and laughed,' said Marianne.

Elvis had started filming his fourth movie, *King Creole*, when news of the summons he had been dreading finally arrived at the Wilshire.

'Elvis was sitting down with all of his cronies at this big dining-room table in his suite,' said Freddie Bienstock. 'Colonel Parker came in with the unhappy news that Elvis had been drafted and he had to go in the Army. One of the boys jumped up. "What the hell is going to happen to us?" he said to the Colonel. "I gave Elvis the best years of my life." At that point, Elvis got very sore indeed. It was the only time I ever saw him really angry.'

Elvis returned to Graceland for Christmas and his call-up papers were delivered by hand on 20 December 1957. Uncle Sam had claimed his most famous recruit. Paramount managed to secure a sixty-day deferment to enable him to complete the movie.

'They were grabbing him off the set to get him in the Army,' said Carolyn Jones, who co-starred with Elvis. 'I had one of my bouts of flu on that picture. We went down to New Orleans and I caught a bug. When we came back to Paramount to finish the indoor scenes, I had a high fever and they were saying, "We don't care if you're dying, he's going into the Army." So I was doing love scenes with him, with a temperature of 104, saying into his ear, "Oh God, I hope you've had a shot of penicillin. You're never going to make it." And he was very nice and kind.'

Two things happened to Elvis while he was in the Army that were to shape the rest of his life: Gladys died soon after he went in, and he met Priscilla just before he came out. Gladys had taken to drinking vodka during Elvis's long absences in Hollywood, often accentuating the effect with amphetamine-based diet pills. The single trip she made to

California with Vernon, driving both ways because she was terrified of flying, only added to her anxiety. She had cirrhosis of the liver, developed hepatitis and died of a heart attack on 14 August 1958, while Elvis was completing his basic training at Fort Hood in Texas. He was still in bits when, as a private first class, he arrived at Bremerhaven with the 32nd Battalion of the US Third Armoured Division in the *General Randall* on 1 October.

At first, the Germans were sceptical about the arrival of the dangerous American they called 'Lardhead' or 'the Yowling Boy' on their soil, but he gradually won them over with his natural southern charm. 'Would you like to meet Brigitte Bardot?' a reporter asked him at his first press conference. 'Yes, I would,' Elvis grinned. 'But she's engaged,' the reporter shot back. Elvis saw the trap and explained: 'I meant I wanted to meet her as a performer.' According to the German press, he came across as 'likable', 'modest' and 'a well-mannered, intelligent young man'.

German teenagers besieged the base at Friedberg, and whenever his Spearhead platoon went on manoeuvres, Elvis had to slip out quietly to prevent fans blocking the road. 'The only way to avoid people is to post him out in some field under a tree at two o'clock in the morning,' said his sergeant. Elvis took Dexies [Dexadrine] to keep him awake on these lonely dawn patrols.

The last thing he was looking for was trouble. Grieving for his mother, he moved Vernon, grandmother Minnie Mae Presley, Red West and a couple of the Guys to a rented house at Goethestrasse 14 in Bad Nauheim to see him through his tour of duty. His respect for his father and grandmother and his devotion to the memory of his mother endeared him to many older Germans. He also befriended two GIs: little Charlie Hodge from Decatur, Alabama, and tough Joe Esposito from Chicago.

Elvis astounded the Germans by doing his share of dirty jobs, standing in line on pay-day to pick up his $135-a-month wages, showing respect for rank with eager 'Yes, sirs' by the dozen, while still managing to be popular with the other men. Off-duty, he zipped around in *Der Elviswagen,* a white BMW sports car, but instead of antagonizing the local constabulary, he drove so carefully that they asked him to lend his name to a road safety campaign. He was even spotted queuing up to donate blood to the German Red Cross.

However, Elvis came close to over-stepping the boundaries of acceptable behaviour when he dated Vera Tschechowa, a respected teenage actress. He spent one four-day leave with her at her home in Munich and attracted a *Blitzkrieg* of abuse from her fans. Once again, he was 'a cheap, uncouth, American gangster'. But Vera defended him loyally 'Elvis is very much misunderstood,' she said, posing on his arm. 'He is a sensitive, honest and good-hearted friend.'

However, Elvis took the hint and looked around for an American girl to share his spare time. Two months before he was due to leave for the States, a friend called Currie Grant brought to Elvis's home Priscilla Ann Beaulieu, the 14-yearold step-daughter of a newly arrived Air Force officer. It was a blind date that was to have momentous consequences. For his part, Elvis was much taken with this dark-haired young girl who seemed so at ease with him and his family. One of the first questions he asked her that first night was: 'Who are the kids listening to in the States?'

'Why, everyone is listening to you,' the ninth-grade student replied truthfully.

'What about Ricky Nelson?' Elvis wanted to know.

RCA had released several pre-recorded songs to keep the Elvis name alive during his Army service, but he was desperate to make up for lost time and the careers of Ricky Nelson and the new generation of rock singers were an important factor in planning his re-entry. Although Elvis thought that Priscilla was 'the most beautiful girl I have ever seen', he knew that she was too young for a serious relationship. Besides, he was about to return to making movies in Hollywood. Secretly, he wondered whether Ricky was still going steady with the gorgeous girl he had brought with him to the Wilshire. One thing that had not escaped his attention during his exile was the flowering of Marianne Gaba. Her looks had by now excited the attention of Hugh Hefner and his fellow connoisseurs at *Playboy*. The magazine had an eager following among US troops in Germany and Elvis read it like any other homesick GI.

'I was a Playmate centrefold in 1959 and I was chosen as Playmate of the Decade,' Marianne told me at her Beverly Hills home. 'But it was actually very, very mild – just a little tushy showing. It would be nothing now, but it was a big deal in those days before the sexual revolution. I went steady with Ricky for three years until 1960, and then Elvis came out of the Army and made *GI Blues*.'

Elvis returned in March 1960 to find that the United States had changed as much as he had. The decade began with Fidel Castro's revolution in Cuba and it would end with Jimi Hendrix's finale at Woodstock. Elvis wasted no time.

During a 24-hour recording session in Nashville, he recorded the No. 1 hit *'Are You Lonesome Tonight?'* and *'It's Now or Never'*, an adaptation of the Neapolitan love song *'O Sole Mio'* (which Colonel Parker claimed to me later was his suggestion). Then he flew to Miami to appear on Frank Sinatra's *Welcome Home Party for Elvis* in a six-minute guest appearance for which the Colonel demanded, and got, a record fee of $125,000. 'Elvis, I tell you something, it's great,' smarmed Frank, who had insisted that Elvis wear a look-a-like tuxedo on the show. 'I'm glad to see the Army hasn't changed you.' Sinatra had once called Elvis's music 'a rancid-smelling aphrodisiac', but that no longer applied. Elvis even sang one of Frank's old songs, *'Witchcraft'*, while Sinatra warbled along with *'Love Me Tender'*. Elvis smiled like good guys should and laughed all the way back to Hollywood.

The plot for *GI Blues* involved Elvis playing Tulsa MacLean, an American soldier stationed in Frankfurt, who tries to win a bet with his buddies that he can bed a long-legged cabaret singer called Lili. The fact that Juliet Prowse, who played Lili, was engaged to Sinatra didn't prevent Elvis from commenting: 'She has a body that would make a bishop stamp his foot through a stained glass window.' When Elvis tried his luck with Juliet, he was quietly but firmly told that Frank wouldn't like it. He backed off and switched his attentions to Marianne Gaba.

'I had the part of a German waitress in a frilly outfit,' she said. 'I had about twenty lines, most of which were cut. One evening, somebody came up to me and said, "Elvis would like to go out with you." So I said, "Oh, of course," and they said, "Can he have your number?" and I gave it to him.'

Marianne had just become engaged to Michael Starkman, a young stockbroker who worked for Prudential Securities. She told him: 'If Elvis asks me out, you will have to understand: I love you and we are going to get married, but back in high school I remember watching him on TV and I have to go out with him.'

'Well, you have to do what you have to do, right?' stammered Mike, swallowing his fear. This was the stuff of which bad Hollywood movies and tabloid headlines were made: ELVIS PRESLEY STOLE MY GIRL.

'We'd only been engaged for a week and I was very jealous and upset,' recalls Mike, who became senior vice president at Prudential. 'I threatened to call off the engagement, but Marianne said to me, "If I don't go, I'll resent it forever." So she went.'

'Elvis did call and they sent over a gold, bullet-proof limousine to my little apartment right at the back of Saks, three blocks from the Beverly Wilshire,' said Marianne. 'My roommate gasped, "Oh, my God, look at that big gold thing – it's as long as the block!" The windows were dark so I didn't know if Elvis was in there or not, but it turned out that he wasn't. When I asked where we were going, the driver said, "To the Beverly Wilshire." I thought, "Oh aye, aye, he thinks I'm going to jump into bed with him."

'There were so many screaming people outside the Wilshire that I had to go in through the back entrance. Elvis had two floors, the 8th and the 9th, and there were people everywhere, maybe twenty men and a few girls running around. Then something happened which told me what type of person Elvis really was.

'They were all ordering food from room service because it was too big a hassle to go out. Everybody was ordering escargots and Chateaubriand, all these fancy, expensive things, and they asked Elvis what he wanted, and he said, "Peanut butter, jelly and mashed banana on white bread." And I thought to myself, "Oh my God, he is just a homespun, sweet young man." He didn't need all this stuff; he wasn't trying to impress anybody. After a while, he told everybody to leave, and there I was in the room with Elvis alone.

'He brought out his guitar and he started playing and my heart was pounding. He was wearing a pretty shiny silk shirt and I was in skin-tight toreador pants. We sat and we necked for a long time. Oh, gosh, yes, he was adorable and a fabulous kisser. It was before birth-control pills and I was certainly afraid that, if I went to bed with someone, I would end up embarrassing my mom and dad who were working back home in Chicago to support me to be out here. But he never even suggested it.'

Mike spent the most nerve-wracking evening of his life with his brother, the artist Shel Starkman. 'I was with Mike and it was serious stuff,' said Shel. 'This was an historical moment. His fiancée was out with Elvis Presley, the sexiest guy in the world. Mike was devastated. He was almost in tears.'

Unaware of this drama, Elvis carried on as though everything was under control. Around midnight, he was ready for some action.

'He had another car come and we were driven to Cyrano's near the Playboy Club on Sunset,' said Marianne. 'I remember driving in the limousine and there were girls looking at him and it was so funny to watch the reaction when he pulled the tinted windows down. People would just look at him and go absolutely crazy. They'd start screaming and try to follow. It was like he was toying with them. He would laugh and roll the window up, then he'd want the same reaction and he'd roll it down again. He'd wait two seconds until someone drove up, see him and go absolutely crazy.

'They must have called Cyrano's to tell them that he was coming because, although everything was taken, they had put a table for us right next to the stage. I can't even remember who was playing. We left before the show finished and he dropped me off at my home.

'Michael rang as soon as I got back in, about 2.00 am, and my roommate said he had been calling every hour on the hour. He made me promise that, if Elvis asked me out again, I wouldn't go. So I told Elvis that I had a boyfriend and couldn't date him again.

About two months later, Michael and I were staying at the Desert Inn in Las Vegas, about to get married at the Little Church of the West. Michael ran into Colonel Parker and told him that we were getting married. The Colonel must have told Elvis because a big hound dog, bigger than life-size, turned up in our room. A note around its neck read: "To Marianne, with love from Elvis and The Colonel."

I kept this huge thing in my bedroom for the first year of my marriage and then my husband said, "Either that goes or I do." So it went.'

Hal Wallis and the studio were delighted with the success of *GI Blues* because it extended the base of Elvis's appeal. 'I think possibly some of his fans might have outgrown him, but there were others to take their place,' he said. But like many early Elvis purists, John Lennon was dismayed: he hadn't outgrown Elvis, Elvis had betrayed him. 'He was disappointed in the way Elvis had changed,' said Bill Harry. 'John said he was saddened that Elvis had turned into just a middle-of-the-road singer.'

In truth, the change had gone much deeper than Elvis's singing style. When he first returned to Memphis, he was asked: 'Do you have any advice for boys of your age who are going to put in a certain amount of duty in the services?' Elvis replied wisely: 'Well, the only thing I can say is to play it straight and do your best because you can't fight 'em. They never lost yet.' He strongly advised against 'trying to be an individual or trying to be different'.

King Creole had marked the last rendition of the rock-age rebel, and *GI Blues* confirmed in John's eyes that Elvis's capitulation to the military amounted to total surrender. It was the equivalent of watching your greatest ally go over to the other side. But, by now, John had plans for his own career, big plans that would take him on a ten-year roller-coaster ride to the top and down again. 'I came out of the sticks to take over the world,' he boasted.

When Elvis flew across the Pacific to make *Blue Hawaii* in 1961, he was delighted to find himself once again in the company of his old friend Patti Page.

'In Hawaii, we would sit around at the Coconut Palm Hotel after dinner,' Patti remembers. 'Elvis would bring out the guitar and we would all sing any song that he or I remembered from childhood, as well as gospel songs and hymns.

Elvis always seemed happiest when he was performing because he liked the acclaim, and I was happy for him, but I always noticed the sadness. I couldn't define it when he was young and we never had a deep conversation about it, but he would just say casually, "My Mama liked that song" or "My Mama loved that dish of food." I liked him very much from the start and I've always thought he had a talent that was never really brought out as far as it could have been.'

4

THE HOUSE THAT ROCK BUILT

Baby let's play house

JUST EIGHT years after 'That's All Right (Mama)' had teased and tantalized a new generation of white youth, fame had made Elvis a virtual recluse in his down-home mansion. Surrounded by an imitation southern countryside that was quickly yielding to fast-food fortresses, Elvis souvenir shacks and advancing columns of one-armed gasoline pumps, he rarely dared to venture out alone.

But a few days before Christmas in 1962, he did just that. Elvis turned the black Cadillac off Highway 51 and was instantly admitted through the 'Music Gates' at No. 3764. Sitting beside him was Priscilla Beaulieu, tired but elated after her flight from Germany. She took in a nativity scene that had been set up on the lawn for the Christmas festivities, and then, enthralled, she entered the big house called Graceland for the first time.

Of all man's temples dedicated to the love of a woman, none surpasses the Taj Mahal, but Elvis had done his best for Gladys with Graceland. In August 1957, he had paid $100,000 for the colonial-style mansion set among towering oaks in fourteen acres of rolling countryside at Whitehaven on the outskirts of Memphis. Just one mile north of the Mississippi border, it was about as close as you could get to Tupelo and still call yourself a Memphian.

Built in 1939 by Dr Thomas Moore and his wife Ruth, Graceland was named after a favourite aunt of theirs, Grace Toof. What the house lacked in historical significance, it made up for with presence, once Elvis had finished with it. The limestone facade and the four Corinthian columns of the massive portico were illuminated with pale blue spotlights, which gave Graceland an aura of gentrified grandeur, even if Gladys had kept chickens in the backyard.

Priscilla, just 17 years old, loved the look of the house and she was excited at the prospect of spending her first Christmas with Elvis. To help her sleep that first night, he gave her two large red 500-milligram Placidyl tablets. She woke up two days later. Now the King himself was fast asleep, the famous face in repose.

At 27, Elvis was at his most handsome. The dyed black hair, cut shorter for his movie roles, was slightly ruffled, but the classical features remained unmarked. The sideburns were neatly trimmed, the spit curl somehow less pretentious. Even the sneer had temporarily departed from the celebrated lower lip. Elvis slept, seemingly at peace.

He lay in a pair of midnight blue pyjamas on a double king size bed, the black silk sheets crumpled. The decor of his bedroom was Rockin' Fifties, the furniture black and white. Heavy blue drapes shut out the pale wintry light, but the black velvet ceiling sparkled with a constellation of tiny spotlights. At the foot of the bed, several TV sets were permanently turned on. The pictures danced and changed silently, the sound turned down. On the bedside table was a photograph of Gladys in a silver frame, and another of Jesus.

Outside, two stone lions guarded the portico of the mansion. Fairy lights twinkled in strands wound down the length of the white columns. The curved driveway swept through bare trees and the rolling lawn down to a group of fans clustered outside the Music Gates.

To the faithful millions that last Pre-Beatle Christmas, Elvis Presley was still the undisputed King of Rock 'n' Roll, and the fans accorded him the worship due to such show business majesty. No other rock star, white or black, had ever come close. The singer who rated second to him in record sales was the country singer/guitarist Johnny Cash and they weren't even competing in the same race. It seemed Elvis just couldn't lose.

At the start of December, the catchy Otis Blackwell/Winfield Scott offering 'Return to Sender' was riding high in the US charts, and Elvis had had three other *Billboard* successes during 1962: 'Can't Help Falling in Love', 'Good Luck Charm' and 'She's Not You'. RCA had abandoned the echo chamber and the rocking guitar in favour of a more mellow, romantic lyricism with only occasional flashes of the old boogified blues. The new style suited Elvis and, more important to the money men, it appealed to a wider audience. The Hillbilly Cat of Western Bop had transformed himself into a sophisticated balladeer who was fully aware of his vocal and erotic powers.

The movies released that year – *Follow That Dream, Kid Galahad* and *Girls! Girls! Girls!* – all followed the tried and tested exploitation formula that had already seen millions queuing at the box office. The studio system worked for Elvis whatever medium he was using, whether it was at RAC Victor, United Artists or Paramount.

In Hollywood terms, Elvis was bigger than Valentino had ever been, and if his acting skills failed to compare with those of his heroes Tony Curtis, James Dean and Marlon Brando, no Elvis movie ever made a loss at the box office. 'A Presley picture is the only sure thing in show business,' growled Hal Wallis. The money kept rolling in.

On Christmas Eve, snow fell at Graceland and Elvis's happiness seemed complete. He gave Priscilla a poodle puppy, which she named Honey. She gave Elvis a musical cigarette case that played 'Love Me Tender'. They ran outside to play in the snow like a couple of kids. Nothing was going to spoil their dream.

In London, early in 1962, a young record store executive called Brian Epstein was having no success whatever in attracting interest in an unknown group he had just signed under their latest stage name, The Beatles. The bosses of the big West End record companies scoffed when he told them in all seriousness: 'My boys are going to be bigger than Elvis.'

It sounded ridiculous. Even the top flight of British stars – Cliff Richard, Billy Fury and Frankie Vaughan among them – had failed to make more than a tiny impression on the US market. No one, least of all a British challenge, had ever got near Elvis.

The sages of Denmark Street, Britain's Tin Pan Alley, listened to a demo tape that the baby-faced manager had brought with him and politely showed him the door. But Brian Epstein had listened when John Lennon told him: 'Elvis is finished, but he doesn't know it yet.' He was convinced that he and John had spotted a gap in the market and that the Beatles were the group to fill it. Brian had kept trying. Finally in May he secured a recording contract with the EMI organization for the Beatles to record on its unglamorous Parlophone label. No one except Brian and the Beatles, certainly not the King himself, his young sweetheart nor the fans shivering at the Music Gates, knew that Elvis Presley's reign as the music industry's supremo was about to end in the most unlikely manner. The Mississippi was about to run into the Mersey.

Like the young pretenders to the King's throne, Epstein came from Liverpool, the great transatlantic port on the east side of the Mersey estuary. Historically, it had one vital connection with Memphis: Liverpool was linked to the Old South by iron chains. In the 18th and 19th centuries, fast-moving clippers had brought raw cotton from the southern states to the Lancashire mills, and then carried woven goods to Africa, where they picked up cargoes of slaves for the American plantations. The misery of human bondage was given voice in the blues. In the second half of the 20th century, Liverpool gave birth to its own bluesy sound: the Mersey beat, which created the Beatles and Beatlemania.

Bill Harry, founder of Mersey Beat newspaper, remembers: 'John Lennon and Stuart Sutcliffe were my closest friends at Liverpool College of Art. John used to dress like a Teddy boy and had a wild reputation. But he was a wonderful line drawer, who could give an amazing feeling of a fat bird or a shaggy dog with just a few lines. Stuart was a fantastic artist. 'The three of us used to go to the local college pub, Ye Cracke, and talk about the American cultural domination of Britain in films and music. We had hardly any money at all, just our student grants of £24 a year, and all we could afford were halves of bitter. We made a vow to make Liverpool famous: John with his music, Stuart with his painting and me with my writing. 'Next door to the art college was the Liverpool Institute, which Paul McCartney and George Harrison attended. They used to rehearse in the art college with the Quarry Men.' At John's insistence, Stuart had joined the band as bass guitarist, even though he was a second-rate musician. Paul and George objected strenuously, but being mere grammar schoolboys, they had to give in to their persuasive leader. Stuart wore dark glasses and played with his back to the audience to hide his lack of expertise.

'In 1958, they weren't regarded as one of the top Liverpool groups,' said Bill Harry. 'We were booking them for art college dances, although they didn't have a proper sound system. Stuart and I were on the Students' Union committee, and we voted for union funds to be used to buy them PA equipment. They didn't even have mike stands, so John's girlfriend Cynthia and the other girls used to sit opposite them on chairs holding brooms with the mikes attached to the handles. John used to make Cynthia dress up like Brigitte Bardot. He had a life-size poster of Bardot pasted to the ceiling of his bedroom.

'Pete Best, whose mother ran the Casbah Club where the Quarry Men sometimes played, joined as drummer in August 1960, shortly before the group made its first trip to Hamburg.' The Beatles were very much a last choice for Germany because Allan Williams, the owner of the Jacaranda

who recruited the acts, didn't think all that much of them. He had asked Gerry and the Pacemakers, but they wouldn't do it, and he asked Rory Storm and the Hurricanes, but they were booked into Butlin's. So in desperation he took the Beatles.

They played in Hamburg for four-and-a-half-months and came back tremendous. 'When they appeared in December 1960 at Litherland Town Hall, the posters announced "THE BEATLES DIRECT FROM HAMBURG". All the local girls thought they were a German group, and said to them, "For Germans, you don't 'arf speak English with a Liverpool accent.' "

In Hamburg, Stuart Sutcliffe had fallen deeply in love with Astrid Kirchherr, a blonde with the film star looks of a Mae Britt, who was a regular at their first venue, the Indra Club. Their romance signalled the end of Stuart's friendship with John, who was consumed with jealousy that anyone should come between him and his best friend. When the group returned to the club for a second engagement, John made his dislike plain whenever Astrid turned up, taunting her with oblique references to Hitler and the Third Reich. 'The group was George on lead guitar, Stuart on bass, John and Paul on rhythm guitars and Pete Best on drums,' said Bill Harry. 'Paul didn't like this. Originally, he wanted to be on lead guitar, but he knew he couldn't match George. So the only other thing was bass guitar. 'The Beatles were on stage with Tony Sheridan at the Top Ten Club one night when Paul and Stuart had a big fight after Paul made some comment about Astrid. Paul was surprised at how tenacious Stuart was, although he was only slight. They whacked hell out of each other and the audience loved it. They thought it was part of the act. After that, Stuart got out of the group.'

He tossed away his guitar, picked up his paints and joined his sweetheart in the attic flat she occupied above her parents' house. John forgave him and wrote moving letters telling him how bad things were at home in Liverpool. 'I've only got one ciggy to last until Thursday,' he wrote in one letter. Plagued by headaches ever since he had been attacked and kicked in the head during a fracas outside a pub in Bootle, Stuart collapsed with a fatal brain haemorrhage at Astrid's home just as his art career was taking off again.

Bill Harry asked John to pen a few lines about the group, and in the rustic style he sometimes liked to mimic, he told of the 'Dubious Origins of the Beatles': 'Why Beatles? It came in a vision – a man appeared on a flaming pie and said unto them, "From this day on you are Beatles with an A." Thank you, Mister Man, they said, thanking him.' In fact, it had been Stu, a devotee of Buddy Holly and the Crickets, who had suggested that the group should change its name to the insect-like Beetles. John agreed, but substituted the famous 'a' for the second 'e'.

Bill Harry took some copies of the first issue of Mersey Beat around to the Whitechapel branch of NEMS (North End Music Stores) and politely asked to see the manager. 'Brian Epstein came down and said he'd take a dozen copies,' said Harry. 'He phoned me that afternoon and said he'd sold out and ordered another twelve dozen. The Beatles were all over the cover. Epstein kept inviting me back to his office for sherry to find out more about what was happening. I asked him to write the record review column for me. He started writing about classical music and jazz, and I told him it had to be about rock'n' roll, so he started doing Elvis Presley and Billy Fury. 'When he became famous, Brian liked to claim that he had gone in search of the Beatles after a young fan, Raymond Jones, had requested a copy of 'My Bonny' at his family's record store in Liverpool's city centre on a Saturday late in October 1961. Jones gave the singer's name as Tony Sheridan and his backing group as the Beat Boys. Brian said he discovered that the track had been recorded in Hamburg, but that the Beat Boys were, like Sheridan, from Liverpool.

Playing as the Beatles, the backing group were currently appearing at the Cavern, a jazz club in the cellar of a converted warehouse only a few minutes from his store. Brian dropped into the club on 9 November 1961 with his personal assistant at NEMS, Alistair Taylor, and was astonished by what he saw. 'They smoked as they played, and they ate and talked and pretended to hit each other,' he remembered. 'They turned their backs on the audience and shouted at them and laughed at private jokes.' Afterwards, he met John, Paul, George and Pete Best, and listened to their copy of 'My Bonny'. 'I don't know why I asked them to come round and see me, although I'd loved their act,' Brian recalled. 'They had some indefinable charm.' Alistair Taylor remembers that day in November very clearly indeed. 'That was the day I turned down two-and-a-half per cent of the Beatles,' he said. 'Brian and I went on to lunch at Peacock's and he asked me what I thought. I said it was going to take money and I couldn't put any up. Being Brian, he said, "I'm not asking you to. If you come with me and we sign them up, I'll give you two-and-a-half per cent of the Beatles' earnings." And I said no, I just wanted a better salary. It was the most monumental gaffe of all time.'

'I had no idea of being a manager,' said Brian. 'But it somehow happened in conversation and we felt we ought to have a contract. None of us had ever seen such a thing so I got one drawn up. It was iniquitous and enslaving in my view, although many stars work under such terms, I know now. So we tore it up and drafted our own. I still haven't signed it.' He never did.

Bill Harry, a reliable witness to the rise of the Beatles, is definite about their first encounter with Epstein: 'Nobody has ever heard of Raymond Jones, and even after all the publicity, he never showed up. I arranged for Brian to go down to the Cavern to see the Beatles. I phoned up and said that Brian Epstein from NEMS would like to come down, and he was so nervous that I told them to make sure there was no hassle about letting him in. When he got there, they announced from the stage that Brian Epstein from NEMS was in the audience. 'The Beatles laughed because they knew him. They were in his shop all the time going through his records. Brian was there while queues of kids were coming in to buy Mersey Beat, which had the Beatles all over it. He also sold tickets for rock concerts and there were posters advertising the Beatles at the Tower Ballroom. After all that, how could he possibly make out that he never knew them? But people keep going along with the false story.'

Brian's first action as manager was to tackle the group's unruly appearance and Hell's Angel image. 'The Beatles were very much John Lennon's group – it was his band – and they were a rough and-ready, hard-swearing lot in black leather doing tough R&B music,' said Bill Harry. 'Brian wanted that to change and smooth them out to make them more acceptable. So he sent them all these neat little typed-out memos saying, "Do not smoke on stage, do not swear on stage, do not talk to the fans." John didn't like all *this because he thought he was being channelled into a false image, but Paul loved it. Paul was doing numbers like 'Till There Was You' from Music Man and 'A Taste of Honey' and all these sweet numbers, whereas John was into rock.*

'Brian got his tailor to run up mohair suits for them. What he was effectively doing was changing it from John's group into Paul's group. When he eventually realized that he was becoming estranged from John, he took him on holiday to Spain and explained why the group needed to change. And he was right. In their old rough way, they were more exciting and better as a group, but Brian made them acceptable.'

However, the rough edges were still showing when I first met the Beatles – completely by accident and just before the explosion that would rock the music world to its very foundations.

5

THE COLONEL MEETS THE COMPETITION

All shook up

On my arrival in Los Angeles with the Beatles on their first U.S. concert tour in the summer of 1964, after many transatlantic telephone conversations, I finally met Colonel Parker face to face. Early one morning he sent a car to pick me up from my hotel and take me to the Westwood apartment where he had been laid up with a bad back for two months.

In his lavishly furnished first-floor suite at the Beverly Comstock, I found him taking business calls from a hospital bed. As I arrived, he was just agreeing a deal for the sale of half-a-million framed colour portraits of Elvis. The photographs of the Colonel himself did not do him justice. Pale blue eyes and plump nose sat in a moon-shaped face like ornaments on a pudding, and his ample chins told a story. Yet even semi-crippled, he exuded the ferocity of a rogue elephant. (He later informed me that the elephant was his favourite circus animal.)

When he finished making money over the phone, he welcomed me cordially, and I asked him for news of Elvis.

'He's long wanted to meet the Beatles, but he arranged ages ago to spend this break between filming in Memphis,' said the Colonel, ever the diplomat.

Although he had not been out of the apartment for eight weeks, he insisted on getting up and taking me down to his offices at the Paramount Studios. Before we left, I phoned Brian Epstein, who invited us to have lunch with him at the Beverly Hills Hotel that day.

At Paramount, an illuminated sign above a doorway advertised Elvis's latest picture. The walls of the outer office and the corridors that connected it to the outside world were decorated with Elvis likenesses: billboards for Presley films, advertising material for Presley records, posters for Presley lipstick, handbags and pyjamas. The centrepiece was a cardboard replica of the cellblock in *Jailhouse Rock*.

The walls of his own office were covered with pictures of Parker with famous politicians and celebrities: the Colonel with President Johnson, the Colonel with the Speaker of the House, the Colonel with Frank Sinatra and, of course, with Elvis himself. He pointed his cane at the rear wall behind his cluttered desk. 'This here is my dead wall. When anybody dies, I move their picture over here. All these people are deceased.'

Later, we drove to the Beverly Hills Hotel, where Brian was staying. There were cries of 'Elvis' and 'Beatles' as the two most famous rock managers in the world shook hands warmly in the foyer. Over lunch, the thing that seemed to concern Brian most was the tight security necessary to protect the Beatles. The Colonel wasn't impressed.

'You don't have to protect the Beatles the way we protected Elvis because, with them, there is no jealousy,' he snorted. 'You don't have to fear the boyfriends because your artists are characters loved in a different way. The boyfriends would throw things at Elvis on stage. We never had to send in the police to get them – the girls always got them first. Your problem is to protect the small fans from getting hurt in the crush. We never had them so little.'

'Will Elvis ever tour again?' a clearly rattled Brian interrupted.

'Put it this way – I'd like him to tour again someday because I'm a showman, but at the moment we can earn more money and entertain more fans by making films. One day you will discover the same situation with the Beatles . . .

'Elvis has required every moment of my time, and I think he would have suffered had I signed anyone else, but I admire you, Brian, for doing it your way with other performers as well. Obviously you have a different organization, but remember, too, that when Presley soared to fame I was 44. When the Beatles happened, you were 28. That helps.'

When the Colonel recalled how he had launched Elvis in the early days by doing rough jobs like selling tickets at dance halls, Brian retorted: 'So did I, in little Lancashire towns. I took around my own posters and sold tickets when they were earning less than £20 a show.'

Whatever the rivalry between their superstars, I noted that the two managers displayed a fair degree of one-upmanship themselves.

The following afternoon, which was hot and humid, I took the Colonel to meet the Beatles. We drove to their rented mansion in Saint Pierre Road, Bel Air, in a station wagon loaded with presents. 'I put on a tie 'specially for these guys,' said the Colonel.

The Beatles had made no such concessions. They had just finished lunch when we arrived and were still in trunks after a morning swim. John regarded the Colonel with barely disguised curiosity. I prayed that he wouldn't sabotage the deal I was carefully piecing together.

The Colonel made himself at home at the dining-room table where the remains of lunch were waiting to be cleared away. He told the Beatles: 'Elvis phoned me this morning to say he was sorry he wasn't here to greet you, but he'd welcome you at Graceland if you'd like to stop over in Memphis.'

Ever hopeful, the Beatles discussed the idea, but Brian shook his head with the sort of reluctance he would adopt to turn down £50,000 deals. 'I don't think our schedule will permit,' he said solemnly. The Colonel shrugged. Secretly, I believe he was relieved. He knew Elvis's state of mind and he wasn't physically well enough himself to deal with his recalcitrant client.

From a huge box, the Colonel handed out his presents like a midsummer Santa Claus. For each of the Beatles, there was a table lamp in the shape of a covered wagon and a valuable leather gun-belt. Brian got a gold one and the Colonel gave me a silver one spangled with rhinestones – all signed 'From Elvis and the Colonel'. Ringo dashed into the kitchen and borrowed a cowboy hat from the chef. The Beatles already had imitation six-shooters and a bizarre gunfight started around the dining room.

'Bang, bang!' said Paul, aiming his gun at the Colonel. 'You're dead!'

John found a more symbolic target. He pointed his gun at his own head and shouted: 'Bang!'

'I wish we had real guns,' said George.

John caught the implication and frowned.

Was this really happening, I asked myself? Had one of the shrewdest operators in the music business been able to reduce these four famous and talented men to a bunch of junior school boys? Parker didn't hang around to find out.

'And these are from Elvis personally,' he said pointing to a parting gift still in the large box from which he'd produce his cowboy souvenirs. Inside were six sets – one for each of us – of all the albums Presley had made up to that point. How personal could you get? 'Have fun,' said the Colonel, finally taking his leave.

That evening, Paul, George and Ringo went across to Burt Lancaster's neighbouring mansion to watch Peter Sellers' latest movie, A Shot in the Dark. Once the film had ended, they ventured down to the Whiskey-a-Go-Go on Sunset. John had stayed at Beatleville, the name we gave any temporary residence, to receive Bobby Darin and Sandra Dee.

After they had departed, John and I were watching TV in the living-room when Jayne Mansfield and a male companion appeared unannounced in the open doorway. We were both in a mad, mischievous mood. 'Only two Beatles

left around here?' she asked, disappointed. 'Why it's the Jayne Mansfield,'
said John, greeting the blonde star of The Girl Can't Help It as though he
was really impressed. 'And Mickey Hargitay,' he said to the complete
stranger with her. 'Good to see you.' 'Oh, silly,' giggled Jayne, loving it.
'Mickey's my ex. This is another friend.' 'I'm John,' said the lone Beatle.
'And this is our friend Chris. The others have gone to the Whiskey-a-Go-
Go.' 'Well, let's go and join them,' she giggled again, breathing in deeply.
'No, thanks, I'm staying in,' said John. 'Would you like a drink?' 'I'll
have a cocktail,' said Jayne, fluttering her eyelashes. 'I'll get it,' I
volunteered.

I'd never mixed a cocktail in my life, but I went into the kitchen and started
to examine the bottles. John followed me. 'What do you put in a cocktail?' I
asked.' A drop of that, that, that and that,' he replied, pointing to every
liquor bottle on the shelf. 'And then you pee in it.' I poured gin, vodka, red
wine and several liqueurs into a large glass, added ice and handed it to John,
who added some liquid Lennon. Jayne pronounced the drink a real
humdinger and got even more excited when John told her it was a Beatle
Special. Playfully, she tugged at John's Beatle haircut and asked: 'Is this
real?' John hated to be touched by a stranger. Dropping his eyes, he returned
the compliment.' Are those real?' he asked. Ms Mansfield took a deep
breath and replied: 'There's one way to find out.'

Her companion interrupted by flourishing a pack of tarot cards. In return
for the hospitality, he said, he would read the cards for John. 'He's going to
tell you your destiny . . . and mine,' breathed Jayne, her massive bosom
heaving in John's direction.

No one knew at this stage that Elvis had been one of Jayne's conquests. She had bedded him after the Colonel had deliberately demanded an astronomical fee for him to appear in The Girl Can't Help It. The Colonel didn't want Elvis to share the billing with Little Richard, Eddie Cochran, Fats Domino and a host of other rock stars. After their one-night stand, Jayne asked Elvis if he would reconsider. 'Ask the Colonel,' Elvis yawned. The Colonel refused to budge, but Elvis gave Jayne a pink motorbike as a consolation prize.

John tolerated the tarot reader while he went through a glib recital of the group's much chronicled success. Then he drew a card that made him stop. He dropped the cards with an expression of mock horror and exclaimed: 'My God, this is terrible. I see an awful ending to all this.' At this point, John lost his temper. He was wildly superstitious and his anger covered up his fear about what fate might have in store. Out!' he ordered America's most famous living sex symbol, taking her and her companion by the arms and propelling them through the doorway. His sudden hostility stunned them so much that they went with barely a murmur. Incensed, John suggested we join the other Beatles at the Whiskey-a-Go-Go for some real cocktails. 'What a phoney that guy was,' he said, relaxing in the cab. 'He told me things everyone knows, then tried to scare me witless.'

It wasn't easy to get into the club. Thousands of fans were being manhandled by the police outside, but John was easily recognizable and we were shoved through the door. Inside, another thousand patrons plus a score of photographers were jostling to join George and Ringo. Paul had found better things to do and had gone off on his own.

No sooner were we seated than a familiar voice was heard above the clamour. 'Hi, you guys – fancy seeing you here!' Jayne Mansfield swanned into view with a photographer in tow and squeezed her breasts into the middle of our group.

John studiously ignored her, but the cameraman snapped a picture of three of the Beatles apparently out nightclubbing with Jayne Mansfield. To show his disgust, George flung the remains of his Scotch and Coke at the photographer. An ice cube hit one of the spectators, the actress Mamie van Doren, in the face. As Gentleman George tried to apologize, John whispered to Jayne what had really been in the Beatle Special. Before she could hit him, we all made an undignified dash for the exit.

The ironic thing was that the 'phoney' tarot card reader had got it absolutely right. Both John and Jayne died violent deaths, the actress being decapitated in a car crash in New Orleans only two years later. The next time John and I discussed predestination, he remembered that day and worried even more about his future. By this time, he was heavily into numerology under the tutelage of Yoko Ono, and he was obsessed by the number nine, the date of his birth. 'Jayne was born on 19 April and she died on 29 June,' he said. 'April is the fourth month and June is the sixth. Add them together and you get ten. I was born on 9 October, the ninth day of the tenth month. She died two months after her birthday, which means I'm going to die on a day with a nine in it, in December.'

A much more welcome guest than Jayne Mansfield or any of the other Beatle-eaters was Bob Dylan, who visited them at the Delmonico Hotel when we reached New York.

After midnight one night, I returned there with Neil Aspinall and Mal Evans. We had been to see Spartacus at a cinema on Times Square. Neil quietly opened the door of the Beatles' suite and we entered the outer room. Through the half-opened door of the living-room, a curious ritual came into view. Mal nudged me and said: 'Christ, look at that!' Six chairs were lined up in a row. The Beatles occupied the centre four, Bob Dylan sat at one end and Brian Epstein at the other. As we watched, Dylan elbowed the Beatle next to him and the gesture was passed along the line to Epstein, who promptly fell off his chair. All six broke into helpless laughter. Brian climbed back on to his chair and the procedure began all over again. Brian fell to the floor once more and everyone burst out laughing. 'If I'm not mistaken, the boys have discovered pot,' I whispered as we crept quietly away.

The Beatles had tried hashish before, but this was their first experiment with potent grass. I raised the subject with Brian the following day while we were having coffee in his suite. He didn't look at all well. 'What was that scene about last night?' 'Were you there? I can't remember.' He popped two amphetamines, washed them down with a glass of water and shivered. 'All I can say about the drug culture is: plenty of drugs but not much culture.'

I finished my coffee and left.

I didn't see Brian again for several days and all my enquiries as to his whereabouts were met with mystifying shrugs. Something was clearly wrong. It was John who told me what had happened. 'Brian went out the other night and picked up a sailor. The guy roughed him up and stole his watch, bracelet, pen . . . all solid gold from Asprey's. He's flown back to London to get replacements.' 'What? For the whole lot?' 'Yeah. He thinks people will notice they're missing and jump to conclusions.'

The image-conscious Brian was normally very cautious about his homosexual entanglements. But once he had downed a few drinks and taken some drugs, he would seek out rough trade in the low dives on 42nd Street. The confident young impresario, immaculate in Saville Row's finest, would become a silly, giggly drunk. His technique was to make a pass at another man, not necessarily a homosexual, and risk everything on the outcome. The distinct possibility of being hit added to the thrill. Drugs, both uppers and downers, had started to erode his sanity. Like Elvis, he would throw tantrums, then reward the victim of a black mood with extravagant presents. There is no doubt that part of Brian's problem was his unrequited love for John Lennon. He was obsessed by John's sardonic wit and artistic genius as well as being attracted by his good looks. In many ways, John was the man Brian most wanted to be: he saw John as wildly outspoken, incredibly brave and extremely talented.

Unfortunately for Brian, John was a dedicated womanizer, a veritable conquistador of the opposite sex. The sexual traffic flowing in and out of his hotel bedroom far exceeded that of any of the other Beatles, and his lovers were always female. Since many of the groupies were under-age girls like the one in Las Vegas, John had developed a liking for the professionals. I could relate many instances of this, but one particular night in Paris will make the point.

We were at the George V when John suddenly felt a desire for some exotic female company. An aide (actually it was the promoter Arthur Howes) was despatched into the Champs-Elysees to bring back some street-walkers, but it was 4.00 am and the streets were deserted. When he returned to the suite to report failure, he found John surrounded by eight glamorous women. The Beatle had made his own arrangements with the help of an obliging night porter.

'Take your pick,' he said to the three men who had stayed behind after a business meeting with Brian. 'This one's on John.'

As each man chose one or more of les belles de nuit, John, dressed in a white bathrobe and looking like Caesar in his Beatle cut, stood at the door handing out 100 franc notes to each girl to pay for the services she was about to render.

John, of course, knew of Brian's lust for him and exploited it to get his own way. They had shared a Spanish holiday in the summer of 1963. Brian personally told me that, in Barcelona, he had not got further with John than a single kiss, so he had switched his attentions to a more amenable Spanish bullfighter. John's version was slightly different. He omitted any mention of kissing.

'A lot of rumours floated around about that holiday,' he told me. 'But I just went to sort Brian out. We sat in cafes and talked and talked and talked, mostly about people we'd been in love with. I convinced him that, while I didn't condemn his way of life, I was into women as far as sex was concerned.

'I really didn't want to hurt him by saying something stupid like "I can't stand queers." I could understand what was in his head. By the end of the holiday, he understood me better and the subject will probably never come up again.'

Brian believed that John had never got over the death of Stu Sutcliffe or his mother. 'Much of John's anger towards the world is grief over Stu and Julia,' he said. 'He thinks about death a lot.'

My biggest coup of this tour was to arrange a telephone conversation between Paul and Elvis. After they left Los Angeles, the Colonel frequently phoned me to keep in touch with the Beatles tour progress. When he was unable to get through to the hotel in Atlantic City, he sent a cable asking me to call him urgently. I contacted him and he gave me Elvis's secret number at Graceland. According to my battered notebook, this was '901 EX(PRESS) 7-4427'. 'You can contact the artist through Marty Lacker,' said the Colonel, wary of eavesdroppers. 'He is waiting for a call from you fellows, so don't let him down.'

'How do you do?' enquired Paul when got him through to Elvis. 'I want to tell you we all think it's a drag that we weren't able to get together with you, but it's just one of those things. We would still like to meet you if it can all be arranged.'

Elvis told Paul that he was disappointed, too. 'I've taken a great big interest in your career and wanted very much to have a long chat with you guys,' he said. 'I've bought an electric bass guitar and I'm learning to play it. The darn thing's given me callouses all over my hand.'

'Well, keep practising,' said Paul. 'You'll get used to it. When are you coming to England, then?'

'Soon, I hope. I'm definitely coming.'

'Great! You can count on us having front row seats for your first show.'

'When are you going to invade the Hollywood studios?' Elvis wanted to know, giving voice to one of his greatest fears.

'Oh, you mean make a film?' answered Paul. 'I don't think we will, really. We like it in Britain and there's no need for us to film in Hollywood, although I appreciate it's the natural thing for an American star to do.'

'Well, I guess you've got a manager to take care of that kind of thing anyway.'

'Too true. I've got no brain for business. I couldn't look after a couple of dollars.'

'Talking of dollars in a pretty modest sort of way, I've bought every single one of your records and we play them all the time up here at the house. I like the cover of your new album [the unsmiling Beatle faces depicted in half light on *With the Beatles*]. It's kinda weird and I like weird things. Your faces on that cover remind me of the faces in that movie, *Children of the Damned.*'

This was more like it, a genuine double-edged compliment.

'Talking of films,' said Paul, 'That manager of yours is a laugh. He told us he had an offer from a producer to make a film with both you and us in it. The producer said he was offering a million dollars for Elvis and a million dollars for the Beatles. But Colonel Parker said, "I told him that he had forgotten there were four Beatles and they'd want two million dollars." We thought that dead funny.'

'Yeah, that sounds like the Colonel all right,' chuckled Elvis.

At this point, Paul covered the mouthpiece with his hand and said to John: 'Have a word with him, man.'

'No, thanks,' John answered. 'Can't think of anything to say.'

Paul signed off diplomatically and hung up his extension. I took over the conversation. When I asked Elvis about his Beatle collection, he replied: 'I guess I've got every record they ever made here. I'm looking at a copy of *A Hard Day's Night* right now and I've also hired a copy of the film which we're going to show up here at the house tonight.'

He added: 'That's how I spend most of my evenings, watching pictures privately. Coming down to Memphis and just kicking around this house is the only way I get to rest. We have a lot of fun out here. We have some wild parties. It's a pity y'all couldn't have made it over.'

I repeated the offer to John, who wasn't impressed by the thought of visiting Graceland. 'If he ever comes to England, he can visit *my* country estate,' he said. 'But I bet he won't set foot in England until we're history.'

My friendship with the Beatles was getting me acres of space in the NME, but I still wanted the big story. More hopeful after hearing the invitation to visit Graceland from the King's own lips, I kept in touch with the Colonel until the Beatles visited the US again in August 1965. This was the year that the Queen awarded them MBEs for services to Britain's export drive.

Outraged holders of the award promptly sent their medals back to Buckingham Palace, one pompous Canadian MP saying that he refused to be placed on the same level as 'vulgar nincompoops'. When the Queen asked the Beatles at the investiture: 'How long have you been together?', Ringo replied: 'About forty years, ma'am.' It just seemed like that. John, the anti-war campaigner, found the idea of medals of any kind repellent. He later claimed that he smoked dope in the Palace loo to express his true feelings and he eventually disowned his honour. 'I thought you were supposed to do something brave in war to get one of these,' he told me. 'Well, there's never been any chance of me doing that. This is just a political gimmick to make Harold Wilson [then Prime Minister] look good.'

More important to John was the fact that President Lyndon B. Johnson had sent 3500 US Marines into Da Nang, the first American fighting troops to be committed to the field in South Vietnam. He hated war in general and Vietnam in particular. When Johnson announced at the end of July that he was sending in another 50,000 troops, John burst out: 'Who does he think he's kidding? That was the idea all along.' John threatened to stage a one-Beatle boycott of the States, but luckily for me, he packed his bags along with the rest of us.

We flew to New York on TWA's flight 703 on August 14 1965 for their second full length U.S. tour which was to start with their record-breaking performance at Shea Stadium.

I kept my fingers crossed for events in another city on the other side of the United States . . . .

6

AN AUDIENCE WITH THE KING

I gotta know

OUR party arrived in Los Angeles shortly before midnight on August 23, 1965. The following morning I had an appointment: I was to be collected outside my hotel, the Beverly Hillcrest, by Colonel Parker at 11.30am. I was early and nervously paced up and down, glancing at my watch. But I had no need to fear he wouldn't show. With his assistant Tom Diskin at the wheel of a shooting brake, he arrived on the hotel forecourt right on time.

Parker was wearing a beach shirt and slacks that looked as though they had been bought off the peg at a chain store. He had on a white Panama hat, and was holding a cane topped with an elephant's head. We set off for Paramount.

Leaning forward from the back seat to make myself heard over the traffic noise, I said: 'It's very good of you to see me again.'

The Colonel held his hat on in the wind, streams of smoke trailing from his cigar.

'Let me tell you, son, I never give interviews. Nor does Mr Presley. *Never!* Ain't that right, Mr Diskin?' He glared at Tom Diskin, who nodded his head in agreement. 'It's one of the unwritten rules of Parker Management. Only tell the press what *you* want them to print. Never let *them* ask the questions. 'The Colonel paused to exhale more smoke. 'One day I'm gonna write a book. My own story. I'm gonna call it "*How Much Does It Cost if It's Free?*"

'So has everything got a price, I asked?'

'Not necessarily so,' said the Colonel philosophically. 'A couple of city slickers from New York came to see me the other day. Million-dollar merchandising proposal. Lot of money.'

Tom Diskin was already nodding in agreement so I suspected he had heard this story a hundred times.

'At the same time, a friend of mine from the carny days dropped by. He'd fallen on hard times. Wanted to sell me a few hundred balloons. Fifty dollars. I asked Mr Diskin to show these New York guys in, then I said to my old friend, "I'll tell you what – I'll give you twenty-five." I bartered with him for some time before we agreed a price.

'The city slickers were standing there with their mouths open. They can't believe what was happening. I could have given him the fifty he wanted or even five hundred, but I quibbled. Once we'd agreed a price he left. The New York types couldn't believe it. They were furious. One of them said to me . . .'

At that moment the shooting brake turned neatly under the giant Paramount arch. The Colonel acknowledged salutes from the security guards with a wave of his big cigar. He continued his monologue in a Brooklyn accent: '"You kept us waiting twenty minutes to do a million-dollar deal while you bought some balloons for a few bucks?"'

He made smoke to indicate his disdain at this attitude as the shooting brake passed through the studio backlots.

'I told him I didn't like his tone and I'd decided not to do business with them. "That's OK," this guy says. "It's not your name we want on our products. It's Mr Presley's."

'"Fine," I said. "Go find Mr Presley and ask him." Do you take my point?'

'Sure,' I said, fairly confident I'd got the point. 'You're the only one who can make a deal for Elvis.'

The Colonel triumphantly alighted as the shooting brake jerked to a halt outside his suite of offices. 'I knew you'd miss the point. You screwed up there, son. Sure, I do all Mr Presley's contracts. See this here ring?'

He held up a heavily jewelled ring, which carried the initials TCB.

'Mr Presley gave me this ring. See those initials? TCB –"Takin' Care of Business".' [It seemed churlish to tell him I was aware that similar rings Elvis gave to those he regarded as true friends bore the initials TLC for Tender Loving Care. So I didn't.]

He stood next to me, drilling me with his clear blue eyes.

'But the point of the story, son, is that you can't put a price on a man's pride. Remember that.'

I entered the inner sanctum of the Colonel's little empire just as I had done on several occasions the previous summer. It was high noon.

'Let's eat,' said my host.

Tom Diskin entered with a large tray of food from the Colonel's private cookhouse. He set it down on a space the Colonel had cleared on his desk with a sweep of his cane. I pulled a chair up to the desk and surveyed the meal. There were pieces of some meat surrounded by huge amounts of vegetables.

'What's the best deal you've ever done for Elvis?' I asked, the hospitality making me reckless.

The Colonel tossed his cane down on the desk, removed his hat and seated himself in a swivel chair.

'Hard to say,' he said, beginning to eat hungrily. His prodigious appetite had become a talking point long before Elvis started to blimp out on food. 'When I discovered our record company was promoting other artists' records on the sleeves of Mr Presley's albums, I billed 'em $100,000 for the advertising space. And they paid up.'

'The word is that Mr Presley pays you 50 per cent of each deal,' I ventured.

The Colonel tried to hide his annoyance behind a show of bravado. '*Wrong!* You screwed up again. I pay *him* 50 per cent.'

He fixed me with a look that could only be described as malevolent.

'How are you enjoying the desert rat?' he enquired politely. I froze in mid-bite on what I had imagined to be a tiny chicken leg. The Colonel roared with laughter, a great belly laugh that filled the windowless room.

'You just qualified as a member of the Snowmen's League,' he said.

'The what?'

'The Snowmen's League. I'm the Potentate. You snow people and then melt away before they can find you. It has a very exclusive membership, including some former Presidents of the United States.'

He gave me a gold-coloured medallion attached to a piece of checkered ribbon. The words 'COL TOM PARKER SNOW AWARD' were inscribed around the circular rim. I've kept it as a treasured memento along with the cowboy belt and the western wagon.

After lunch, the Colonel, holding a sheaf of papers, led me across the lot. He opened a door and motioned me inside.

'Wait here, son. I'll only be a few minutes.'

After the noon blaze of the California sun, I had to allow my eyes to adjust to the sudden gloom. The soft light provided by a single lamp did little to illuminate the surroundings. I walked slowly into the room and made out an armchair, a coffee table, a settee. A TV set flickered in one corner. I sat down on the armchair.

A few moments passed before I realized that I was not alone. My eyes moved across the dark green carpet to a pair of highly polished black cowboy boots studded in silver. Elvis Presley was sitting in the armchair, legs outstretched. So this was it.

Everything had come down to a few square feet in one small room. It was hard to believe that the man quietly sizing me up from his armchair was Elvis the Pelvis, the most celebrated, exciting . . . and, according to some, the most notorious, performer in the history of popular entertainment. This was the same Elvis who had instigated rock 'n' roll riots and inspired a generation of teenage rebellion, the same Elvis who had caused broken love affairs and triggered reckless adventures, the same Elvis who was the maker of young dreams and the breaker of juvenile hearts. Here within easy reach was the world's most outrageous rock-age rebel and jukebox tearjerker turned cult hero and movie matinee idol: just one man, so many myths. When it came to the moment of realization, the indisputable fact that this same Elvis was really only human flesh and blood blew my mind.

'I wasn't expecting . . .' I stuttered. 'The Colonel told me . . .'

In the half-light Elvis smiled gently. 'Yeah, I know. That ol' man sure does like to ring the bell. You and I spoke on the phone last year. You're the guy who knows the Beatles.'

He rose slowly, a tall incredibly handsome man, dressed in a green shirt with puffed sleeves clipped in at the cuff and a pair of tight slacks. He walked to the chilled water dispenser, poured himself a glass of H20 and started drinking. Then he moved closer.

'I didn't realize you were back in Los Angeles,' I said.

'We got through filming in Hawaii sooner than expected, and came straight back to finish the picture in the studio,' he said. 'My girlfriend drove up around the Beatles' place yesterday and said there was a heck of a lot of fans outside. Those guys can't be getting much peace at all. The Colonel tells me you want me to meet 'em. That right?'

With Elvis now on his feet and towering over me, I felt awkward and strangely insecure.

'It would make a great . . . I mean, they respect you. They want to tell you . . . to say thanks.'

He gave a low laugh. It was a great sound.

'What you really mean is that it would make a great story for your newspaper. Reporters are always tryin' to get me to do things. It's phoney as hell. Anyway, go ahead – *shoot!*'

I could feel panic rising in my throat. This was the moment I had been praying for, yet now that it had arrived, I was totally unprepared.

'Look, my mind's gone blank. I have so many questions to ask you and I can't think of a single one.'

Elvis laughed that great laugh again.

'That's OK. I seem to have that effect on people. At least you're honest about it.' He paused and fixed me with his pale blue eyes. 'Well, I gotta question for you.'

He sat down in his chair, facing me across the coffee table.

'This John Lennon. How good is he? What I really mean is: could he have made it on his own?'

'He's a bright guy. Very bright. But the Beatles are a group. None of them could have done what you've done on their own.'

Elvis nodded slowly, taking it in.

'I hear he's a fag. Is that right?' he said using the American term for homosexual.

Now it was my turn to laugh.

'No, that was a misunderstanding,' I informed him. 'He asked a security guard at a hotel to get him some fags. He meant cigarettes. That's what we call them in England. Fags.'

Elvis shook his head.

'English sure is a weird language.'

'If you'd agree to meet them, you'd find they're OK.'

Elvis's next remark gave me an insight into how the manager manipulated his famous client.

'Colonel says they're just after the notoriety. Want to be able to boast that they're knocking me off my perch.'

'No, the meeting was my idea. I've been one of your biggest fans for years. I've known the Beatles since the beginning and they're no big deal to me. They still can't believe what's happening.'

'Yeah, I can identify with that. It happens so quickly it takes your breath away.'

'Will you do it?'

Elvis shrugged. 'Depends. I'll do what the Colonel recommends. He hasn't been wrong so far, though sometimes I wonder. I reckon I could be doing better things, but the Colonel has a policy about remaining loyal to the film companies. They pay me a million dollars-plus in addition to investing $2 million in each picture we make. If fifty million people can see me do a TV spot for free, they won't need to go to the movies. I won't go on the road without the Colonel – I never have done and I never will. And he says he can't do it. His back hurts pretty bad, and he thinks he would break up before a tour was half completed.'

This was true behind-the-scenes stuff: Elvis Presley explaining himself on what he clearly regarded as a pretty major career move and without his manager in sight.

Right on cue, however, the door swung open and the Colonel was framed against the harsh afternoon light. Ignoring his famous client, he said to me: 'We'll take our coffee in the executive dining suite.'

Outside, I had to run to keep pace.

'Thanks for setting up the meeting with Elvis. I really didn't expect . . .'

'Mr Presley?' he drawled. 'I didn't see no Mr Presley. 'Slow to appreciate the favour that had been bestowed upon me, I persisted: 'Back there. In the room . . .'

'It must be the sun gettin' to you. I already told you: Mr Presley does *not* talk to journalists.'

Like a maverick bullock the Colonel veered off the lot into the dining complex. We passed through a cafeteria section where extras, stage hands and the lower ranks of the studio hierarchy dined. Parker marched on, ignoring the occasional 'Howdy, Colonel.' I received an affectionate greeting from Suzanna Leigh, the British actress filming *Paradise*,

Hawaiian Style with Elvis and seated at one of the cafeteria's plastic-topped tables. I returned her wave and wanted to stop, but the Colonel kept walking, and again I had to sprint to catch up. We had entered a medium-range restaurant. Here, there was waitress service.

'Who was that?' asked the Colonel.

'Who was that? You're kidding!' I said, amazed. 'That's Suzanna Leigh, she's in the movie you're making here with Elvis. She's his co-star isn't she?'

With perfect timing, we finally arrived at the executive dining room where only producers, directors, studio heads and the most valued stars fraternized. There were checkered tablecloths, crystal water jugs, even a *maitre d'* dancing attendance.

'Well, you see where she's eatin',' he replied.

Maybe the sun was getting to me because I drew level and spoke loudly.

'Let's stop playing games, Colonel. Is Elvis going to meet the Beatles or not?'

Various big shots froze, forks in mid-air, when they heard the Beatles' name. The Colonel, however, knew exactly how to play to his audience.

'You can tell Mr Epstein that Colonel Parker will be delighted to listen to his little proposition.'

After coffee, I visited the closed set of *Paradise, Hawaiian Style* on Stage 5 where Parker had me photographed with Elvis – but only on condition that Suzanna Leigh was in the picture too saying 'It might do her some good in England.' I sensed he was feeling guilty about the way he'd rebuffed her after the cafeteria encounter. So he had a heart after all.

Later that afternoon, I took the Colonel up to the Beatles' rented house at 2850 Benedict Canyon above Beverly Hills. They asked him, yet again, about Elvis's career. 'Elvis is unavailable for personal appearances because of his film commitments,' he explained patiently to the Beatles. 'I've just sent his gold Cadillac on a tour of America. Matter of fact, it's so successful I'm thinking of putting his gold suit on tour too.'

As he left, he assured the Beatles that they would meet Elvis, subject to me being able to fix a convenient time and place. This was the best news I had heard on any of my three trips to the States. Things were finally starting to move in the right direction – and quite fast for a change.

The following day, the Colonel and I circled the pool at the Beverly Hills Hotel, and approached Brian Epstein who, clad in swimming trunks and a white towelling robe, straddled a Lilo outside a cabana. His fresh, babyish face coloured red by the West Coast sun, Brian looked happy and relaxed. The Colonel grasped his outstretched hand and said: 'I'm sure we can work something out.'

Lunch was served poolside. Brian and I ate lobster salad and drank chilled Chablis. 'One of life's little pleasures,' Brian said, mixing his own salad dressing from stoppered bottles of olive oil and vinegar.

The Colonel had chosen chicken, saying: 'I'm mighty partial to chicken. I started out with this little sideshow – dancin' chickens. Now chickens are not by nature Fred Astaire, so how did I make 'em dance? Well, you'd dance if you were standing on a hotplate. I'd start each week with seven dancin' chickens and finish with just one.' He flourished a chicken leg. 'A fella's gotta eat!'

Parker laughed heartily at his own joke. Then, suddenly serious, he said, 'Let's get down to logistics.'

'As you know, my boys are staying in Benedict Canyon,' began Brian.

'Yeah, I've been there. Could present security problems,' the Colonel decided, automatically ruling it out. The air space above the house had already been declared a no-fly zone after two fans hired a helicopter and dived into their swimming pool from it.

'There are going to be security problems wherever they meet,' Brian replied, colouring visibly. He liked to get his own way as much as the Colonel.

'Mr Presley lives in a secure part of Bel Air.'

'So you insist that *we* visit *you*. Have I got that right?"

"Insist" is a strong word. Listen, Brian (he had a bit of a problem with his 'r's so it always came out as 'Bwian'), you're in *our* country. If Mr Presley were in *your* homeland, *we'd* come to *you*. We'll be the hosts in the United States. That's the way of it.'

'You have a point. OK. I've got to go to New York but I'll be back on Friday. What about Friday night?'

The Colonel whipped out a diary and scribbled a note in it. 'Friday night it is. August twenty-seventh.' He snapped the diary shut and pocketed it. 'Only one stipulation. No publicity – apart from what Mr Hutchins writes in his newspaper after the event.'

116

'That's going to be tricky, Colonel Parker,' said Brian. 'Fleet Street is here in force. They'll go crazy.'

The Colonel turned to me. 'That's your job, Chris. Lay down a false trail. Give the competition the slip.'

I nodded my assent and suggested to Brian that he include in our group a chirpy chap called Tony Barrow who worked for Epstein's company as a publicist. He would be there to ward off any journalist who managed to break through the security cordon. Brian agreed and Barrow clearly did his job since one scribe who subsequently wrote about 'being there' was never in the house – unless he had managed to lock himself in Elvis's wardrobe! Of all the stories in my short, though busy, career, this was the one I most wanted to myself.

The Colonel still wasn't finished: 'And another thing. No cameras, no pictures of any kind and no tape-recorders. That agreed?' He offered his hand to the man who loved the Beatles.

'Anything else?' asked Brian, failing to disguise his irritation but shaking the Colonel's hand before it was withdrawn. 'By the way, Colonel, what *is* Mr Presley's address in Bel Air?'

Caught unprepared, the Colonel blustered: 'That will have to remain classified information. I'll send one of my men to pick your boys up.'

'That's ridiculous,' Brian exclaimed.

The Colonel rose abruptly to his feet. 'If that's the way you feel, I'd as soon call the whole damn thing off, only we've shaken on it. Anyway, I'm doing this as a personal favour to my friend Mr Hutchins here.'

I jumped up and reassured him: 'I'm sure we'll manage, Colonel. It will be all right on the night.'

Back at 2850 Benedict Canyon, the Beatles received the news from Brian with mixed feelings. They had waited so long that it seemed too good to be true. 'I bet he cancels,' said John. He listened to the account of my audience with the King, and even though I omitted the personal references that Elvis had made about him, he professed to be unimpressed.

'I'm fed up with meeting celebrities,' he said wearily. 'Most of them are disappointing, and I bet he's the same.'

The day after their arrival in LA, the Beatles had attended a party hosted by Capitol Records, which was carpeted wall to wall with some of the most famous people in Hollywood. The guest list included Steve McQueen, Julie Andrews, Richard Chamberlain, James Stewart, Rock Hudson, Gene Kelly, Edward G. Robinson and Jane Fonda. However, once again, the group had been displayed as novelties rather than real people in their own right.

Brian flew off to New York for his business trip and I stuck close to his boys. Neither Ringo nor I could swim but we both tried to learn a few strokes in the pool. John borrowed my camera and took some holiday snaps of Paul wearing Mal's glasses and a nervous Ringo surveying the deep end. We played pool in the games room, Ringo deliberately using the blunt end of the cue. 'This is Ringo time at the table,' he said when someone pointed out his mistake. 'I play my way.' He was starting to become more assertive.

The eve of the long-overdue rendezvous found me driving in the shooting brake along a winding, hilly street in Bel Air with the Colonel and Tom Diskin. We had been touring the salubrious residential district for some time, more or less going round in circles. I now knew the Colonel's guilty secret: he had never actually been to Elvis's home.

'Just carry on up this hill, Mr Diskin,' the Colonel instructed. 'Let's see, Bellagio Road. Every goddam street around here is Bellagio. It's up here some place. We want Perugia Way. Number 565.'

Consulting a road map of the area, I located Perugia Way at the top of Bellagio overlooking the Bel Air Country Club.

'Ah, yes, the country club,' said the Colonel. 'I remember now.'

Finally, the shooting brake pulled up on the crest of a steep hill outside the high-security gates of 565 Perugia Way. A Rolls-Royce, two Cadillacs and three Harley-Davidson motorcycles were parked in the driveway under a row of palm trees. The courtyard leading up to a panelled front door was lushly planted with petunias, tiny hedges, a profusion of ferns and strips of well-tended lawn. The house, a two-story mansion, was built into the hillside. Most of it was hidden from the roadway by bowed garden walls seven feet high, covered in tropical creepers.

'All right, Mr Diskin,' the Colonel ordered. 'Let's head back to civilization.'

I had hoped to go inside, and said so. The Colonel, however, had a management rule to cover just such an eventuality:

'Never interfere with the client's private life. Mr Presley leads his life and I lead mine. We're strictly business. Friday is business and this is Thursday.' And we drove away to the more familiar territory of Beverly Hills.

'The Colonel is a wily old fox,' Seymour Heller, Liberace's manager, told me later. 'He didn't get too close because he didn't like a lot of the things that Elvis did, drugs or whatever, and he didn't like his friends.'

The house at 565 Perugia Way had once been owned by the Shah of Persia and Rita Hayworth, although not at the same time. It was built around a circular, glass-roofed games room, fifty feet in diameter. A pool table, an illuminated jukebox and California-style furnishings were now visible from the front door. According to an account delivered by a member of the Memphis Mafia, new arrivals to Elvis's home would follow a maid across the thick white shag carpet of the foyer, and pass through the living-room, where a huge painting of Elvis, Gladys and Vernon outside Graceland dominated one wall above a fireplace. The adjoining den was the King's notorious party room.

'I'm gonna buy a horde of chorus girls and make 'em dance on my bed,' Elvis had promised himself in *Jailhouse Rock*. Now, it seems, he was living out that fantasy.

'At party time, he would sit in the centre of a horseshoe-shaped couch near another fireplace, watching TV,' the indiscreet former employee continued. 'His face was chubbier now, his waistline slightly more rounded, but he was still extremely handsome. Perhaps a dozen young women would be seated on the couch, six on either side of him. His cousin Gene Smith, Sonny and Red West, and Lamar Fike, an overfed Southerner whom Elvis called the Great Speckled Bird, would prop up a cocktail bar, ready to cue the laughter that such occasions required.

'The girls would be either starlet types with heavily made-up faces and puckered lips or wholesome groupies in jeans. Every one of them would jockey for the best position to catch Elvis's roving eye. He would look around and appear to fix one girl – say, a pert brunette – with a knowing stare. She would instantly smile until she realized that he was looking at the peaches and cream blonde next to her. The smile would vanish. No one would speak to Elvis unless Elvis spoke to them. Sometimes, something on TV would amuse him, and he would laugh.'

He was, however, far from amused about the impending arrival of the Beatles. His insecurity came out in several outbursts: he didn't like the movie he was shooting (it was 'the worst yet'), he didn't like the soundtrack ('Queenie Wahine's Papaya . . . *yuk!'*), he didn't like the way the Colonel and the studios had transformed him into an 'entertainer' rather than a singer who could also act dramatic roles, like the one he had played in *Flaming Star* ('What's an entertainer? A nice guy that everybody loves, and that ain't me'), and he didn't like the fact that everywhere he went, it was Beatles, Beatles and more Beatles.

He complained of having 'a hole deep down that I can't fill no matter what'. Not having had a hit single for more than three years only made matters worse. The Colonel, I discovered later, was having a terrible time controlling him. At one point, it was touch and go whether Elvis would actually open the front door to admit his guests, the rivals.

7

PRESLEY ENTERTAINS THE PRETENDERS

One night . . .

FRIDAY night, 27 August 1965. The bar of the Beverly Hillcrest hotel was crowded with newshounds in search of an exclusive. It was already early Saturday morning in London and the big Sunday newspapers would soon be screaming for some action on the Beatle front.

I was drinking alone, keeping the biggest secret of my life carefully under wraps. My friend Don Short, a reporter with the *Daily Mirror*, detached himself from one group and, drink in hand, joined me. 'Porky' Short was a chubby, prematurely balding man with the glow of a relentless bon vivant. But he had a wicked news sense and he sensed that something was up.

'I've spoken to Brian,' he said, leaning into the bar to suggest confidentiality. 'Something's going on. He wouldn't tell me what. It's Elvis, isn't it? Elvis meeting the Beatles?'

'Brian's in New York,' I replied. 'Anyway, why ask me? If I knew anything like that, I wouldn't be sitting here, would I?'

'I'm asking you because you're in with both Brian and the Colonel. Come on, Chris. Remember, we're pals.' I knew there was only one way out of this corner:

'Okay, okay. Just keep it to yourself, right? Elvis is meeting the Beatles tonight. But security is tight. I can't get you in. You'll have to find your own way.'

'Just give me the address.'

I levered myself off the bar stool, whipped out a pen and scribbled on the back of my bar check.

'Pick up my tab. If anyone asks, I've gone to the movies.' As I left, I secretly hoped that Porky enjoyed the striptease show at the address I'd copied down from a board above the bar payphone.

Parker collected me from the back of the hotel and we headed for LAX to pick up Brian Epstein on his return from New York. His flight arrived on time and he was soon aboard Parker's station wagon with Tom Diskin at the wheel. There was an ominous silence in the vehicle as Diskin swung it on to the San Diego Freeway. The Colonel broke it by asking Brian: 'Everything set your end?'

'Well, it was when I left New York,' was the tetchy reply.

'Just checkin',' said the Colonel, clearly enjoying the fact that he was now in charge. Through the windscreen, a street sign read 'SUNSET BLVD'.

'We change cars here,' commanded the Colonel. Everyone piled into a white limousine parked beside the kerb. When we reached Benedict Canyon, we switched cars again, this time into a black limousine with one of the Memphis Mafia at the wheel.

'Sure you weren't followed?' demanded the Colonel.

'Not unless they're hiding in the trunk,' the Mafioso answered sourly.

'Go check,' remonstrated the Colonel. 'We can't be too careful.'

The limousine swept past cops looking out for intruders until it reached the five-bar gate which marked the entrance to No. 2850, Mulholland Drive, Benedict Canyon. Already alerted to the news that the managers were on their way, we watched as John, Paul, George and Ringo emerged from the house and climbed into the back of their own limousine driven by Alf Bicknell, the amiable British chauffeur who had accompanied them to America. Thoroughly enjoying the intrigue, the Colonel shouted like a wagon master: 'Roll 'em!'

Parker's alert to the LAPD, who already had adjacent roads closed to all but those who could prove they were residents while the Beatles were holed up in the Canyon, proved effective. Police motorcycles pulled into the road to prevent anyone from following the limousines with their precious cargo, and moved ahead to block roads at approaching junctions in order to allow the vehicles to proceed without having to pause.

Halfway down the Canyon, the motorcade veered off to the right re-joining Sunset Boulevard near the iconic stone archway into Bel Air.

More police cars blocked the roadway, holding up traffic. Red lights flashed and the crackle of police radios sounded in the night. Then the road started to curve and rise steeply. This journey had been uphill all the way. Now, I was praying it would be a smooth ride back down.

A short driveway off Perugia Way led down to the grand front entrance of number 565. The white painted house was spectacularly floodlit seemingly in preparation for the great event it was to host on this balmy summer evening. I watched as the four boys from Liverpool – three from council house homes – stepped from their limousine to stand and stare at the elegant property before them. Perhaps, I wondered, Elvis had felt the same when he first viewed it. After all, he had been raised in a two-room shack in the one-horse town of Tupelo, Mississippi with no indoor bathroom, and this house had several. All five men had come such a long way and never was it more clear than at this moment.

As the electronically controlled wrought iron gates closed silently behind us, our group finally moved towards two towering palm trees guarding the front door where Elvis's main man, the ebullient Joe Esposito, stood waiting to greet his boss's guests. The large diamond set in the ring on his left hand (a gift from Elvis), glittered in the bright lights as he shook hands with each of us. After some brief banter with Colonel Parker – this man, after all, had to serve two masters – he led us into a two-storey entrance hall which featured a magnificent double staircase. This was luxury living at its finest. As recently as early 2015 the house was on the market for $18.5 million.

I patted the breast pocket of my jacket to make sure I had not forgotten the notebook in which I would secretly record (on frequent visits to the loo!) the fine detail of what I saw and heard over the next few hours. Missing for many years, that notebook recently resurfaced during a house move of my own and allows me access to information I had previously failed to recall. Needless to say it is now stored in a safe with other valuables such as the postcard reproduced on the cover of my earlier book, THE BEATLES: Messages from John, Paul, George and Ringo, and some historic letters from both Brian Epstein and Colonel Parker.

By now John, Paul, George and Ringo were surrounded by the Memphis Mafia – the men from Tennessee who made up Elvis's Praetorian Guard, remember. I caught John's eye and for once he looked as though he didn't know how he should behave: this was not the world of rock'n'roll he was expecting. I was about to offer him some reassurance when the ever-smiling Esposito delivered the dramatic invitation the Beatles had waited so long to hear: 'Come and meet Elvis'.

And with that he led the group into a vast living room where The King, smiling broadly, rose from his place on a horse-shoe couch suntanned and seemingly relaxed – although looks could be deceiving – he was wearing a scarlet shirt beneath a close-fitting black jerkin, it's high Napoleonic collar rising above his sideburns (I was to be told later that he changed three times before finally deciding on that outfit). He greeted each Beatle and their manager with a handshake and a pat on the arm before introducing his bride-to-be along with his bodyguards' wives. Priscilla Beaulieu was pure Hollywood starlet: her black bouffant towered above her forehead and she was heavily made up with thick black mascara, midnight blue eyeliner, red blusher and what I chose to describe as Heartbreak Pink lipstick. She was wearing a figure-hugging cream jacket with long pants and there was a jewelled tiara on her head.

As an entry in my precious recovered notebook reminds me, John attempted to introduce some Lennon humour into the moment by addressing Elvis in a Peter Sellers/Inspector Clouseau accent. Elvis shot me a puzzled glance but the biggest star in the world never stopped smiling. Gesturing his guests to take their seats he pointed to a table groaning with party food:

'Help yourselves if you're hungry.'

It was after 10pm, however, and Paul politely told him we had all eaten. Nobody was here for the food. Instrumental music was coming from a juke box in the corner. A television was switched on but the sound was off.

What does one say at a rock summit of this proportion? None of us seemed to know. Paul made some complimentary remarks about the house which Elvis responded to pointing out that in the daytime they would have been able to enjoy a view from the rear window (more of a glass wall) 'right across the golf course – not that I play, you understand'.

Next, Elvis picked up a gadget to switch channels on the still-silent TV. George was to remind me later that it was the first time any of us had seen a remote control – back home we were still getting used to colour television.

'I hear you guys had a little trouble on the plane ride to Portland,' said Elvis slipping more comfortably into his role of host.

'Yeah, like one of the engines caught fire,' replied George. 'But I've known worse. Another time, when we were flying out from Liverpool, the window next to me blew in.'

'I took off from Atlanta once,' recalled Elvis. 'The plane only had two engines and one of them failed. Boy, I was really scared. That time I thought my number was up. We had to take out pens and things – any sharp objects from our pockets and rest our heads on pillows between our knees. When we landed, the pilot was wringing wet with sweat even though it was snowin'.'

'Yeah, we've had some crazy experiences on tour,' interjected Paul. 'Once a guy ran on stage, pulled the leads out of the amplifiers and said to me, "One move and you're dead!"'

'It can be pretty scarin' sometimes,' said Elvis clearly doing his best to make Epstein's boys feel they'd all been friends for years. 'I remember once in Vancouver, we'd only done a number or two when some of the fans rushed the stage. It was lucky the band and I got off in time – they tipped the whole damn rostrum over.'

'I suppose it's easier for us,' said John.

'When the fans went for you, you were up there all alone. With us, it's four against everybody and we can at least draw support from each other.'

The banter went on until Elvis, shifting uncomfortably in his seat, said:

'But enough of that near-disaster stuff, we're all alive and well – and here. I thought we'd sit and talk about music. You guys up for a jam session?'

Four mop-topped heads nodded affirmatively and someone went to fetch the instruments he'd assembled for the occasion.

While the electric guitars were produced and plugged into amplifiers scattered around the room and a white piano was pushed into view, Colonel Parker bellowed from behind a hurriedly assembled roulette wheel table: 'Ladeez and gentlemen, the casino's open. Anyone who doesn't play a musical instrument is welcome.'

Brian needed no further encouragement: gambling had become his thing. Roadies Neil Aspinall and Malcom Evans and one or two members of the Memphis Mafia had moved to the cocktail bar for drinks and tough-guy talk and while others moved towards the latest Parker operation, I stayed close to the music – this was a session I would one day be able to tell my grandchildren about and I wasn't going to miss a single note.

Elvis picked up the bass guitar he'd been learning to play, John and George began tuning the two rhythm guitars and Paul sat down at the piano.

'Sorry there's no drum kit Ringo, we left that back in Memphis.'

'No worries,' responded the drummer, 'I'd rather play pool.' And with that he joined Jerry Schilling and Sonny West at the pool table.

It was beginning to look, and sound, like the party I had always planned for it to be.

While they sorted songs they all knew, Elvis played a few notes on his bass and addressed himself to Paul:

'Still not good huh… but I'm practicing.'

'Elvis lad,' replied Paul, 'you're coming along well. Keep up the rehearsals and Mr Epstein over there will make you a star.'

I shot a nervous glance at the Colonel, but with a cigar showed into one side of his mouth and a fistful of dollars in his grip,' he hadn't heard the remark although Brian had, and pulled a face. Phew! That was close.

And so Sergeant Presley's Lonesome Heartbreak Band was ready to play. In front of a privileged audience of just a couple of dozen people, a billion dollars' worth of talent was lined up to give its one and only performance.

'What's it gonna be?' asked Elvis.

'Let's do one by the other Cilla – Cilla Black,' said Paul, leading into *'You're My World'*.

'This beats talking, doesn't it,' said John. He could never resist making some obscure or barbed comment just when things were going well.

The Bel Air All-Stars proved to be just as good as one might have expected, slipping easily and freely into their individual roles. Elvis's voice rose, richer, deeper and more powerful than the others, his left leg pumping in time to the beat. You could feel the magic and he did it so naturally. Paul, on the piano, joined Elvis in some vocal duets, George worked in some of his neat little riffs and John, even if he was just going through the motions, didn't let the side down. I started to relax a bit and enjoy the piece of music history being enacted in front of my eyes.

Simultaneously, the roulette game proceeded and Ringo shot pool surrounded by six excited children while the wives and girlfriends watched the jam session with rapt expressions. Each time there was a lull, I slipped off to the bathroom to scribble the notes the Colonel had forbidden me to make but knew perfectly well I would.

Elvis was getting into the spirit of the evening. 'This is what you guys gave me for my thirtieth birthday,' he said. 'It made me sick.'

Then he laughed as he led them on bass guitar into *I Feel Fine*.

'Why have you dropped the old stuff? The rock?' asked John, for once with feeling. 'I loved the old Sun records.'

For a moment, Elvis looked uncomfortable. This was one line of questioning he must have expected but clearly had not looked forward to.

'It's true I'm stuck with some movie soundtracks but that doesn't mean I can't do rock 'n' roll anymore,' he said perhaps a little testily. 'I'd love one day to go back on the road just like you all are doing.' And in the only reference I heard him make alluding to matters financial, he added: 'Plus I have to put food on the table, just like you. A lot of tables…'His voice trailed off as he looked across at his gambling manager, a sad expression on his face.

John caught the change of mood and in a bid to swing it back, reverted to his Clouseau accent: 'Zis is ze way it should be... Ze small homely gathering wiz a few friends and a leetle muzic.' A perplexed Elvis shook his head.

The next couple of hours slipped by and I felt I could relax even though Elvis – no fool him – asked me on one of my returns from a note-taking session in the bathroom, 'Somethin' wrong with your bladder?'

It was well after midnight when *it* happened: John on a stroll around the house once the music making had stalled, spotted an illuminated table lamp. It was made in the style of a western wagon, just like the ones the Colonel had presented to us on his gift dispatching visit to the Beatles the previous year. This one, however, was different: emblazoned on its canvas cover was the slogan, in bold capital letters, ALL THE WAY WITH LBJ. Sadly, it was the flame which lit a fire set to burn inside him for the rest of his days.

To John, Lyndon Baines Johnson was nothing less than a warmonger responsible for the slaughter of innocent civilians in what he – John – regarded as a civil war between the Vietnamese people. John's mood could change in an instant, and that is exactly what happened at the party Elvis Presley threw for the Beatles that night.

He reacted a little later when he heard Elvis, answering a question from George, say: 'Making movies gives me a lot of free time. We finished one – I won't say which – that took just fifteen days to complete.'

'Well, we've got an hour to spare now,' said the Beatle with the shark-infested mouth. 'Let's make an epic together.' To some it might have sounded like a joke but now he was probably seething inside.

Elvis looked stunned, but held his tongue. John had been too clever to mention Vietnam outright, knowing that this would only lead to a political argument in which he would be hopelessly outnumbered. His technique in situations like this was to make people look foolish over something they believed in. By putting Elvis down over his movies, he was also belittling the King's support for the Vietnam War.

In hindsight, I would classify that crack from John as the final insult, the one that started the feud for real. Before that, the disputed territory between Elvis and the Beatles had been about record sales in the marketplace, public acclaim at the box office and headlines in newspapers. Now it would become a highly personal conflict, which had nothing whatever to do with music but everything to do with politics: a stand-off between Elvis, the staunch American patriot, and John, the vehement anti-war protester.

The former tank corps sergeant got up from the couch and went over to Sonny West and Alan Fortas, a former football player known as Hog Ears. Only Elvis and the Memphis Mafia dared call him that. He was clearly disturbed but far too polite to say what was going on in his head. I learned later that he told his pals he thought John was stoned which was quite probably true.

The atmosphere now was strained. Had I been looking for a sensational 'feud' story then I was surely on the brink of one now, but that had never been the intention. I had merely wanted to set up a meeting between the greatest music stars on Earth and cover it so that people could read about it in years to come. Had Brian Epstein and I thought it through we might have realised that John would probably misbehave. As it was, the mood he was in made his anger about America's actions in south east Asia overcome his love of rock'n'roll.

For the rest of the night – and we stayed at Perugia Way until around 2am – the hosts did what they could to put their guests at their ease. Elvis, no fool, chided me again about my frequent visits to his bathroom – he'd spotted the notebook. Having won on the tables, Parker promised to buy Epstein a cocktail cabinet 'Because I can see you like your drink', and the latter said he would have a Shetland pony dispatched to California 'to remind you of your circus days, Colonel'.

Ringo told Elvis he would be welcome to enjoy their hospitality if he cared to call over to Benedict Canyon the following day. He didn't take up the offer and he never spoke to John again.

As we stepped out into the Bel Air night, the Colonel turned to me and said: 'Tell the fans it was a great meeting.' John overheard him and said something to the contrary.

The happiest note was struck by chauffeur Alf Bicknell: 'He called me "sir",' he said almost crying with delight. 'Elvis Presley called me "sir"!'

Needless to say, Elvis did not visit the Beatles and he never spoke to John Lennon again. John, however, was soon talking about Elvis in glowing terms, which I knew to be totally at odds with his true feelings.

'There's only one person in the United States of America that we ever wanted to meet – not that he wanted to meet us! And we met him last night,' he said. 'We can't tell you how we felt. We just idolized him so much. The only person we wanted to meet in the USA was Elvis Presley. We can't tell you what a thrill that was.'

Privately, John later gave friends a different opinion. 'It was just like meeting Engelbert Humperdinck,' he was to say later. Asked to comment, Paul would only say that Elvis was 'odd'. Yet, coming from the most diplomatic Beatle, that word spoke volumes.

The close encounter in his own home simply added familiarity to Elvis's contempt. For months, he raged against the Beatles in general and John in particular.

Priscilla recalls finding him soon afterwards, stoned in the back garden, gazing down the escarpment to the greens of the Bel Air Country Club, where a sprinkler system was in operation.

'Can you see 'em, Sattnin?' he asked her.

'See what, honey, the water?'

'The angels out there.'

'Angels?'

'I have to go baby. They're calling me. They want to tell me something.'

Elvis started to walk down towards the 'angels' on the lawn and had to be gently led back to the safety of his house.

By autumn, the Colonel knew that Elvis had to say something to his fans about the Beatles. He persuaded him to make the following delicately-worded statement:

> People have said my absence from personal appearances has given the Beatles their big opportunities. I know nothing about that. As for the Beatles, all I can say is – more power to them. I have watched all their television appearances over here. I don't think I should say what I feel about them. It wouldn't be fair to fellow entertainers.
>
> I'll say the Beatles have got what it takes and in great abundance and that they've been given a heck of a vote of confidence. I'm sorry, but I have to be diplomatic and I'm honest about it. They are entertainers like myself and I guess they're as dedicated as the rest of us. Which, in the long run, is all that matters. I wish them luck.

John told me: 'I'm not sure who's the bigger bullsh***er – him or me. The vendetta that had begun at 565 Perugia Way still had a long way to go.

There was to be no winner.

8

SIR ELVIS?

Too much

THE MEETING in Bel Air had proved that the Colonel was a great fixer. He had what Las Vegas called 'juice', casino slang for the right connections. Anyone in show business who had ever crossed swords with him knew that for a fact.

Following their initial skirmishes, Brian frequently called him for help. Sometimes the Colonel offered his advice whether the Englishman had sought it or not. The Colonel was evasive on this point when I asked him who had placed the call, late on the afternoon (Pacific time) of 6 August 1966, during one of the Beatles' darkest hours – Brian Epstein or himself? Not that it really mattered. The distressed tone that was usual in Brian's voice in such situations had been the memorable thing. An avid news-watcher, particularly when a story concerned other entertainers, the Colonel was well aware of the big trouble the Beatles were in.

Five months earlier, John had obliged his journalist friend Maureen Cleave with an interview for London's *Evening Standard,* in which he remarked that the Beatles were 'more popular than Jesus'. The quote had gone virtually unnoticed when the *Standard* published it, but the full interview had just been reprinted in the American magazine *Datebook*, with the seemingly blasphemous one-liner, 'Bigger than Jesus', splashed across the front cover. The Beatles were about to start their third major tour of the US, and John's *faux pas* was flashed across the nation like news of a major catastrophe.

What John had actually said was:

'Christianity will go. It will vanish and shrink. I needn't argue about that; I'm right and I will be proved right. We're more popular than Jesus now. I don't know which will go first, rock 'n' roll or Christianity. Jesus was all right but his disciples were thick and ordinary. It's them twisting it that ruins it for me.'

Although he was still recovering from glandular fever, Brian had left his sickbed to fly to New York in a desperate attempt to salvage the tour. He had evaded questions fired by journalists awaiting his arrival at Kennedy Airport only by promising to give a full-scale press conference at his hotel, the Sheraton, the following day.

Brian admitted to me later that he had been tense as he discussed with Elvis's manager the best strategy to employ with the now-hostile media. The older man hardly needed to remind him of the advice he had already given him on several previous occasions: that the Beatles should not give interviews in which they confided their private, innermost thoughts. 'You have to think of the fans, Brian,' he had said. 'The fans don't want their idols mixed up in controversy.'

'Controversy' was an understatement for the situation facing Brian. The pop manager was about to become a Daniel in the lions' den. His intelligence sources provided bleak news from all fronts.

Parker watched from his office in L.A. as promoters who had booked the Beatles to appear in stadiums across America were being bombarded with protest calls.

Tickets remained unsold; cancellations were rising. The office of Nat Weiss, Epstein's friend and New York lawyer, had received dozens of complaints, mainly from the Bible Belt, warning that John would not go unpunished for his sacrilege. More than thirty radio stations announced that they had banned Beatle records. Even those dubious defenders of the faith, the Klu Klux Klan, were marching to the crackle of Beatle records burning on bonfires.

'Tell the boy to apologise,' advised the Colonel.

'He refuses to apologise for something he didn't say.'

'What are you planning to do?'

'I'll cancel the tour if necessary.'

'That'll cost you plenty.'

'I've already checked and I've been told it will cost us a million dollars, but I don't care. I'm not going to put the boys' lives at risk even if it costs $10 million. This is developing into a holy war and I'll cancel . . . unless . . .'

'Unless what, Brian?'

During his transatlantic flight, Brian had feverishly examined his options, and he now ran one possibility past the Colonel. It had not escaped Brian's attention that the centre of the most fanatical anti-Beatle activity was Memphis, Elvis's home town and the so-called 'buckle on the Bible Belt'. Even now, Memphis city council was meeting to discuss a possible ban on the group's concert because of the Jesus remark.

Brian now wondered aloud whether Elvis, a devout (if prodigal) Christian, might be prepared to help out. Perhaps he could issue a statement saying that John's quote had been misunderstood, that he had said 'more popular than Jesus', not 'bigger than Jesus', and was really a good chap: a God-fearing Beatle.

By this time, nothing fazed the Colonel. He was used to being asked to lend Elvis's support for one purpose or another. And he was used to saying no. On this occasion, however, he saw an opportunity to test his rival's mettle. It was Epstein's winding-up remark he found irresistible: 'And needless to say, if there is anything *we* could ever do for *you* . . .'

The Colonel must have smiled to himself. He so admired titles and the honours that invariably went with them (so much so that he had bestowed one on himself even before two obliging governors no less, in Tennessee and Louisiana, had seen fit to approve it). He had, for instance, been greatly impressed the previous year to read that the Queen had presented the Beatles with medals at Buckingham Palace. He believed that the Beatles' MBEs had been cleverly engineered through Brian's contacts in English society, soon after Brian had struck up a close friendship with the Queen's sister, Princess Margaret.

Now it was the Colonel's turn to wonder aloud. Perhaps somebody could suggest to Her Majesty that an honorary award for Elvis might be in order. It would be Britain's way of showing its appreciation for such a fine, upstanding and much loved American. If Lennon were to be elevated to St John, why not Sir Elvis Presley? The Snowmen's League was in session and the Colonel was in the chair.

Brian said that he had tried to explain that he really had not had a hand in the Beatles' royal honour.

'These things are worked out between the prime minister and the monarch,' he told the Colonel. 'You just can't negotiate them in the way it might be possible to swing a show business award.'

By now, Brian was convinced that the old showman was playing games with him. He couldn't seriously believe that he could pull strings to get Elvis an honorary knighthood. Or could he? The Colonel had performed the seemingly impossible on so many occasions and now here he was challenging his rival to do the same.

Brian's next call that night was to John Lennon. Whether or not he told him about Parker's proposition is unknown, but *something* shifted the Beatle's previously intransigent position. His most stubborn client agreed to make a conciliatory statement to the press:

'I'm not anti-God, anti-Christ or anti-religion,' John said soon after the Beatles reached Chicago. 'I was not saying we're greater or better. I believe in God, but not as an old man in the sky. I used "Beatles" because it was easier for me to talk about Beatles. I'm sorry I said it really. I apologise if that will make you happy.'

The tour went ahead, only for the Beatles to be unnerved by an anonymous death threat, saying that they would be shot in Memphis. There were some tense moments when firecrackers exploded at the Mid-South Coliseum during the concert, but apart from that, there were no hitches.

With his love of intrigue, the Colonel has never owned up to what he failed to pull off for Elvis, but he acknowledged to me that 'there are many things you know about from knowing us that I can't stop you from writing.'

By the time he was selling Elvis in the mid-Fifties, there was already a secrecy about his *modus operandi* and a mystique about the man himself that many people found infuriating and not altogether edifying. It was tempting to some to dismiss him as nothing more than a carny hustler, a man who dyed sparrows yellow and passed them off to suckers as canaries or who sold foot-long hot-dogs with bits of frankfurter sticking out at either end and none in the middle.

The Colonel played along with this stereotype because it suited his purposes. In fact, it was his own invention, and he was often guilty of spreading these stories himself. Beatles roadie Neil Aspinall remembered this classic: 'He told us about an aged circus lion that had lost its teeth. The Colonel had a set of false teeth made up and he put them in the lion's mouth every time it had to go on show. But first, he smeared them with a bit of mustard. The lion was constantly irritated in its mouth and would roar *aaaargh!* as though it was really fierce although it was fifty years old and could hardly move. But the Colonel was such a bullsh***er anyway, he was probably making it up.'

However, many people who heard these stories swallowed them whole and accepted the Colonel on face value. What you saw, they said, was what you got: an overfed, moon-faced huckster who had somehow got lucky and was now revelling in playing the big shot. Big, bluff and boastful, he looked like a man who had just eaten a plate of self-congratulation for lunch.

However, I had come to realise that his public persona was simply a front, a mask to hide the real person. Men of the world such as Frank Sinatra, Sid Bernstein and Henri Lewin, the Hilton Hotel boss, knew this instinctively. 'He was the first man who did not call the star by his full name – just *Elvis*,' Lewin told me. 'You know, Sinatra copied that ten years later. The Colonel was tough. If he had died first, I'm convinced Elvis's career would have ended. The Colonel was the one who made this thing last.'

There was more to the Colonel than met the eye and he went to great lengths to disguise it. Two of his most useful props were the cigar and the hat, both of which gave the impression that he equated power with size. It was noticeable that, as his ability to influence events developed, his cigars grew longer and the brim on his hats increased in width. Over the years, he graduated from small Dutch cigars to large Havanas, and from battered trilbys to stately, ten-gallon Stetsons.

In other ways, he seemed to be incredibly small-minded. The audience of 55,600 people that Sid Bernstein had packed into Shea to see the

Beatles in 1965 might have been bigger than any Elvis got until ten years later, but the important thing to the Colonel had been who had the hot-dog concession. The Beatles drew phenomenal crowds, but according to Elvis's manager, it was the detail that made the difference. Raised in the heyday of the carnival, the Colonel had learned a simple truth: if enough nickels and dimes went in the same direction, you counted the profit in millions of dollars. He was a happy man if he could print a million Elvis photographs for a nickel each and sell them for a dime.

'The Colonel was very shrewd – he got money from everywhere, even the photos,' said Sid Bernstein. 'I would see the Colonel stand in the lobby and sell photos. When I worked with him from '72 to '74, he was charging a buck a time.'

For Bernstein, the Colonel was an acquired taste. 'At first I did not like him – I thought he was an egomaniac but quite a good twister, you know,' he said. 'One day he took me to lunch at Plato Reserva, which is a very wonderful Italian restaurant in Little Italy.

'"Sid, you don't like me very much, do you?" said the Colonel.

'"What makes you say that, Colonel?"

'"I can tell."

'"You're right, Colonel."

'"I want you to understand something. Elvis Presley is my client, he is the biggest act in the world, my one job is to protect him and, if that offends anybody, then I am sorry but, understand, I'm just here to take care of my client. I was born to do that and this is my job and I hope I do it as well or maybe better than any man.'"

Sitting there over the pasta, Bernstein had had a sudden change of heart. 'From that moment on, I respected him,' he said. 'I got to like him and understand him and we became good friends. He was the greatest manager that ever lived.'

The bigger picture tended to confirm this. The Colonel made movie and merchandising deals that brought Elvis $5 or $6 million dollars a year, and when the movie money dried up, he sold him on a Las Vegas tablecloth for another $5 million for just ten months' work spread over five years. And that was before he had shifted a single Elvis mugshot, souvenir programme or statuette.

If Brian Epstein prided himself on knowing what people wanted, the Colonel's genius was in persuading them to buy what they didn't need. As a salesman, he had few equals.

But Brian was a fast learner and he came to appreciate the Colonel's skills and to regard him as something of a mentor, even if he remained a mystery. Brian told me he consulted him on numerous occasions, particularly on matters of security, such as the successful getaway from Dallas airport in the laundry truck. On other occasions, Brian booked rooms for the Beatles in several hotels, just as the Colonel had advised him to do, to throw unwelcome newshounds off the scent. He even considered another of the Colonel's suggestions: to have them lie down on canvas-covered couches to be smuggled in and out of hotels by furniture removers. But these were all tricks of the trade. The Colonel guarded his personal secrets jealously, and for good reason. He had never intended the world to discover that he had been born not Thomas Andrew Parker in West Virginia, as he had allowed others to believe, but as a Dutchman of humble origins.

Jack Kelly, one of the two Los Angeles private investigators hired by Vernon Presley, had turned up a wealth of material about the Colonel during his enquiries.

'In further checking the Colonel, I have determined that my original information on him was slightly awry,' Kelly informed me in one of several written reports. 'The correct spelling of his name is Andreas Wilhelmus von Kujik and he was born on 26 June 1909, at Breda, Holland.'

Two days after the Colonel's birth, his father Adam von Kujik had gone to the Breda town hall to register it, a blacksmith and a shoemaker acting as witnesses. Andreas (later it was shortened to the diminutive Dries) was Maria van Kujik's fifth child and there were to be four more. The man who was destined to manage the biggest star of the 20th century, and to become as wealthy as the American dream would ever allow, had been born to the unpretentious van Kujiks in their apartment over some stables on a modest Breda street called Vlaszak.

Young Dries made a pet goat the star of his own mini-circus, charging friends a small fee for admission. That was before he learned to crack a whip and make huge draught horses trot slowly around the stable yard, turning about on command.

Jack Kelly's report picks up the story:

Dries left Holland in 1927 to avoid military service, spent a few months in England, and then went to the West Indies. He entered the US in 1928. He sold hotdogs in a carnival [the Royal American, which toured Canada and the US by railroad] until 1931 when he enlisted in the US Army, supposedly serving in Panama for a while. He was discharged in 1936 with a small pension for a back injury. That same year he wrote home for the last time and told his family that he had legally changed his name to Thomas Andrew Parker.

He next surfaced in 1940 when he was the dogcatcher of the Humane Society of Tampa, Florida. He started booking shows at the weekend into a little theatre in Tampa. It was during this period that he met the country & western singer Eddy Arnold and became friendly with him. In 1945, he convinced Arnold that he could expand his career [which he did] and became his fulltime manager.

The Colonel had first gone to Las Vegas with Arnold in 1944 after doing a deal with the William Morris Agency. That same year he signed Arnold to the RCA record label, and the deal took off with a massive hit, the million-seller 'Bouquet of Roses'.

The Colonel had based himself in Nashville and, after securing Arnold's Vegas and RCA deals, bought a sprawling eleven-room, one-storey house on Gallatin Road in Madison, Tennessee, operating his business from the garage. The Colonel's assistant in those days was the dapper Tom Diskin, who remained with him throughout Elvis's career, just as the Colonel stayed faithful to RCA and the William Morris Agency, subsequently committing Presley to both.

Jack Kelly's report continued:

> Through his association with Arnold, he met and became known to all the performers and bookers of country & western, including Hank Snow. Now Snow at that time was one of, if not the biggest, country & western stars.
>
> In 1954, Parker and Hank Snow formed a company called Jamboree Attractions, which booked touring shows starring country & western performers. This probably is the single most contributing factor for the spread of country & western music throughout the US. Formerly it had been confined to the South and Southwest.
>
> In 1954, Parker was in Texarkana, Texas, scouting for some new acts for his Jamboree Attractions when he first saw Elvis Presley performing. That was all the Colonel needed and the rest is history. Checking with the FBI and Interpol does not reveal any criminal record under either his given or adopted name.

Loyalty was the Colonel's watchword. 'You gotta be loyal to people,' he had once told me. 'When you are loyal to them, they're loyal to you and everybody gets to make a buck or two.'

In 1966, the Colonel had reason to doubt Elvis's loyalty to him, but he acted with great self-control. Elvis had fallen under the influence of Larry Geller, a self-styled 'hair nutritionist' and spiritualist from New

York. Geller, who had started cutting Elvis's hair in 1964, coaxed him into reading such esoteric books as *Through the Eyes of the Masters*, *The Wisdom of the Overself*, *Cosmic Consciousness*, *Cheiro's Book of Numbers* and Paramahansa Yogananda's *The Autobiography of a Yogi*. Elvis lapped up the new knowledge and started to ask questions about the direction his own life was taking.

Geller guided him to the Self-Realization Fellowship Centre on Mount Washington in the Hollywood Hills. As the Colonel and the hard core of the Memphis Mafia watched in alarm, Elvis started changing in definable ways, not all of them conducive to the old, free-spending lifestyle that had guaranteed that he would have to work almost constantly to pay the bills. He experimented with marijuana and LSD, saw Stalin's face in some clouds over the desert ('the Anti-Christ'), and heard Jesus's voice in birdsong. He was definitely moving to a higher plane of consciousness.

When Elvis had an accident in the middle of the night at his new home, 10550 Rocca Place in Stone Canyon, the Colonel moved in for the kill.

'He was taking downers that were making him slur quite a bit and, from what I understand, were responsible for him having a fall at home, hitting his head,' said Sonny West. 'He may have even taken the prescribed amount, but he got up to go to the bathroom when he shouldn't have.

'He had in his employ a barber to cut his hair to have him looking nice for the movies, who was also bringing him all kinds of spiritual books.

'At that time, Elvis had those books burned and the guy was dismissed and that was it.'

In fact, Geller was not dismissed, although the spiritual texts that he had encouraged Elvis to read were blown to the four winds in a very occult bonfire. The Colonel also ruled that one of the Guys had to be present whenever Geller cut Elvis's hair. This put an end to the cosy téte-a-tétes that the guru had enjoyed with his employer, and so he quit. However, Elvis invited Geller to join his personal entourage when he started touring again in the Seventies.

His head recovered from both the fall and the mystic mindset, Elvis went on to make *Clambake,* in which he stars as a rich man who trades places with a poor man so that people will accept him for himself. Geller must have found that highly amusing.

29 USA

ROCK & ROLL SINGER, 1935-1977

ELVIS

FROM BOYHOOD TO NATIONAL HERO: Elvis was to grow into the national figure his country would honour with a postage stamp just like the UK has always done over the centuries with its monarchs. But Elvis Presley's first performance (*below*) was singing *Old Shep* as a very junior cowboy at the Mississippi-Alabama country fair and dairy show talent contest. He came 5th.

HUMBLE BEGINNINGS:

Elvis was born on January 8, 1935 in the two-room shotgun shack (*below*) which was built by his father Vernon. The abode was set in woodland on the dusty old Saltillo Road (now Presley Heights) on the east side of Tupelo. Mississippi. When Elvis was asked if that was the wrong side of the tracks, he answered 'In Tupelo there wasn't really a right side of the tracks. No one was eating too good. We never starved, but we were close to it at times.'

Following the death at birth of his twin brother Jesse Garon, Gladys took special care of her surviving son with the result that Elvis was bullied by boys in the neighbourhood who called him a 'Mommy's boy'.

THE FORMATIVE YEARS: Elvis at 15 (*above*) sitting on a Memphis sidewalk with his first dancing partner, neighbour Betty McCann.

MODERN STUDIOS

MEMPHIS *Recording* SERVICE

706 UNION AT MARSHALL   TELEPHONE 37-7197

January 6 _____ 195_4

Elvis Presley

462 Alabama Street

Memphis, Tennessee

STATEMENT

DATE	QUAN.	DESCRIPTION	AMOUNT
01/04	1	Acetate Master 0812-A and 0812-B	$ 8.25

SUN RECORD CO.
UNION AT MARSHALL
MEMPHIS, TENN.

—0812-A/B—
Acetate Masters
Master Protection
Metal Masters
Metal Mother
Stampers
Studio Time Elvis Presley
Talent

Paid

Paid

DISC   "WE RECORD ANYTHING—ANYWHERE—ANYTIME"   TAPE

**Big Stage Show
5 Big Stars
ALVIS PRESLEY
(That's Alright)**
★ ★ ★
BILLY WALKER
(Thank You For Calling)
★ ★ ★
PEACH SEED JONES
(If You Don't Someone Else Will)
★ ★ ★

CITY AUDITORIUM

**SAN ANGELO
Wednesday, Jan. 5th
8:00 P.M.**
Adults $1.00 Children 50¢

MAKING A START: Elvis paid $8.25 to Sam Phillips' Memphis Recording Service (later he Sun label) for the acetate on one of his earliest recording sessions. He put down two songs, *I'll never walk alone* and *It wouldn't be the same without you.* He was appearing at various local shows but was so little known they frequently spelled his name wrongly - see 'Alvis' in the flyer on the right, others spelled Presley with two 'S's. They soon learned.

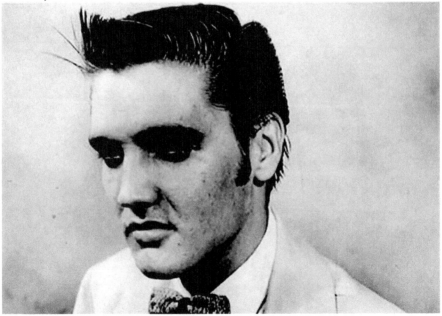

EARLY REWARDS: There were two early rewards for Elvis when he started to get successful. The local boys who had once called him a 'Mommy's boy', began to seek him out to join their football games and (*lower picture*) he was able to buy his parents a single-storey ranch-style house on Audubon Drive, Memphis, where his mother parked the pink Cadillac he bought her but which she never learned to drive. He lived there for 13 months before buying Graceland for $100,000.

WORRIED MUM: Gladys Presley was never happy when Elvis was on the road and would often cry as he left home for a gig. She said she could never get over the fear of him being hurt in a road accident or robbed of the money he brought back. She began to drink heavily and became deeply depressed despite the comforting of husband Vernon. It did not, make any difference to Elvis's wild stage performances (*below*).

THE ELVIS PRESLEY SHOW
STARRING
IN PERSON

ELVIS
PRESLEY

WITH AN ALL STAR CAST
THE JORDONAIRES
PHIL MARAQUIN
FRANKIE CONNORS
BLUE MOON BOYS & Others

RCA Victor Recording Star
HEAR HIM SING
"HEARTBREAK HOTEL"
"BOUND DOG"
AND THE OTHER GREAT
RECORDING HITS

FLORIDA THEATRE
JACKSONVILLE · FLORIDA
FRI · SAT AUG 10 · 11
MATINEE AND NIGHT SHOWS

THE FINAL FIFTIES TOURS
ALAN HANSON

FIRM FRIENDS: If there was one man in the world who could talk to Elvis in a man-to-man way it was Tom Jones. "If he was talking rubbish Tom would tell him without fear of harming their friendship, Elvis respected him,' said Lamar Fike. Elvis called on Tom to witness the Welshman's Las Vegas debut in 1967. There was never any shortages of VIPs on the film sets. Here (*below*) Elvis and Colonel Parker are with Tennessee Williams, the late Laurence Harvey and producer Hal Wallis.

TIME TO DRESS UP: Elvis gets fitted for a new jacket by his long-term tailor, Bernard Lansky and (*below*), always known for his gentle sense of humour, he cracks Sammy Davis Jnr up during some dressing room banter.

ARMY BOUND: Elvis joined the U.S. Army in March 1958 - but he had to get a haircut first. When he returned from Germany at the end of his military service, manager Parker was there to greet him as he stepped off the train in Memphis.

SEEING THE BEATLES OFF: Elvis was photographed seeing John, Paul, George and Ringo off from his Beverly Hills home after their historic meeting in August 1965. Author Hutchins, who arranged the meeting, is standing in front of him.'

(Below left) Elvis's cook Mary Jenkins and *(right)* Elvis and his father with his new stepmother Dee Stanley and her sons. Elvis called her 'The wicked stepmother' a title she justified when she wrote two vile books about him following his death.

LEADING MEN: Elvis makes a point to Fred Astaire while Frank Sinatra looks on. That's No.1 man Joe Esposito between Presley and Sinatra. (*Below*) The King shakes hands with the President after calling on him (albeit unexpectedly) at the White House in December 1970.

MAGIC MOMENTS: (*Left*) A classic scene from what many regard as his greatest movie, *Jailhouse Rock*. (*right*) Elvis paid $10,000 to present to Muhammed Ali this elaborate dressing gown he had made 'specially for him. Ali wore it 'to dazzle Ken Norton' when they met for a heavyweight championship fight in March 1973. Below Elvis shows his musicians the gold disc he had just been awarded for *Heartbreak Hotel*.

The Sun

HE WAS 42 AND ALONE

KING ELVIS DEAD

A massive heart attack at sundown

DUCHESS DIES TO HALT TV SERIES — Page 2

Daily Mail

ELVIS, KING OF ROCK, DIES AT 42

Daily Mirror ELVIS

PRESLEY IS DEAD

Was king of Rock killed by drugs?

THE COMMERCIAL APPEAL

Death Captures Crown Of Rock And Roll
— Elvis Dies Apparently After Heart Attack

Memphis Press-Scimitar FINAL

Memphis Leads World in Mourning For Elvis Presley

A Lonely Life Ended On Elvis Presley Blvd.

THE END OF A LEGEND: It required more than forty limousines to transport relatives, friends and celebrities in Elvis's funeral procession on August 18, 1977 - two days after his tragic death. Initially he was buried next to his mother in Memphis's Forest Hills Cemetery, but later both were moved to the Meditation Garden at Graceland for fear grave robbers would strike in the public burial ground. When he died two years later, Vernon Presley was buried alongside them.

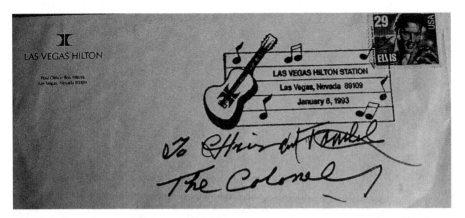

Over the years the Colonel wrote me a number of letters, writes author Hutchins. Thoughtful as ever he even sent me an envelope addressed to 'Chris and Family' (above) with the Elvis Presley stamp on it the day the stamp was issued - the day which would have been Elvis's 58th birthday.

But the most moving of all his letters, sent from his office in Madison, Tennessee, on October 13, 1981. began: 'Friend Chris, Thank you for your letter dated September 29th. As you know I have a fractured shoulder and take special treatment exercises.'

I had asked him if it was true that Elvis never toured overseas because, being an illegal immigrant, he - Parker - had no passport. His response was: 'Chris, I am going to be blunt with you. I know you have been a friend for many years, and so have I [sic]. In answer to your question about the passport, that is total bunk. First of all Elvis at all times made the final decision if he wanted to go on tours, not me. We presented the tours to him and on several occasions tours of Japan and England were talked about but we never got a final OK [from him]. I used to receive complaints from fans about why Elvis did not come to England and I told them to tell Elvis to let me know when he wanted to go as I was tired of hearing from them that Elvis wanted to go but I would not let him. This was ridiculous as he could do whatever he wanted with his career. As for me not being able to go, if so, it meant nothing for we had plenty of people available on my staff to do so.

'As to your question on drugs, I can't help what you read in books as there are so many untruths in the many books which have come out, which I understand as they are all printed to make money with some information coming from some people who should say the nice things Elvis did for them . . . I did whatever I could do for him in the best way I could. He was his own person and did not accept any influence on his personal life from anyone . . .

'My association with Elvis had nothing to do with his or my personal life. I will endeavour one day to let the world know the many good deeds this man did for the people that are now helping to tear him down. If they knew all these bad things they sure waited until he passed away to talk about it but they are not remembering all he did for them.'

He concluded his letter by saying what he had written 'comes from one friend to another who I feel can understand.'

9

MARRIAGE, DEATH . . . AND REBIRTH

Witchcraft

FOR HOURS, Elvis concentrated on the lyrics of new Beatle records as they were released, trying to detect any anti-American propaganda or coded messages about drugs. When *Sgt Pepper's Lonely Hearts Club Band* was released in the summer of 1967, he thought he had hit the jackpot.

One of the songs, 'Lucy in the Sky with Diamonds', contained just such a reference – to LSD – in its title. John had actually borrowed the line from his young son Julian, who said it was the theme of a painting he had drawn at nursery school, but to Elvis, *Sgt Pepper* provided positive proof that what he had suspected all along was true. The Beatles, now shaggier than ever with large drooping moustaches, were the bellwethers of America's great unwashed druggie flock.

This was a difficult time for Elvis. The Colonel, it is widely believed, had decided that marriage would be a good career move for him and had arranged a secret wedding ceremony in Las Vegas. Elvis married Priscilla at the Aladdin Hotel on 1 May, squeezing his nuptials and the briefest of honeymoons in between filming scenes for *Clambake*. George Klein, however, believes that it was Elvis's idea all along and that the Colonel did not apply any pressure on him.

'I was one of fourteen people in the room – I was a groomsman,' said George. 'Elvis had called me from California on 4 March to tell me that he was going to get married. There I was, sitting on one of the greatest secrets in show business of all time.

'The weekend of the wedding, I flew out to LA and then to Palm Springs in the Lear Jet that Elvis had chartered. It was me and Elvis, Priscilla, and Joe Esposito and his wife Joanie. We flew from Palm Springs to Vegas and the rest of the wedding party followed in another plane. We got into Vegas late at night, maybe two or three o'clock in the morning, and Elvis and Joe went to the registrar to get the wedding licence. It's open all night long and actually Elvis went down there at 4.00am so that they wouldn't be crowded. We got about three hours' sleep and they had the wedding about ten o'clock in the morning. After the ceremony, we went downstairs to a reception, where the rest of the party were waiting.

'Elvis got married because he was in love with Priscilla. They had been dating for a long time, and he felt that it was the right time. He also wanted a family. I don't think the Colonel had anything to do with it; that's a misconception.'

The last thing that Elvis wanted as a wedding present was yet another collection of soar away Beatle hits, but that is precisely what he got: the group's greatest-ever creative masterpiece, a *tour de force* so dazzling in its musical concept and so brilliant in its technical execution that it would revolutionize popular music.

The *Sgt Pepper* album also provided convincing evidence of a subtle change in the Beatles' attitude towards Elvis. It was Paul's idea to feature dozens of celebrities, both living and dead, on the most famous record cover of all time.

'We want all our heroes together here,' he said. 'If we believe this is a very special album for us, we should have a lot of people who are special to us on the sleeve with us.'

Each of the Beatles was asked to submit a list of twelve favourite heroes and heroines from throughout the ages for a tableau to be created by the artist Peter Blake and photographed by Michael Cooper. When the lists were handed in, one obvious name was missing: Elvis Presley.

Stu Sutcliffe, Lennon's dearest friend was there, along with Bob Dylan and Dion from the pop world, Marilyn Monroe, Mae West and Diana Dors (but not Jayne Mansfield), Tony Curtis, Marlon Brando and Lawrence of Arabia (ironically three of Elvis's own heroes), W. C. Fields, Marlene Dietrich, Carl Jung, Edgar Allen Poe and Fred Astaire. Oh, and Albert Einstein. Two of John's candidates, Adolf Hitler and Jesus Christ, were ruled ineligible on the grounds of taste.

Elvis noted the omission of his own face as he scoured the line-up searching for incriminating clues. The face that attracted his eagle eye was the bearded, patrician figure of Karl Marx, practically the godhead of Communism, who was standing between Oliver Hardy and H. G. Wells. If anyone had doubted that the Beatles were Reds, here was the proof. In the United States, *Sgt Pepper* sold more than 2.5 million copies in three months and won four Grammy awards, further confirmation in Elvis's eyes that American youth was held in dangerous thrall.

Brian Epstein took the unusual step of holding a special press launch party for Sgt Pepper at his London house in Chapel Street, Belgravia, on 19 May 1967.

The more I saw of him, the more I understood why the Beatles – and Paul in particular – were concerned about his mental health. We dined frequently at Overton's, a restaurant in St James's. He would pore over the menu, carefully choosing his dish of the evening and instructing how he wanted his vegetables cooked or his salad prepared. He would then pop a handful of pills, insisting that I join him in what he called 'our little helpers'. The uppers were appetite suppressants, and by the time our food arrived, neither of us wanted to eat. Time after time, the food would be sent back to the kitchen with 'Mr Epstein's compliments to the chef', but never an explanation as to why it had barely been touched.

On just such an evening, he explained his absence over a prolonged period: he had been detoxed in an expensive west London rehab. 'I've been in the Priory getting over a slight problem,' he confided. 'You see that chap over by the door? He's my bodyguard. He's supposed to protect me from myself, if you've ever heard such nonsense. Anyway, he doesn't let me get any blues, so I hope you are carrying plenty.' Alas, I had a new career of my own to develop and I had sworn off unhealthy substances. Brian was furious, but at least he ate his dinner.

Bidding me goodnight, he said: 'I'm off to a party where I know they'll have lots and lots of little goodies. I do hope my shadow doesn't get too tired.'

In the event, that is exactly what did happen. Brian stayed awake for three days and three nights, a feat his bodyguard could not match. He finally dropped from exhaustion at Brian's country house at Kingsley Hill in Sussex. Brian gave him the slip and made his way back to Chapel Street. Inside his house there, he indulged himself until his heart could take no more.

On 27 August 1967 – the second anniversary of the Beatles/Elvis meeting he had helped me arrange – the butler knocked on his bedroom door but failed to get a reply. The door was broken down and Brian was found dead. He was lying on a single bed, dressed in pyjamas, some correspondence he had been reading spread out over a second, unoccupied single bed beside him. Police found seventeen bottles of pills by the beds, two in a briefcase and eight in the bathroom. Death had been caused by bromide poisoning due to 'an incautious self-overdose' of a prescribed drug called Carbrital.

The news reached the Beatles in the Welsh seaside resort of Bangor, where they had gone to be indoctrinated in the art of transcendental meditation. Pattie Harrison had met the Maharishi Mahesh Yogi after a lecture on spiritual regeneration at Caxton Hall and had fallen under his spell. She had told George about the power of Indian mysticism and he had converted the other Beatles, who had become interested enough to go on a spiritual retreat that weekend.

Their lack of public reaction to Brian's death owed as much to the teachings of the Maharishi, who assured them that death was simply part of the process of reincarnation, as it did to the fact that they knew Brian had previously tried twice to commit suicide because of clinical depression.

A message bearing Elvis's name arrived, which expressed 'deepest condolences on the loss of a good friend to you and all of us'. There were no prizes for guessing who had really sent it.

John was grief-stricken, although he appeared blissed out in the company of his giggling guru. Cynical though he might be, he had a very soft spot for Brian, whom he regarded as a protected species. Not only was Brian one of the few people safe from the Lennon lemon acid, John didn't like anyone else putting Brian down and that included the other Beatles.

John – the Liverpool Lip – was the most cutting person I ever met, even with royalty. He didn't like Princess Margaret because of her airs and graces, although he knew that Brian adored her. It had been Margaret who said that 'MBE' stood for 'Mr Brian Epstein'. In response, John changed her name to 'Priceless Margarine'. He told me about a time when he thought he had heard the Queen's sister remark that Beatle fans had inconvenienced her arrival at a cocktail party.

'I said I didn't know why she had bothered to turn up if our bloody fans were a nuisance to her,' he said. 'I didn't say it to her directly, but I'm sure she overheard me. I just hope I hadn't misheard her!'

John had to go along with the Establishment for the sake of the group, "but he would rather have been one of the Stones, whom Andrew Oldham had groomed to be as anarchic as they liked. However, when John and Andrew did get together, weird things started happening.

'The Stones were still dying in the North so I decided to go and see the Beatles, the opposition, playing in Liverpool,' Andrew told me. 'After the show, I had the pleasure of being driven back to London in John's psychedelic Rolls-Royce. I'm not saying we weren't on acid and I'm not saying we were. I was high on the event, anyway, because it was a welcome home concert after they conquered America. Somehow, we got into hysterics about what would happen if the car windows suddenly shattered. John said, "It would be great – we'd have to wear the bear suits." It would be interesting to analyse that statement to find out what he meant.

'I later tried to buy that Roller from John because I believed it had two sets of windows. I was just so stoned that I hadn't realized that the windows were shut at one stage of the journey and open at another.'

Elvis was beginning to change for the better because of an impending birth. Priscilla had become pregnant soon after the wedding and, with the arrival of his first child approaching, the father-to-be was fired by a new enthusiasm. For the first time since 1957, he abandoned Hollywood schmaltz and went back to his roots in blues and country & western, recording 'Big Boss Man', 'High Heel Sneakers' and 'Guitar Man' during a highly charged session at the RCA studios in Nashville.

Lisa Marie Presley was born in Memphis at 5.01 pm on 1 February 1968. 'Nungen, us has a baby girl,' Elvis lisped to his wife. Had Lisa been a boy, he would have named his son and heir John Baron Presley. But he had never been prouder than when he took mother and baby home, first to Graceland and then to the West Coast to 1174 Hillcrest Drive on the Trousdale Estates in Los Angeles. As soon as Priscilla was fit enough to celebrate, Elvis decided to take her to see Tom Jones, who was playing to packed houses at the Flamingo in Las Vegas.

In 1966, I had left the *NME* to set up my own public relations company, and Tom was my first client. I had contacted his manager Gordon Mills after seeing Tom's picture in a women's magazine, in which he was wearing an apron and washing dishes, with his wife Linda drying up. Mills agreed to meet me for lunch, and I outlined the following strategy: Tom should seldom be available for interviews and photographs; no attention should ever be drawn to his marriage; his sexuality should be projected both on and off stage; we should exploit and even exaggerate his successes so that both fans and promoters would start to think of him in the same light as Presley and Sinatra.

I walked out of the restaurant as Tom's image maker for the princely sum of £25 a week, all Tom could afford at the time. I immediately began planning to promote him in America in much the same way as the Colonel had sold Elvis there. I had learned a lot from the Colonel during my trips with the Beatles, and I frequently sought his advice once Tom started to happen in front of American audiences. Women adored the miner's son born Thomas Jones Woodward in Pontypridd, South Wales. They threw their panties, bras and room keys at him, – and he didn't always throw them back.

The sudden decision to see Tom on stage was typical of Elvis's competitive nature. He wanted to see for himself what all the fuss was about. One Saturday afternoon in April 1968, Joe Esposito phoned me from LA to request a table in Elvis's name for the midnight show. The place had been sold out for weeks, but I arranged for an extra table and chairs to be set up directly in front of the stage. At fifteen minutes to midnight, Elvis and Priscilla walked through the casino to the lounge, having flown to Vegas in a private jet. To make sure they didn't feel lonely, eight companions had tagged along for the ride. No expense was spared when the King took his Queen on a night out.

The lights were still up and the crowd buzzed with excitement at the sight of America's rock royalty. To catch Elvis in a public place was a rarity. To catch him with Priscilla at a rival performer's show was really hitting the jackpot. With a huge jewelled cluster underpinning her stacked raven hair, and clad in an off-the-shoulder black sheath dress, Priscilla did not disappoint them. She looked top-heavy, but stunning.

Tom stepped on stage to a tremendous reception and gave it everything he had. When he did the first up-tempo number, *Don't Fight It*, Elvis slapped the table and rolled his head in time to the beat. Several times during the song, he turned to comment to Priscilla, a broad smile on his face and a long thin cigar clamped between his teeth.

Later in the act, Tom announced: 'Ladies and gentlemen, we have in the audience tonight a man I have admired for many years, Mr Elvis Presley.' The audience cheered Elvis, who stood up to wave and take a bow. 'OK, that's enough – sit down,' Tom commanded jokingly. When Tom finished with *Land of a Thousand Dances* the wildest number in his repertoire, Elvis jumped up and led the audience in a standing ovation. After the curtains had closed, I took Elvis and Priscilla backstage to meet with Tom, who was soaking wet in his stage suit. Elvis took Tom's hand in both of his and offered his congratulations.

'Say, Tom," he said, 'we should do a show together at either end of the stage with the Beatles backing us up in the middle.'

Tom screwed up his nose at the mention of the Beatles.

'What's wrong with the Jordanaires?' he quipped.

As members of both entourages packed in, the two stars moved into a smaller dressing room to escape the crush.

'You've lost a lot of weight,' Tom told Elvis, who was smart in a dark blue yachting jacket and white roll-neck shirt.

'Sure have – I'm on what they call a "drinking man's diet",' replied Elvis. 'You know, I've got some unhappy memories of Vegas. I was at the Frontier in '56 and I died a terrible death. When I came out with those hip movements, man, they just weren't ready for me!' To emphasize the point, he gyrated his pelvis in the famous way that nobody had seen since he had gone into the Army.

'I gotta tell you, though, that that *Green, Green Grass of Home* is really something,' he continued.

'When it was released here, the Guys and I were on the road driving in our mobile home. Man, that song meant so much to us boys from Memphis we just sat there and cried. We called the radio station and asked them to play it again and they did – four times! We just sat there and sobbed our hearts out. 'When it was time to go, Tom and I escorted the Presleys to their long, low, black Cadillac with darkened windows and masses of aerials.

'You see all these aerials?' said Elvis. 'Well, they don't mean a thing – they ain't connected to nothing!'

Back in the charts with *Guitar Man* and inspired by Tom Jones, Elvis agreed to give his first TV performance since he had appeared on Frank Sinatra's show in 1960. The King was back, snarling.

'Been a long time, I tell you,' he said during an informal jam session in the comeback special for NBC-TV. He took the opportunity to hit back at the Beatles, declaring that they hadn't produced anything he couldn't match. 'Performers today have learned to trick things up with choruses and electronic gimmicks – but the beat is still there,' he said. 'It's still what I call rock 'n' roll.'

Elvis was on a winning streak. He recorded no fewer than thirty-six tracks when he went back into the studio, this time in Memphis, in January 1969. Reaching deep into his soul, he dragged up towering performances for *In the Ghetto, Suspicious Minds* and *Kentucky Rain.*

Surprisingly, Elvis included a couple of Lennon/McCartney numbers, *Yesterday* and *Hey Jude*, in his repertoire, but nothing that involved 'electronic gimmicks'. When things were going his way, the vendetta seemed to go into remission, although there were also sound commercial reasons for the decision.

Since the previous November, the Colonel had been planning an enterprise that would put Elvis back in the public eye on his own terms. The billionaire entrepreneur Kirk Kerkorian was constructing a new hotel in Las Vegas, the International. At a cost of $60 million it would be the resort's biggest and grandest and its showrooms would need attractions to match. Kerkorian already owned the Flamingo – where Tom Jones was appearing with Joan Rivers as his support act – and had in charge an executive vice-president of his corporation named Alex Shoofey who was also to head up the International. Thanks to Tom, I had come to know Shoofey and also the Flamingo's entertainments manager, Bill Miller, who was an old friend of Parker's.

I was lounging by the pool one afternoon when I got a surprise call from Shoofey: 'Colonel Parker is coming up to Vegas tonight to talk some business. We're having dinner together and he said to tell you that he'd like you to join us for coffee at the end of the meal. For some reason he wants you to be the first to know what's happening.'

The dinner took place in the VIP section of the Flamingo's splendid dining room just a mile from where the International was reaching for the sky on Paradise Road. By the time I reached their table the cloth adorning it was covered in penned scrawl. Ever the showman, the Colonel had turned that cloth into a giant contract. I stared in amazement: I was looking at an historic document, for this piece of tableware was the contract for Elvis Presley's stage come-back. Soon after Barbra Streisand had opened the hotel, he was to be the headlining act, the king of rock'n'roll performing in a town where he had previously flopped.

It was a deal to suit everybody: the International would get world-wide publicity, Elvis would be able to do what he had witnessed Tom Jones doing in the very hotel where we were sitting, and the Colonel would get month-long stints in Vegas to enjoy his first love: gambling. Part of the cloth was folded under so I could not read the numbers Elvis and the

Colonel were to get but I imagine that no Vegas artist had ever been promised a bigger pay day.

I was still in a daze when the Colonel led me to the casino where he taught me to shoot craps. He won and I lost but I made up for my losses the next day when Alex Shoofey cornered me in the coffee shop and offered me a deal. I was to handle publicity – 'in England' as he quaintly put it – for Elvis's come-back in Las Vegas and that meant being there on opening night 'with a few of your best journalist buddies – it's the Colonel's idea.' How neat was that? I was to be paid for being in on the big occasion and Parker hadn't even had to ask me himself.

Three months prior to the start of his first stint that August, Elvis turned up at the International building site to add his name to the contract and there wasn't a tablecloth in sight. 'Elvis won't even start thinking about what he's going to sing or wear until we've finished *Change of Habit* [his last movie],' Joe Esposito told me. 'No, he's not nervous. The first two or three nights he'll get butterflies, but he'll take it all in his stride.'

Watching Elvis perform live on stage was something I had dreamed about since hearing 'Heartbreak Hotel' for the first time. I didn't realize then just how close I would get to the eye of the hurricane.

10

SUPPER WITH TRUMAN CAPOTE

Viva Las Vegas

ELVIS spent his weekends away from Priscilla at his secluded home in Chino Canyon Road, Palm Springs. Between games of Scrabble, motorbike racing and entertaining his friends, he had come under another, more benign, influence.

In the desert resort, he struck up the most bizarre friendship of his life with one of his neighbours. Of all the people whom Elvis had ever encountered either by choice or by accident, he had elected to befriend one who seemed to inhabit an entirely different planet: the writer Truman Capote. Capote of *Breakfast at Tiffany's* and *In Cold Blood*, Capote with the ultra-sophisticated taste, waspish New York wit and camp lisp, Capote the son of an alcoholic mother who had committed suicide. They made an odd couple, the King and his friend Tru-boy.

Only five feet three inches tall, the baby-faced social butterfly was more accustomed to flitting from one society beauty to another, cross-pollinating them all with the latest gossip from the others. But in his company, Elvis was able for the first time to face up to the truth about his own childhood and the mother he had idolized above everything.

His high-pitched voice lowered to a confidential whisper, Capote described his own mother Nina's drinking binges and her endless string of lovers in the southern hotels he had called home before she abandoned him into the care of her cousins in Monroeville, Alabama, at the age of four.

'My mother was a very beautiful girl and only seventeen when I was born. She used to lock me in these rooms all the time, and I developed this fantastic anxiety,' Capote would tell Elvis. 'I pounded and pounded on the door to get out. That did something to me. I have great fear of being abandoned by some particular friend or lover.'

When he later, in New Orleans, asked a witch to turn him into a girl, she had answered: 'I hear a baby crying.' The image provoked memories from Elvis's own distant past. He remembered Gladys's mournful sobbing and heard a small voice crying in the dark of that cold Mississippi shack: 'What wrong, Mommy?' The spirit of his twin brother Jesse Garon was never far from Elvis and his mother. Gladys drank moonshine to drown her grief that Jesse had died at birth; Elvis cried tears of guilt because he had been the twin to survive. Capote helped him to uncover the root cause of his insecurity.

The writer seemed to understand this intuitively. He was, he admitted, an alcoholic and a drug addict, first with prescribed medication and later vast amounts of cocaine. Asked why he drank and drugged, Capote replied: 'I can tell you in exactly one word: anxiety. I think certain people have a feeling of anxiety. A lot of analysts call it "free-floating anxiety". You know it doesn't mean anything, but it's always there.'

Just as Elvis had done, Capote collected doctors who would supply pills for insomnia, anxiety and copious other ailments, real and imagined. By nature, he loved to isolate himself, scribbling furtively with his pen in a ruled exercise book behind locked doors, his booze and pills close at hand. But perversely, he also craved the spotlight. 'Every single person who's really been close to me in my life has been a recluse,' he said. 'I can't imagine why I'm attracted to them when my attitude is "Let's go to a party."'

Elvis totally identified with that feeling: he was himself a classic case of the loner who needed to be the centre of attention. 'I get lonesome right in the middle of a crowd,' he once said. The way Capote explained it made sense of a lot of the contradictions in his life.

It was indicative of Capote's personality that he should take a shine to both Elvis Presley and his arch-enemy, who became known as John Ono Lennon. 'Elvis was nice, I sort of liked him,' Capote said. 'And I liked John Lennon a lot. He was very intelligent. He was a sensitive, very good-hearted person. I couldn't stand her. The Jap. She was always paranoid. The most unpleasant person that ever was, in my opinion.'

Capote wasn't the only one to take a dislike to Yoko Ono, who had met John at the Indica Gallery in London in November 1966. They kept their affair secret until John sent Cynthia away on holiday in May 1968 and Yoko promptly moved into the marital home. When it happened the other Beatles believed her influence over John contributed to the band's break-up, a claim that he hotly denied. It was ironic that it should be John, the Great Beatle Protector, who had introduced a *femme fatale* into the group. Elvis lapped up the gossip from London whenever he saw his friend Truman.

As Elvis's date at the International drew near and the butterflies started to circle, he pleaded with Capote to be there.

'He was going to open this big hotel in Las Vegas,' the writer recalled. 'He was making some sort of comeback. He hadn't appeared in public in a long time and he invited me to come up and see it 'cos I had never seen him work. In fact, I really had never heard any of his records either. So he said if I would come up, he would give this dinner party for me. I was more curious as to who in the world he would invite to this dinner party than I was about anything else, so I went with a friend. The one and only time I've ever been to Las Vegas.'

Steeped in Fifth Avenue chic, Capote hated even the thought of Las Vegas. Uncultured people making whoopee in brash casinos offended his aesthetic taste. Nevertheless, Elvis was his friend, and his curiosity had been aroused. He packed his tuxedo, buttoned his cardigan, put a fedora on his large round head and, cigarette holder clamped firmly between his even teeth and took off for Nevada.

The scene that greeted him at the International eclipsed any previous display of vulgarity it had ever been his misfortune to witness. The single world 'ELVIS' covered the hotel's huge marquee, fair warning of what was to come inside. The Colonel had excelled himself. In the lobby, the casino lounge, the restaurants, everywhere, he had Elvis show posters,

Elvis Styrofoam hats, Elvis balloons, Elvis hound dogs, Elvis teddy bears and other kitsch Elvis souvenirs. With the management's connivance, he had turned the entire hotel into a tacky Elvis sideshow. His senses reeling, Capote headed for the bar.

Elvis had been so anxious about the reception he would receive at his first live performance since the Fifties that he had invited a host of old friends, including Sam Phillips, to attend the first night. In my new capacity as the hotel's 'England PR man', I was there, too.

Anyone who thought Elvis's performance in the NBC special had been a carefully staged one-off for the cameras was to be pleasantly surprised. He put more effort into recruiting his band, led by the guitarist James Burton, rehearsing his two backing groups – the Imperial Quartet and the Sweet Inspirations – and choreographing his own stage moves than for any other performance in his entire career. He had worked so hard that he had shed fifteen pounds in the run-up to opening night, and when I saw him before the show, he was thinner than I had ever seen him, as well as extremely nervous. But, once he got in front of the audience, the butterflies started to fly in formation.

His rock band, backed by the hotel's twenty-five piece orchestra, thundered the defiant *Baby, I Don't Care* as the gold curtain lifted to reveal the man himself. Priscilla rose from her table near the front of the vast, multi-level showroom and led 2000 people in a standing ovation before her husband had even sung a note. Dressed in a black karate outfit slashed to the waist, he let rip with a very fast and very short version of *Blue Suede Shoes* before going into *I Got a Woman*. Then he paused, drank some Gatorade and, looking around the huge amphitheatre decked out with a Roman colonnade, murals of Greek ruins, some Louis XIV waxwork figures and a flight of celestial cherubs, said: 'Good evening, ladies and gentlemen. Welcome to the big, freaky International Hotel, with those weirdo dolls on the walls, and those funky angels on the ceiling . . . and man, you ain't seen nothin' till you've seen a funky angel.'

Elvis, of course, had seen some very funky angels in his time, but no medication impaired his style that night as it would in the years ahead.

It was a fabulous show with something for everyone. Dressed in a flared black karate suit – appropriate because his stage movements had been largely choreographed by his karate instructor Mike Stone – and looking thinner than he had been in years, he gave us his new hit singles to show that he meant business. His hair almost Beatle length, he did *Yesterday* and *Hey Jude* to show he was just as good as the Liverpool Four. *Johnny B. Goode* was for Chuck Berry to show he recognized a true master, and *Mystery Train* was for his own mentor Sam Phillips. He closed with *What'd I Say?* but came back with *Can't Help Falling in Love* for Priscilla, as an encore.

After the curtain had gone down to tumultuous applause, Elvis hugged a tearful Colonel and changed hurriedly for a press conference. Asked about his movie career, he said: 'I couldn't dig always playing the guy who'd get into a fight, beat the guy up and in the next shot sing to him.'

Did he regret doing so many soundtrack albums? 'I think so. When you do ten songs in a movie, they can't all be good songs,' he said. 'Anyway,

I got tired of singing to turtles. I get more pleasure out of performing to an audience like tonight than any of my film songs have given me.'

Inevitably he was asked about his rivalry with the Beatles. 'I well remember my meeting with the Beatles and have recorded *Hey Jude* for my next album,' he replied. 'They are so interesting and experimental, but I liked them particularly when they used to sing "She was just seventeen, you know what I mean?"'

On that enigmatic note, Elvis adjourned upstairs to entertain Truman Capote at the only dinner party he ever threw for anyone.

'We saw the opening show, and the dinner party was in between shows,' Capote recalled. 'I can't say that I was at all impressed by his performance. So we went to this apartment he had there in the hotel, and the dinner party consisted of about eight young men and one old friend of mine who had flown all the way from Honolulu, mainly because she was a fan of Elvis's. She loved Elvis, and guess who it was? Doris Duke.'

Elvis and Doris had become friends in Hawaii where the heiress, another reclusive figure hiding from the world behind dark glasses, high walls and security guards, had been holed up at her Shangri-la estate. Doris had embraced mystical Eastern religions and, like Elvis, meditated daily and believed in reincarnation. They had become very fond of one another. Tall, slim and middle-aged, Doris was the sole heiress of the tobacco mogul James Buchanan Duke who, in 1925, had left her $80 million. She could be a reckless spender – she had the dubious distinction of having taught her friend Imelda Marcos the art of shopping – but was also so astute financially that her fortune had multiplied to an estimated $1.5 billion.

'So we had this dinner party,' said Truman Capote. 'This table was full of orchids up and down, and everything looked very fancy in a gauche, peculiar way. But the dinner was incredible. It was all kinds of different things, fried pork and fried chicken and fried catfish.'

In honour of his guest, Elvis had ordered the chef to prepare a meal in the southern style. Capote, however, had actually spent most of his life eating French and Italian cuisine in the better restaurants of New York City and wondered what on earth he was eating. His *bon mots* might have been lost on the rugged and be-ringed members of the Memphis Mafia, but no one cared. The King was back where he belonged, and an hour or so in the company of a small, dainty gentleman he obviously admired was a small price to pay. For once, Elvis was really happy.

I did not hear from the Colonel for three days and the media men I had brought over from the UK on the promise that they would get to meet Elvis, were getting restless. Then, finally, I received Parker's summons: 'Mr Presley will see you now – and bring your London buddies.' With no time to prepare for whatever lay ahead, the *Evening Standard* columnist Ray Connolly, the *Daily Mirror* writer Don Short, the photographer Terry O'Neill and I headed for one of the International's multi elevators.

The lift whisked us to the 30th floor where Elvis, still dressed in his stage outfit was waiting. As the ultra-observant Mr Connolly wrote later: 'A silver bracelet bearing his name dangled from his wrist. It struck me as funny that one of the most famous people on earth needed a bracelet to remind him who he was.'

The Colonel hovered in the background, keen to ensure that no one asked a wrong question. Never one to tolerate creative people (and that included songwriters and film directors) getting too close to his boy and putting ideas into his head, his very presence ensured that this was a court rather than a deeply meaning exchange of intelligence. Accordingly he accepted compliments about his newly-slim physique and acknowledged the 'good work' being done by the Beatles who had sent him a Good Luck telegram. The Colonel scowled when Ray Connolly dared to ask Elvis 'Why did you make all those crummy films', but before he could intervene the star answered that he was in a rut; he had signed a contract and couldn't get out of it. Actually I had asked Parker if it was true he never read a script before agreeing a movie deal: 'Why should I?' he had answered, 'They're not going to pay him a million dollars a picture and then give him a lousy script.'

Bearing in mind that Alex Shoofey had tasked me with getting the hotel some good press, I was relieved when the subject turned to his gig at the International: 'We didn't decide to come here for the money, I'll tell you that. For the last nine years I've always wanted to perform on the stage again, it's been building inside of me since 1965 until the strain became intolerable. I got all het up about it and I don't think I could have left it much longer. The time is just right. The money – I have no idea at all about that. I just don't want to know. You can stuffit.'

That did not remain a truism, however. The tablecloth contract made no allowance for inflation and Elvis told his manager he was not pleased to learn four years later that he was being paid the same amount as he had for the original engagement but, like the film contracts, there was nothing could be done about it.

Dissent was in the air.

Truman Capote was not the only important figure Elvis had met in Palm Springs. He buttonholed Vice President Spiro T. Agnew and regaled him with a diatribe against the forces trying to destroy America, *his* America.

Richard Nixon's deputy had come to the desert in late November 1970 to relax in the winter sun. In the event, he was warmed by Elvis's fervour.

Elvis explained that his fears were motivated not only by the murder of the actress Sharon Tate and other ritual killings by the self-styled Manson family, which had stunned America, but also by threats against his own life. He was a wealthy man with the means to protect himself, Priscilla, Lisa Marie and members of his extensive entourage, he told the Vice President. But the time had come for people in the public eye like himself to stand up and be counted. He, for one, was really, willing and able to tackle the problem of violent dissent head-on.

Elvis tried to give Agnew a Colt .357 snub-nosed magnum for his own protection, but the politician explained that, as a public official, he could not accept gifts from citizens. He was, he said, quite happy with the protection already afforded him by the Secret Service.

When Agnew returned to Washington, he mentioned the meeting to White House staffers. Then, embroiled in the problems of the Nixon administration – and an investigation into his own crooked past – he promptly forgot all about it.

Elvis, however, had been deadly serious. He started using the alias 'Colonel John Burrows' to shield his identity while on tour, and collected as many as thirty badges from law enforcement agencies, ranging from the LAPD to the Royal Canadian Mounted Police. He carried at least two guns, one in a shoulder holster and another strapped to his leg. After the Sharon Tate murders, he slept with a gun under his pillow and breakfasted with a gun beside his plate. The Memphis Mafia carried so much hardware that they resembled a SWAT team.

Sharon Tate had been eight months' pregnant when she and four others were murdered at the Beverly Hills home she shared with her husband, film director Roman Polanski. The bodies were mutilated with knives and the word 'PIG' smeared in blood across the front door.

The murders took place on 9 August 1969, just as Elvis was hitting his stride in Las Vegas. The next night, the killers executed supermarket tycoon Leno LaBianca and his wife Rosemary. The words 'HELTER SKELTER' and 'DEATH TO PIGS' were daubed in blood at the LaBianca residence. These vicious, mindless acts inspired enormous fear among the rich and famous of Los Angeles. Elvis ordered security stepped up around his imitation French regency home on Hillcrest Drive. 'It could have been us,' he told Priscilla. 'We're getting outta here.' He put his house on the market and moved his family to more secure premises at 144 Monovale Road, between Bel Air and Beverly Hills.

Almost immediately, details began to emerge of a weird sect called 'The Family', the members of which took LSD and other drugs, practised Satanism and listened to Beatle records. Their leader, a drifter called Charles Manson, who had dubbed himself 'Jesus Christ', recruited young dropouts from the streets and took them to a desert hideout, where they were blooded in crude techniques of assassination. By December, Manson and three young women disciples had been arrested and charged with the murders.

When the Manson trial began in the summer of 1970, it was claimed that the bearded, long-haired hippie had been motivated by the lyrics of *Helter Skelter*, one of the tracks on the Beatles' *White Album*. The prosecution believed there was a definite link between the murders and the Beatles' music. Manson, himself a song writer, proclaimed that the Beatles were prophets who, through the words of *Helter Skelter*, were predicting the outbreak of a race war in the United States. He interpreted the title as meaning 'Armageddon'. According to Manson, when *Helter Skelter* came, the Black Panthers – led by Rocky Raccoon (the name of another track on the *White Album*) – would rise and kill the Piggies (the title of a third track). Added together, the Beatles' songs represented a signal for Manson to start the slaughter.

Asked about the Manson allegations, John replied: 'Well, he's barmy. He's like any other Beatles fan who reads mysticism into it. I don't know what *Helter Skelter* has to do with knifing somebody.'

In fact, it had been Paul McCartney who had penned the words to *Helter Skelter*, about an innocent fairground ride. *Piggies*, which Manson saw as an incitement to murder members of the White Establishment, was actually a George Harrison composition and the line, 'What they need is a damn good whacking', came from something his mother had once said.

But the notion that the Beatles were more dangerous than ever stuck in Elvis's mind. It was at this point that he was personally involved in a double threat of kidnapping and assassination. Inside Elvis, something snapped.

He had only a few more nights to run of his third successful season in Las Vegas when a security officer at the International Hotel received a telephone call. The date was 26 August 1970. The anonymous male caller claimed that criminals known to him were planning to kidnap Elvis and hold him to ransom. The caller said that he had been approached to take part in the conspiracy, but had opted out.

Kidnapping being a Federal offence, the Las Vegas Police Department immediately contacted the FBI. Barely had the agency started to act on the first call when a second one was received the following day when I was visiting the Colonel in his office on the fourth floor of the hotel.

This call came from a man with a southern accent, who advised the Colonel to treat the threat of the kidnapping as a matter of urgency. Not a man to panic, Elvis's manager did just that before regaining his usual sang-froid and guiding me into the casino to chance our luck at craps.

FBI agents were still processing this call when yet another threat arrived. This time, a caller warned that Elvis would be shot on stage. The would-be assassin was named as a woman who had tried unsuccessfully to sue Elvis over the paternity of her child.

The FBI files that I was able to examine twenty years later contain the following report:

> Call was received at twelve noon, stating that this individual who is going to kill Presley has already departed from Los Angeles airport and has apparently made a reservation for the Saturday evening performance of Presley. The potential killer, a woman, is carrying a pistol fitted with silencer.

The files further show that J. Edgar Hoover issued instructions that he should be kept informed about any developments.

Elvis was alternately fearful and furious about the threats. He might have prophesied his own death in a Manson-style slaying, but to be the target of two simultaneous attempts was defying even destiny. When he was told of Hoover's concern for his safety, he calmed down a bit. The great man himself was on the case. He had found a saviour.

Everywhere I went, the hotel seethed with FBI activity. Fans in Elvis T-shirts and clutching one or other of the Colonel's cuddly toys swarmed excitedly through the hotel's corridors bumping into the well-padded shoulders of men in grey suits and snap-brimmed trilbys. It was clear from the beads of sweat on usually-confident Joe Esposito's brow that even he was nervous. When he became fidgety, I knew he was scared. He held himself personally responsible for Elvis's safety, and things were getting out of hand.

Elvis's bodyguards, some of them 'specially recruited for the new crisis, were given photographic ID cards not only to identify themselves to the hotel staff and members of the public but also to enable them to recognize each other. As they were all armed to the teeth, there was a very real danger that one of the new faces might be shot by mistake for getting too close to Elvis.

Elvis refused to abandon his act, but he went on stage with a gun tucked in the back of his trouser waistband. If anyone fired at him, he intended to shoot back. As Sonny West and Jerry Schilling were stationed nearby to jump in front of Elvis at the slightest sign of trouble, this could have proved fatal. Elvis had issued other orders as well: 'If anyone gets me, kill 'em before the cops move in. I don't want anyone to become famous for shooting Elvis Presley.'

All the precautions worked, and Elvis closed in Las Vegas without a scratch. But his aides privately reported that he was using more medication and his behaviour was becoming increasingly erratic, even on stage.

Fans were sometimes treated to a rambling version of his life story. I dropped in one night and heard this: '. . . Like to tell you a little about myself. I started out . . . in childhood. I started out when I was in high school, went into a record company one day, made a record, and when the record came out, a lot of people liked it and you could hear folks around town saying, "Is he, is he?" and I'm going, "Am I, am I?" . . . *whew!*. . . .Elvis deterioratin' at the Showroom International in Las Vegas . . . Where was I? . . . Oh, anyway, made a record, got kinda big in my home town, few people got to know who I was, that's w-u-z, was. See? So I started down in the wuz . . .Aw, shucks, what I mean to tell you is I was playin' around these night clubs, alleys and things. Did that for about a year and a half, then I ran into Colonel Sanders . . . Parker,

Parker . . . and he arranged to get me some [Elvis blew his nose] Kleenex . . . he arranged to get me . . . *Whew*, I'm tellin' you . . .. shot to hell, this boy can't even finish a sentence straight . . .Anyway, there was a lot of controversy at that time about my movin' around on stage so I . . . cleared my throat again, looked at my watch and ring and the guy said . . . the guy said? . . . the guy said nothin' . . . *I'm* the guy! I'm telling you, you better get this together, boy, or this is gonna be the last time they let you up on a stage . . .'

There was a lot more of the same embarrassing nonsense. It amounted to one thing: Elvis was losing touch with reality. Sometimes he changed or forgot the lyrics of his songs; at other times, he stumbled around the stage or fumbled with the mike. Not once did the audience lose its reverence. Some fans booked in for all sixty-odd shows a month to catch the King for better or worse.

Presley was actually in physical pain. According to Charlie Hodge, 'Elvis often needed painkillers after his act. As everyone knows, he could be very physical in his performance, with his karate stunts and so on, and he genuinely used to pull a muscle or damage himself. He did have a high pain tolerance. When they discovered he had an eye condition called glaucoma, I went with him to see the doctor. He said it was so bad that he needed to give him a shot right there, but there was no anaesthetist available. So Elvis said, "Do it!" He grabbed the side of the chair and the doctor just gave him a shot right in the white of the eye. It came up like a tennis ball.'

To celebrate the new, live Elvis, RCA released *On Stage: February 1970*, a collection of songs recorded in Las Vegas, in reply to the Beatles' *Let It Be* album, their 13th – and last.

Suddenly, the most famous group in the world was history. The Beatles had been falling to pieces ever since Brian's death, but the official death knell was sounded on 31 December 1970, when Paul McCartney, who had tried to keep the band together, took out a law suit in the High Court to dissolve the partnership. 'I was stoned all the time and I just didn't give a damn,' admitted John, who now looked like a refugee from a hippie commune. 'Idiots rang up and said, "Yoko split the Beatles." She didn't split the Beatles. After Brian died, we collapsed. Paul took over and supposedly led us. But what is leading when we went round in circles? We broke up then. That was the disintegration.'

Both Elvis and John were showing signs of disintegrating themselves. The chains of addiction had been fitted so subtly that neither realized he was enslaved until he tried to walk away. By then, it was too late.

11

THE KING, THE PRESIDENT . . . AND THE FBI CHIEF

Suspicious minds

FOR ONE fleeting moment, Elvis might have sought help from the President himself. Instead, he sank deeper into his obsession to bust John Lennon and, in the process, sabotaged his own chance to get well.

When I first wrote, in the *Daily Mirror*, about Elvis's visit to Richard Nixon in the Oval Office, eyebrows were raised until official confirmation of the story came forth. It sounded so absurd that many found it hard to believe.

However, papers released from the archives of the Nixon administration and the liberated FBI files show that the truth was even stranger than I had suspected.

It started at Graceland a few days before Christmas 1970, when Elvis adopted the troubled 'users' classic posture towards reality. Driven by an uncontrollable craving to 'get out of it', he started arguing with everyone. He rowed with Priscilla over Lisa, with Vernon over his manic spending and with the Colonel over the arrangements for his next tour. He was restless, difficult, demanding and unreasonable.

After one particularly savage exchange with the Colonel on the phone, he stormed off into the night, dressed in a dark blue suit and cape, and wearing a pair of dark glasses. He was carrying a silver-topped swordstick in one hand and, in the other, clutched the leather valise that contained his medication. He was also armed with a Colt .45 pistol in a shoulder holster and carried another gun, a World War II Colt .45 in a presentation case.

Elvis drove himself to Memphis airport, where he boarded an American Airlines jet bound for Washington. His original intention had been to escape from the demons pursuing him, and to do that in the company of the two men he trusted most in the world: J. Edgar Hoover and Richard Nixon. They would understand his problems. They would save him. But once he had checked into the Washington Hotel under his alias, Colonel John Burrows, Elvis started to lose his nerve. Alone in his bedroom, the large quantity of medicines he had consumed merely brought on an attack of paranoia. He couldn't sit still. He was in an agony of indecision. It was already dark outside and he was too frightened to make a move.

Wherever he went, whether it was in Memphis, LA, Las Vegas or passing through some tiny country town while on tour, Elvis had always lived like a Tudor monarch, rarely unguarded and never left on his own for more than a few minutes. Now he was lonely and terrified, and the enormity of his decision to do something without the physical presence of the Guys at his side started to terrify him. Unable to stand the four walls a moment longer, he dashed to the airport and grabbed a flight to Los Angeles.

Jerry Schilling had quit Elvis's service following one argument too many, and was now working on a film in Hollywood. He got Elvis's call in the middle of the night. The plan had changed somewhat during the long flight west, and Elvis, swearing Schilling to secrecy, outlined his new mission. He told his startled former aide that he intended to see both Nixon and Hoover to demand that he be made a Federal agent in the fight against the dual menace of street drugs and Communism.

However, there was a hidden agenda, which he kept to himself. By becoming an agent, he could legitimize his own usage, which, he continued to fool himself, involved only properly prescribed medication. It would be the perfect cover to protect his addiction.

Schilling agreed to go along with Elvis, with one proviso. He insisted on calling Sonny West at Graceland and having him fly to Washington to meet them. Elvis agreed. He had lost his taste for solitude.

On the early-morning plane to Washington on 21 December, Elvis, polite as ever, struck up a conversation with George Murphy, a Republican Senator from California. They covered Elvis's favourite topics – politics, drugs and the Beatles – and Murphy offered to help. He suggested that Elvis should outline his plans in a personal letter to the President, while he would contact Hoover at the FBI and John Ingersoll, director of the Bureau of Narcotics and Dangerous Drugs, with a view to Elvis working under cover for both agencies.

A helpful stewardess handed Elvis some notepaper headed with the American Airlines logo, and he carefully composed a five-page letter to the President in his own uncertain hand. When the plane landed, he delivered it to a guard at the White House gate. The letter to Nixon, with syntax and punctuation intact, read as follows:

Dear Mr President,

First I would like to introduce myself. I am Elvis Presley and admire you and Have Great Respect for your office. I talked to Vice President Agnew in Palm Springs 3 weeks ago and expressed my concern for our country. The Drug Culture, the Hippie Elements, the SDS, Black Panthers, etc, do not consider me as their enemy or as they call it the Establishment. I call it America and I Love it. Sir I can and will be of any Service that I can to help the country out. So I wish not to be given a title or an appointed position. I can and will do more good if I were made a Federal Agent at Large, and I will help best by doing it my way through my communications with people of all ages.

First and Foremost I am an entertainer but all I need is the Federal Credentials. I am on the Plane with Sen. George Murphy and we have been discussing the problems that our Country is faced with. So I am staying at the Washington Hotel Room 505-506-507. I have 2 men who work with me by the name of Jerry Schilling and Sonny West. I am registered under the name of John Burrows, I will be here for as long as it takes to get the credentials of a Federal Agent. I have done an in depth study of Drug Abuse and Communist Brainwashing Techniques and I am right in the middle of the whole thing, where I can and will do the most good. I am Glad to help just so long as it is kept very Private. You can have your staff or whomever call me anytime today tonight or tomorrow. I was nominated this coming year one of America's Most Outstanding young men. That will be in January 19 in My Home Town of Memphis. I am sending you the short autobiography about myself so you can better understand this approach. I would love to meet you just to say hello if you're not too busy.

Respectfully

Elvis Presley

P.S. I believe that you Sir were one of the Top Ten Outstanding Men of America also. I have a personal gift for you also which I would like to present to you and you can accept it or I will keep it for you until you can take it.

While this letter was silently making its way through the corridors of power, Elvis arranged to visit the Narcotics Bureau, using Senator Murphy's name to gain entrance. Murphy had kept his word and had contacted Ingersoll, but although the director agreed to a visit, he fobbed Elvis off with his deputy, John Finlater. While Finlater told Elvis that he appreciated his concern for the youth of America, he said that he could not issue him with an agent's badge. He was sorry, but it was impossible. The agency simply didn't work that way.

Finlater had other reasons for refusing the King's request. He and his staff knew an addict when they saw one, and Elvis's sweating face, uncertain speech and unkempt appearance tended to confirm that prognosis. But it was the dark glasses hiding from close inspection his eyes with their pinhole-sized pupils that were the real giveaway.

Elvis was devastated. After two sleepless days, he was starting to come down and his world seemed to be collapsing with him. However, there was good news from Jerry Schilling, who had stayed at the Washington Hotel to await a call from the White House. The President's office had duly come through, requesting Elvis to be at the White House at noon. Elvis was elated.

Once his letter had arrived and a check call to the Washington Hotel had confirmed that 'Colonel John Burrows' was indeed staying there, it had become a busy morning at the White House, at least for one Dwight L. Chapin, who sent a memo to Nixon's chief of staff, H. R. 'Bob' Haldeman.

MEMORANDUM

THE WHITE HOUSE

WASHINGTON

December 21, 1970

MEMORANDUM FOR MR. H. R. HALDEMAN

FROM: D WIGHT L. CHAPLIN

SUBJECT: Elvis Presley

Attached you will find a letter to the President from Elvis Presley. As you are aware, Presley showed up here this morning and has requested an appointment with the President. He states that he knows the President is very busy, but he would just like to say hello and present the President with a gift. As you are well aware, Presley was voted one of the ten outstanding young men for next year and this was based upon his work in the field of drugs. The thrust of Presley's letter is that he wants to become a "Federal agent at large" to work against the drug problem by communicating with people of all ages. He says that he is not a member of the establishment and that drug culture types, the hippie elements, the SDS, and that Black Panthers are people with whom he can communicate since he is not part of the establishment. I suggest that we do the following:

This morning Bud Krogh will have Mr. Presley in and talk to him about drugs and about what Presley can do. Bud will also check to see if there is some kind of an honorary agent at large or credential of some sort that we can provide for Presley. After Bud has met with Presley, It is recommended that we have Bud bring Presley in during the Open Hour to meet briefly with the President. You know that several people have mentioned over the past few months that Presley is very pro the President. He wants to keep everything private and I think we should honor his request. I have talked to Bud Krogh about this whole matter, and we both think that it would be wrong to push Presley off on the Vice President since it will take very little of the President's time and it can be extremely beneficial for the President to build some rapport with Presley. In addition, if the President wants to meet with some bright young people outside of the Government, Presley might be a perfect one to start with.

Approve Presley coming in at end of Open

Hour_____

Disapprove_____

As the Watergate scandal in which he was involved later revealed, Bob Haldeman was nobody's fool. In the margin next to the advice Chapin offered in his last paragraph, he scribbled: 'You must be kidding,' but he initialled his approval for the visit nevertheless. On his instructions, a second memo was prepared for Nixon to brief him on the meeting, standard procedure for such appointments. The memo included an impromptu list of useful 'talking points'. The final page of the letter that Elvis wrote to President Nixon on 21 December 1970 The internal White House memo that led to Elvis getting his Federal agent's badge. .

A few minutes before Elvis was ushered into his presence, Nixon rapidly scanned the pages with a practised eye before tossing them to one side. He would, he decided, rely on his own political nous – he wasn't called 'Tricky Dicky' for nothing. Manipulating someone like Elvis Presley would be child's play. With an election coming up in 1972, he might just need a few star names on his team.

Egil 'Bud' Krogh took detailed notes of the meeting and, afterwards, wrote yet another, more selective memo:

Memorandum for: The President's file

Subject: Meeting with Elvis Presley, Monday,

21 December1970, 12.30pm

The meeting opened with pictures taken of the President and Elvis Presley.

Presley immediately began showing the President his law enforcement paraphernalia including badges from police departments in California, Colorado and Tennessee. Presley indicated that he had been playing Las Vegas and the President indicated that he was aware of how difficult it is to perform in Las Vegas.

The President mentioned that he thought Presley could reach young people, and that it was important for Presley to retain his credibility. Presley responded that he did his thing by 'just singing' He said that he could not get to the kids if he made a speech on the stage, that he had to reach them in his own way. The President nodded in agreement.

Presley indicated that he thought the Beatles had been a real force for anti-American spirit. The President nodded in agreement and expressed some surprise.

The President then indicated that those who use drugs are also those in the vanguard of anti-American protest. Violence, drug usage, dissent, protest all seem to merge in generally the same group of young people.

Presley indicated to the President in a very emotional manner that he was 'on your side'. Presley kept repeating that he wanted to be helpful, that he wanted to restore some respect for the flag which was being lost. He mentioned that he was just a poor boy from Tennessee who had gotten a lot from his country, which in some way he wanted to repay. He also mentioned that he is studying Communist brainwashing and the drug culture for over ten years. He mentioned that he knew a lot about this and was accepted by the hippies. He said he could go right into a group of young people or hippies and be accepted which he felt could be helpful to him in his drug drive. The President indicated again his concern that Presley retain his credibility.

[Bud Krogh omitted the fact that, at this point, Nixon spoke into his intercom and ordered that a badge of the Bureau of Narcotics and Dangerous Drugs and a set of credentials be prepared for Elvis and delivered to the Oval Office.]

At the conclusion of the meeting, Presley again told the President how much he supported him, and then, in a surprising, spontaneous gesture, put his arm around the President and hugged him. [The 'surprise' was that Elvis actually broke down in tears.]

In going out, Presley asked the President if he would see his two associates [Sonny West and Jerry Schilling]. The President agreed and they came over and shook hands with the President briefly.

At this meeting, the President thanked them for their efforts and again mentioned his concern for Presley's credibility.

By the time Elvis was being shown to the door, the agent's badge and the appropriate paperwork were waiting in the outer office and Nixon handed them over. The speed with which they had turned up indicated that the Narcotics Bureau's decision to exclude Elvis had already been countermanded before he had even set foot in the Oval Office.

On 31 December, Nixon covered his tracks in a noncommittal letter addressed to Graceland:

Dear Mr Presley,

It was a pleasure to meet with you in my office recently, and I want you to know once again how much I appreciate your thoughtfulness in giving me the commemorative World War II Colt .45 pistol, encased in the handsome wooden chest. You were particularly kind to remember me with this impressive gift, as well as your family photographs, and I am delighted to have them for my collection of special mementos.

With my best wishes to you, Mrs Presley, and to your daughter, Lisa, for a happy and peaceful 1971

Sincerely, Richard Nixon

Mission accomplished, Elvis returned to Graceland proudly displaying his new badge. It was the best Christmas present anyone had ever given him.

Elvis might have been happy, but he had no intention of settling down to a peaceful life. On New Year's Eve, the day Nixon dictated his letter and, coincidentally, the day that Paul began the law suit against the other Beatles, Elvis was back in Washington visiting the FBI, where he pursued his vendetta against John Lennon with all the vigour he possessed.

He had arrived mob-handed the day before with William N. Morris, a former sheriff of Shelby County (of which Memphis was a part), and half a dozen of the Guys. Morris contacted the FBI on Elvis's behalf, and Hoover agreed to the group making a special tour of the Bureau, expressing his regrets that he would not be able to meet Elvis in person. Hoover had his doubts but, like Nixon, was prepared to use Elvis to his own advantage. He would not, however, risk any flak, which a public endorsement of Elvis might attract if things went wrong. He wanted Elvis as a spy, not a Federal agent blessed by his own hand.

Hoover, too, had been gunning for John Lennon for some time, without success. He had tried to prosecute John and Yoko under interstate law for transporting obscene material – the cover of their album *Two Virgins*, which showed them in a full-frontal nude pose – but had been advised by his legal office that such a charge would not succeed in court. In London, however, the drug squad had raided the Lennons while they were staying at Ringo's flat in Montagu Square, with the result that John was fined for possessing cannabis.

His antenna tuned to the possibilities that Elvis's cooperation presented, Hoover ordered an administration assistant to prepare a confidential report on the King's FBI visit. This report details adverse comments that

Elvis had made about the Beatles to FBI officers in a private conversation after the tour.

4 January 1971

From: M. A. Jones

Subject: Elvis Presley William N. Morris Former Sheriff, Shelby County, Tennessee

Bureau tour 31-12-70

Presley and Morris and six individuals who provide security for Presley visited FBI Headquarters and were afforded a very special tour of our facilities in accordance with plans approved by the Director.

Regrets were expressed to Presley and his party in connection with their request to meet the Director. Presley indicated that he has long been an admirer of Mr Hoover and has read material prepared by the Director including Masters of Deceit, A Study of Communism as well as J. Edgar Hoover on Communism. Presley noted in his opinion no one has ever done as much for his country as has Mr Hoover and that he, Presley, considers the Director the 'greatest living American'. He also spoke favourably of the Bureau.

Despite his rather bizarre personal appearance, Presley seemed a sincere, serious-minded individual who expressed concern over some of the problems confronting our country, particularly those involving young people. In this regard, in private comments made following his tour, he indicated that he, Presley, is the 'living proof that America is the land of opportunity' since he rose from truck driver to prominent entertainer almost overnight. He said that he spends as much time as his schedule permits informally talking to young people and discussing what they consider to be their problems with them.

Presley explained that his long hair and unusual apparel were merely tools of his trade and provided an access to and rapport with many people particularly on college campuses who consider themselves 'anti-Establishment'. Presley said that while he has a limited education, he has been able to command a certain amount of respect and attention from this segment of the population and in an informal way point out the errors of their ways.

He advised that he does not consider himself competent to address large groups but much rather prefers small gatherings in community centres and the like, where he makes himself accessible for talks and discussions regarding the evils of narcotics and other problems of concern to teenagers and other young people.

Following their tour, Presley privately advised that he has volunteered his services to the President in connection with an Agent's badge of the Bureau of Narcotics and Dangerous Drugs. Presley was carrying this badge in his pocket and displayed it.

Presley advised that he wished the Director to be aware that he, Presley, from time to time is approached by individuals and groups in and outside of the entertainment business whose motives and goals he is convinced are not in the best interests of this country and who seek to have him lend his name to their questionable activities. In this regard, he volunteered to make such information available to the Bureau on a confidential basis whenever it came to his attention. He further indicated that he wanted the Director to know that should the Bureau ever have any need of his services in any way that he would be delighted to be of assistance.

Presley indicated that he is of the opinion that the Beatles laid the groundwork for many of the problems we are having with young people by their filthy unkempt appearances and suggestive music while entertaining in this country during the early and middle 1960s. He advised that the Smothers Brothers, Jane Fonda and other persons in the entertainment industry of their ilk have a lot to answer for in the hereafter for the way they have poisoned young minds by disparaging the United States in their public statements and unsavoury activities.

Presley advised that he resides at 3764 Highway 51 South, Memphis, Tennessee, but that he spends a substantial portion of his time in the Beverly Hills, California, Las Vegas, Nevada, areas fulfilling motion picture assignments and singing commitments.

He noted that he can be contacted anytime through his Memphis address and that because of problems he has with people tampering with his mail, such correspondence should be addressed to him under the pseudonym Colonel Jon [sic] Burrows.

Hoover already knew Elvis's address and a great deal more besides. Files had been opened on Elvis when his gyrations on stage had attracted official scrutiny back in the Fifties. These files were packed with information about his permissive lifestyle and personal drug abuse. Informants had branded Elvis a pervert who represented a threat to the moral wellbeing of young American women. These files had never been closed.

However, Hoover immediately wrote to Elvis thanking him for his 'generous comments concerning the bureau and me' and assuring him that his offer of help would be kept in mind. The same day he alerted every FBI field office to Elvis's pseudonym and telephone numbers should they need to contact him. Then he ordered a review of all FBI files concerning John Lennon. Elvis had planted a seed in Hoover's mind, which was about to grow into rampant poison ivy. To put it bluntly, Hoover the master manipulator planned to set one junkie to catch another.

The legendary FBI chief was, in fact, nothing like the rugged, crime-busting hero of popular acclaim. Elvis would have been devastated to know that his 'greatest living American' had dodged military service during World War I and that he kept an array of women's clothes in his closet, which he liked to wear on social occasions with his homosexual friends.

Through the press and his own grapevine, Elvis had kept track of John Lennon's movements since his marriage to Yoko Ono on the Rock of Gibraltar on 20 March 1969. The odd couple had spent their honeymoon staging a 'bed-in for peace' at the Hilton Hotel in Amsterdam, the drug capital of Europe. John and Yoko had posed for pictures sitting up in bed, each holding a single tulip. Signs saying 'hair peace' and 'bed peace' were displayed behind them. Heavily bearded and with his hair touching the shoulders of his neatly buttoned pyjamas, John looked like a cross between the Maharishi and Charles Manson. There was no doubt in Elvis's mind, as he surveyed the evidence, that this odious oddball was dangerous.

Every one of his activities came into the category of 'unsavoury', each a calculated insult to 'the Establishment' that Elvis purported to admire. John had returned his MBE to the Queen, he had held an exhibition of erotic lithographs, which Scotland Yard had raided after complaints of obscenity, and the music he was recording with the Plastic Ono Band was full of avant-garde messages in which words such as 'peace' and 'love' were used to subvert the young.

Most disturbing of all was that John and Yoko had been admitted to the United States. They had travelled to Los Angeles supposedly to undergo 'primal therapy' with Dr Arthur Janov, doubtless a front for other 'questionable activities'. Whatever gossip came Elvis's way about John, no matter how fanciful, he fed into the FBI system.

The attention that John had received from the British constabulary indicated to Elvis that the former Beatle's Day of Judgment might arrive much sooner than his appointed hour in 'the hereafter'. It was up to him and the FBI to close the case in the United States. The thought pleased him so much that he decided to take direct action as President Nixon's own authorized drug buster. Colonel John Burrows strapped on his guns and went looking for trouble.

I visited Los Angeles many times during 1971 and moved there the following year. Jan, my then-wife, and I rented the actor Ben Gazzara's house in Holmby Hills, a colonial-style mansion that looked like a miniature Graceland. After the grass-and-acid trips of the Sixties, cocaine had become the fashionable drug. 'You have to line up to get a cubicle in Beverly Hills,' one of the *cognoscenti* told me.

Elvis's cronies hung out at the Luau, a Hawaiian restaurant in Beverly Hills. At other times, I saw them at the Rainbow, a rock club/restaurant on Sunset. Dealers to the stars operated at both venues without the management's knowledge.

When famous entertainers and members of the pop world were inexplicably raided in their homes by the drug squad, the suspicion grew that someone with connections was leaking information to the authorities. It now seems fairly certain that the informer was Elvis, the narcotics agent. Certainly he had the motive and the opportunity.

> *John Lennon himself was never caught in any incriminating situation in the United States. In fact, the only solid piece of evidence that Hoover had against him was that he had been granted a visa to enter the country after being given a discretionary waiver against a drug conviction in Britain. When he arrived with George Harrison and his wife Pattie Boyd, a full-scale FBI alert went out.*

Date: 23 April 1970

Subject: John Lennon, George Harrison, Patricia Harrison

These individuals are affiliated with the Beatles musical group and Lennon will be travelling under the name of Chambers and the Harrisons are using the name Masters. They will remain in Los Angeles for business discussions with Capitol Records and other enterprises. They will travel to New York for further discussions. Waivers were granted by the Immigration and Naturalization Service in view of the ineligibility of these three individuals to enter the US due to their reputations in England as narcotic users.

While Lennon and the Harrisons have shown no propensity to become involved in violent anti-war demonstrations, each recipient [of this memo] should remain alert for any information of such activity on their part or for information indicating they are using narcotics. Submit any pertinent information obtained for immediate dissemination.

The FBI had a star witness to attest to John's drug-taking: the Beatle himself. Around this time, he was talking frankly about his habit. If he had known the hassle that lay ahead, he might have kept his mouth shut. 'I've always needed a drug to survive; the others, too, but I always had more,' he admitted with reckless honesty. 'I always took more pills, more of everything because I'm crazy probably. I must have had a thousand [LSD] trips. I used to just eat it all the time.'

John, George and Pattie came and went without incident, and John applied to re-enter the US again in the summer of 1970, saying he wanted to edit a film and attend a custody hearing in New York over Yoko's daughter by her former husband, Tony Cox. He was granted a visa to enter the US *until September and was then given an extension. When Hoover heard that, he exploded. The FBI files show that, from then on, John was targeted like Public Enemy No. 1.*

'Every agent should remain alert for any activity on his part of a potentially illegal nature,' one memo ordered. 'Lennon is a heavy user of narcotics . . . this information should be emphasized to local law enforcement agencies with regards to subject being arrested if at all possible on possession-of-narcotics charge,' said another. The Lennons were followed and harassed at every opportunity.

Fortunately, they were not without powerful friends of their own. When deportation proceedings were issued against them at Hoover's instigation, John Lindsay, the Mayor of New York, where they were living, spoke out furiously about the treatment they were receiving. In a strongly worded letter to the Immigration authorities, he said that 'a grave injustice' was being perpetrated:

> *The only question which is raised against these people is that they speak with strong, critical voices on major issues of the day. If this is the motive underlying the unusual and harsh action taken, then it is an attempt to silence the constitutionally protected First Amendment rights of free speech and association, and a denial of the civil liberties of these two people.*

Backing John's application for a green card, Lord Harlech, the former British ambassador in Washington and, ironically, a close friend of Princess Margaret, opined: 'When the musical history of our times comes to be written, there is no doubt that the name of John Lennon will be given a most important place in it.'

This was one up to the Walrus, but in Vegas the Hound Dog was barking loudly.

12

ENTER TOM JONES

Let's have a party

WHENEVER Elvis met up with Tom Jones in Las Vegas, it was party time. He would catch Tom's act at Caesars Palace and the two stars and I would invariably adjourn to the Imperial Suite, where Elvis threw more parties than Nero. Even Tom would concede that, for eight years, Elvis was *the* main event in Vegas.

'We'd get a call to let us know that Elvis was coming in and a security guard from the hotel would go to the airport to pick him up and bring him here,' Jim Vernon, the hotel's security boss, told me. 'He'd come in through the north service area at the rear of the hotel in one of our stretch black Cadillacs. The elevator from there went right up to the back door of the 30th floor suite. Secrecy was standard practice. We never let anyone know he was coming in, just the people who needed to know.

'Once he was in the hotel, we had more people to cover Elvis than any other entertainer. There were his people and six of us. They'd tell us if they had heard about a threat to his life, but they took care of their business and we handled certain other things. We escorted him from the suite to the stage and stayed with him during each show. We had people on either side of the stage and in the audience to keep the fans at bay.'

George Ziros, the Hilton's chief chef, remembers when Elvis first played the hotel in 1969. 'He was a tall, slender guy who was always smiling. Before a show, he came down from his suite surrounded by security guards with a towel wrapped around his neck. He was trotting along – not walking – and waving to people. And the people stood up and applauded him because he was really well-liked by everybody.

'He ate his dinner after he finished the second show around 1.00 am. We sent it up from the kitchens, usually Italian food, spaghetti, meatballs, sausage, steaks, chicken or veal. But he had room service as well so he could order anything he wanted. He liked shakes to drink and he never ordered wine, but I have maybe seen him with a beer in his hand, that's all. Later on, he put on weight, but anybody over the age of 40 puts on weight if they don't watch themselves.

'There were always people up there, thirty or forty at a time. The only female one I recognized a couple of times was Ann-Margret. The Colonel would mingle with the crowd after the show, perhaps have a drink and maybe a bite to eat, but I only saw him a few times up in the suite. He would talk to members of the party and then he would just disappear.'

In 1971, Elvis had a new employer when Kirk Kerkorian sold the hotel to Conrad Hilton. 'We renamed it the Hilton Hotel and I was put in charge,' recalls Henri Lewin. 'It was the largest hotel in Las Vegas, with 1500 rooms and it also housed the largest showroom in the country.'

Elvis made history there. It is said that he never played to an empty seat at the Hilton.

'When you have a star who sells out sixty shows in ten minutes, you have a different opinion about the whole game,' said Lewin. 'There was nobody alive at that time who could even come close to Elvis, not Tom Jones, Engelbert Humperdinck, Nat King Cole, Bill Cosby. You name them: nobody ever reached the numbers he did – a total of 2.5 million paying customers.

'He gave two shows each night for twenty-eight days in February and thirty days in August into September, a total of fifty-six and sixty shows a month respectively, for six years. As a hotel company, we didn't care whether the showroom made or lost money. But people who came to see him stayed at the hotel and we were booked solid for the whole month he was there.

'We had to put twenty extra telephone operators on duty just to turn people away. Some people saw the dinner show and the midnight show, two shows in a row, every night for thirty nights.'

On one occasion, Elvis avoided an international incident between the hotel and a group of fanatical fans who had flown in for one show. 'One hundred and sixty girls from a Japanese factory came to Las Vegas just to see Elvis,' said George Ziros. 'Elvis very seldom got sick – once in a while like any other human being – but as the girls were lining up outside the showroom, it was announced that he had been forced to cancel through ill health. The only trouble was that these girls did not speak any English and they were still trying to get in because they didn't want to miss the show. Finally, we got some Japanese interpreters to tell them: "I'm sorry, but Elvis is sick. He can't perform tonight." The girls got so hysterical that some even passed out and others were crying. They were flying back to Japan in the morning and it had been their only chance to see the show.

'Someone told Elvis and he made arrangements with the airlines and the hotel for the girls to stay an extra day. That night, he brought them to the show personally and sat them all in the front row. The girls went crazy, screaming and yelling, when he did his act. It was unbelievable.

Touched by Midas, Elvis sparkled on stage in one of his hand-crafted, jewel-encrusted jumpsuits like the high priest of a fabulous, futuristic cult. Each suit had a name: the Inca Gold Leaf, the Mad Tiger, the Mexican Sundial, the Prehistoric Bird, the American Eagle and the King of Spades. He wore embroidered capes until an excited fan grabbed hold of one and almost dragged him off the stage. After that, he abandoned the capes in favour of colourful scarves, which he tossed into the audience. Around his waist was a thick belt embossed with heraldic eagles and shields, and dripping with gold chains. Around his neck he wore a gem-studded collar, great gold crucifixes and a Star of David or Hebrew *chat*. Over the years, he fused the pomp of a coronation with the passion of a religious revival. Added to the ceremonial was his own anthem, the medley of *Dixie*, *All My Trials* and the *Battle Hymn of the Republic* – known collectively as the *American Trilogy*.

'I gave him a gold rope to wear around his neck, three pounds of pure gold, and he threw it into the audience one night,' said Henri Lewin, whose business card gave his job description as 'MILLIONAIRE'. 'I was there and I got the security guards to catch it. I went up to him after the show and said, "You must be out of your mind. I'm a refugee, I came from nothing and I gave you this gift as a friend. If you want to give something valuable away, go buy it and throw your own stuff away." He said, "Give it to me, Mr Lewin, it's mine." I handed it back and he kept it.'

In terms of audience reaction, no other performer ever topped Elvis, according to Elia Verzilli, the Hilton's theatre manager who had worked in the showroom since its first night. 'In the first couple of years, he was more like a teenager, very lively, very playful, very friendly. He gradually changed over the next six years until he was very heavy and subdued. But everybody liked Elvis, no matter what.'

Security chief Jim Vernon's problem was that some of them liked Elvis too much. 'The main thing was to make sure that he got back to his room all right and nobody bothered him while he was up there,' he said. 'When he went up to his suite, one of our guys stayed outside the door around the clock. No one could get out on that floor unless their name was on a master list, which had been furnished to us. People tried, but they never made it.'

The guard was the first person Elvis's party guests saw when they came out of the lift on the 30th floor, but his jurisdiction ended at the suite's front door. Inside, prescription drugs were freely available, and despite Tom Jones's warnings, Elvis was on non-prescribed medication in the early seventies.' One day you'll overdo it with those drugs and none of us will be around to help you,' Tom warned him more than once.

However, there were intimate moments as well. Elvis confided to his friend that he had never recovered from the loss of his mother. 'Mama died trying to be beautiful for me again,' I heard him say during one visit to Tom's dressing room. 'She would be so proud if she could see me now, a married man with a baby. She'd be a grandmother and that would go a long way to making up for the loss of Jesse.'

Elvis had brought Priscilla with him and I introduced her to my wife. While Tom and Elvis chatted, the two women compared baby pictures of our respective daughters, Lisa and Joanne.

'I found it very hard to accept my daddy's new wife,' Elvis said, referring to Vernon's marriage to divorcee Dee Stanley, the mother of three young boys. 'I still can't get used to the idea of having a stepmother.'

As soon as Priscilla left Elvis, a disturbing picture emerged of his new life. One night, Elvis came to Tom's dressing room when the Welsh singer was showering after a show. Elvis used an adjoining cubicle and they carried on a conversation through the glass partition. After a few minutes, ready to get dressed again, Elvis called one of the Memphis Mafia with a yell of 'Red!'

Red West knew exactly what was required of him. Entering the cubicle, he pulled up Elvis's skin tight leather trousers and, while his boss sucked in his belly, laced them up. Afterwards, Tom went into the cubicle and found a handgun Elvis had dropped on the floor. He was genuinely shocked that Elvis needed to carry a weapon. However, the King constantly talked about being a target. On one occasion, a camera flash flared briefly in a window high up in the Hilton as Elvis was preparing to step into his black-windowed limousine.

'He made us go back in and search the place for that happy snapper,' Red told me. 'Of course, we had to come down and tell him our efforts were in vain and he got pretty mad. Yet five minutes later, he was happily posing for a picture with some chick at a gas filling station.'

Jim Vernon said that Elvis 'never really showed it if he was nervous about his safety'. Red and Sonny took care of any troublemakers who tried to gate crash the Imperial Suite or fanatical fans who tried to mob Elvis down in the lobby. 'They were real protective, but they put up with Elvis's gags,' he said. 'He was a great practical joker who liked to goof around. He loved water fights, either upstairs in the suite or downstairs; he didn't care where it was. He'd get squirt guns and the Boys never knew when he was going to open fire, so they were the ones who wound up getting wet. Elvis was a great guy and a lot of fun to be around. I miss him.'

However, working for Elvis was never easy, as the silver haired Dr George C. Nichopolous – a.k.a. Dr Nick – found to his cost. 'Dr Nick', remembered Joe Esposito, 'came on the scene around 1967 when he got called out to Elvis's ranch for something. George Klein's wife worked for Nichopolous at the time, and she called him out. They hit it off pretty well, and about a year later, he became Elvis's personal physician when we had started the tours. He started to come along on the tours and look after Elvis's health from then on.

'Elvis just had the feeling that he needed a doctor around for himself and for the entourage and for the show people. I mean, it wasn't just Elvis he cared for. He was just used for the road work. Elvis had other doctors who attended him in Las Vegas and Los Angeles.'

'My nights were just horrible,' the later much maligned doctor told journalist Stanley Booth. 'I would go to bed when he'd go to bed, and then he might sleep two or three hours and wake up, and I'd have to go in and try to get him back to sleep. On a tour, I had very little time when I could go and do anything. If he woke up and I wasn't there, he'd go bananas. It got to the point where I was working eighteen or twenty hours a day, sleeping in cat naps.'

(In 1980, the district attorney-general's office in Memphis ordered two of its officers, Larry Hutchinson and David McGriff, to investigate the doctor concerning his most famous patient's drug usage. They interviewed many of the key figures in Elvis's life, including the Colonel, Joe Esposito, Linda Thompson and Sonny West. A grand jury later indicted Dr Nick on ten counts of illegally prescribing drugs to patients, including Elvis, but he was acquitted on all charges at a jury trial. The DA's investigators tape-recorded their interviews, and copies of those tapes are now in my possession. They are quoted in parts of this book.)

For the time being, however, the party was still in full swing, with Elvis and Tom Jones as the centre of attention. Their friendship seemed to be untouched by the fiercely professional rivalry between the two camps. Elvis joined Tom on stage on many occasions and they would fool around in front of the audience, although they never actually sang together. Tom's road manager Chris Ellis was told to keep the spare microphone hidden in case Elvis ever tried to do a duet. Neither star's management wanted to risk a damaging confrontation. Tom's action showed that the mutual admiration society had its limits. He also told me as we watched one of Elvis's performances: 'Look, he's like a big chorus girl up there.'

Nor was Elvis quite the Tom Jones fan he seemed to be, according to Sonny West. 'We would go to his shows and Elvis always would say something to knock him,' Sonny said in his memoirs. 'Tom wears very tight pants and Elvis would always say, "He sticks a damn sock down his pants." He would comment on Tom's singing, and during a performance, he would sing along with Tom, making out that he could hit the high notes, which by then he couldn't.'

Elvis was never critical to Tom's face, but he did ask him once: 'Why do you bother singing the high notes?'

'Why? Because they're in the bloody song,' Tom replied, wondering what point Elvis was making. 'You can't sing it without them.'

'I leave 'em to J. D.,' Elvis explained, referring to J. D. Sumner and the Stamps, his backing group after 1972. 'It's a lot easier that way. The audience sees me with my mouth open in front of the mike and no one knows who's singing what.'

One unpleasant episode gave me a chilling insight into Elvis's temper. In the Imperial Suite, Elvis had sung his favourite number at that time, 'Killing Me Softly with His Song', and he asked Tom if he liked it.

'Yes, very nice,' Tom answered politely.

Elvis interpreted this as a call for an encore and gave his private rendition of the song again . . . and again . . . and again.

'He must have done it about seven times,' Tom groaned later. 'Anyway, he was about to start it once more when Chris Ellis pulled away the stool the pianist was sitting on. Elvis aimed a karate kick at Chris, but missed. Because of the bad atmosphere, we left, and the following day Elvis's doctor told me he had the hump with us.'

Around two in the afternoon, Ellis was asleep in his room at Caesars when the telephone rang. It was Elvis on the line, 'in a menacing mood,' the road manager recalled. 'After a couple of minutes shouting at me, Elvis went off the line and his oriental karate instructor came on saying, "Elvis velly mad. You be here 4.30 sharp to apologise on hands and knees,"' said Chris.

'I asked to speak to Sonny and told him, "If Elvis wants me there at 4.30, I'll be there – but I'll bring a couple of Mafia pals with me and they'll come in shooting." Sonny told me that he would tell Elvis that I had come over but couldn't get in because of the security.'

Tom was working in Houston a few days later when he asked me to get Elvis on the phone so they could sort the situation out 'one way or another'. I placed the call to Elvis's hideaway at Palm Springs and the friendship was patched up. ..

When I asked Tom what would have happened if Chris Ellis had been beaten up, the singer replied: 'I'd have gone over there and rammed his f***ing karate belt right down his throat.'

Time and again, Elvis needed to prove that he was the toughest kid on the block. The captain of an airliner preparing for take-off at Las Vegas airport witnessed one such display of macho behaviour. Standing in the path of the aircraft a man stood holding up an object that glinted in the morning sun. Even from his lofty position on the flight deck, the pilot was able to tell the control tower that he recognized the solitary figure. It was Elvis Presley, a.k.a. Colonel John Burrows.

Elvis had leapt from his stretch limousine, which had forced its way through an airport barrier. The shiny object in his raised hand was the narcotics agent's badge Nixon had given him. Elvis was using his authority to hold up the plane because he believed a passenger he wanted to apprehend might be on board.

The hunt had started after a diamond ring and a picture showing Elvis and a girlfriend had disappeared from his bedside. As one of his entourage was due to fly to Memphis that day, Elvis decided that he must be the culprit.

'Elvis jumped in his car and went to the airport with Sonny and Red,' George Klein, Elvis's DJ buddy, told me. 'As they ran to the gate, a plane was about to depart, so Elvis waved his badge and yelled, "Stop that plane, stop that plane!"

'Through the combination of Elvis Presley, the Federal badge and all the commotion, they stopped the plane and rolled the steps up to the cabin door. Elvis boarded the plane looking for the guy, while Sonny and Red searched the airport lounge. They found the guy reading a newspaper, or rather hiding behind one, and Sonny grabbed him and threw him into the limousine.

'On the way back to the hotel, this guy started using some lines like in an old Hollywood gangster movie: "I guess the gig's up. Yar gonna put me six feet under. Yar gonna wipe me out." Sonny was driving and he almost started laughing, but Elvis was not amused, he was very perturbed. They got back to the hotel and Elvis slapped the guy around pretty good. He had a ring on and it kinda cut his head.'

His right hand heavily bandaged, Elvis told us the story when he came into Tom Jones's dressing room at Caesars that night. 'I didn't want to hurt the guy,' Elvis said, 'but it was the only way to deal with him.'

Elvis spotted a two-pound box of chocolates, which a fan had sent Tom. Invited to help himself, he did just that. He ate the lot, stuffing chocolates into his mouth with his good hand. Once he started, he couldn't stop. A possible sign of cocaine usage.

'The only time I'm aware of Elvis receiving drugs other than from a doctor was when he was using some cocaine,' Sonny West told the DA's investigators. 'As far as I'm concerned, all the other drugs that he took he got from doctors. He did not go out on the streets and buy drugs. He got all the prescriptions he needed from doctors, but he did use some cocaine that he got from a pusher in Nashville.

'When Red found out about that, he went round there and threatened this fella with harm if he got any more coke for Elvis. Red did scare the guy; he was afraid of Red. Elvis found out about it and threatened Red with his job if he didn't leave that guy alone. He said he needed it.'

Elvis also got liquid cocaine from one of several doctors he used, according to Sonny. 'Elvis used that with cotton balls he put into his nostrils,' he said. Sadly, the King was killing himself, albeit softly.

13

RAQUEL, SMOKE AND MIRRORS

You seemed to change, you acted strange

BY THE TIME she hit Las Vegas, Raquel Welch was the most upfront lady in show business. Wearing a mini-dress shorter than a British summer, she disembarked from a limousine at the Hilton.

'I was going to play Vegas and I walked into the hotel, where they asked me if I would like to see Elvis's show,' she told me. 'I was with my choreographer and they put us in the celebrity booth. Colonel Parker came over to say hello, and he said to me, "Would you like to see the boy afterwards? OK then, I'll tell him you're coming backstage." I couldn't believe this man was talking about a prince of his profession, the Valentino of our day. "*The boy*"? He'd "*tell* him", not *ask* him? I'm sorry, but this man was talking about his star as if he were white trash.

'Again, I was disappointed when Elvis came on. Again, he looked more like Wayne Newton than Elvis Presley. Somebody had put the lid on all that raw talent and I thought it was the saddest thing. He had this ridiculous outfit on and the hair was sprayed so that not a strand of it moved.

'After the show, I was taken backstage to the dressing room and I had to believe the man before me was Elvis Presley because it was as if the real him wasn't there. There were mirrors all around the room. He started showing me his rings and stuff, and then, when I was talking to him, I realized that he wasn't looking at me but at himself in the mirror behind me.'

However, it was more than vanity that made Elvis catch his own reflection. He lived in terror that he might be losing his looks, and in the company of stunning women like Raquel Welch, he needed to reassure himself. This is why he preferred the heavily macho presence of Red and Sonny West and overtly masculine friends such as Tom Jones.

Sonny had noticed a change in Elvis during 1972, when his weight started to cause problems. 'He had been keeping his weight down since he opened in Vegas in '69 and he looked real good – he never got over 170-175 pounds,' he said. 'Then in 1972 he started putting on some weight and he started withdrawing more. He went on a diet because he was getting ready to go live via satellite to over twenty-five countries around the world in January 1973. He lost weight and he looked good, but the night after the show, he got totally out of it in Hawaii. I'd never seen him like that.

'At one time or another, we all talked about it, Red and myself and Joe, Dave, Lamar, Jerry – all of us talked about it: "Man, what's he doing to himself?" When we saw him in Memphis on several occasions similar to this, we felt he was getting his drugs in Memphis. I also know that there were times when he left Memphis and went to Las Vegas to replenish his supply.'

Elvis flirted with death so often that Sonny came to believe he had divine protection. He had once overdosed in Palm Springs during a night with a young lady and he came close on at least one other occasion in Las Vegas. Doctors were invariably called in to give Elvis a reviving shot whenever he went too far, but Sonny believes that other forces were at work as well.

'Elvis seemed to be able to project to all of us around him that nothing was going to happen to him. After several close calls, it became even more believable that, maybe, this man wasn't going to die of anything but old age. It always seemed like the hand of God lifted him up out of it in the nick of time. So there is such a thing as a guardian angel.'

On many occasions, the guardian angel took the human form of Linda Thompson, who was 23 when she became Elvis's girlfriend after Priscilla left.

'In '74 he almost choked to death on an apple core in Las Vegas,' said Sonny. 'He had taken quite a bit of sleeping medication and he went to sleep while eating the apple. The core was in his throat, and Linda reached in and got it out. If she hadn't been there, he probably would have choked to death. He was laying on his back, 'sound asleep, and he probably didn't know he was choking. His mind was telling him he couldn't breathe, but he couldn't do anything about it.'

Linda remembers that night vividly.

'The problem for us was controlling the sleeping medication, making sure that he didn't choke on his food,' she said. 'That was always a problem. On several occasions, he would fall asleep while eating, and we'd have to take the food out of his mouth to stop him choking. Sometimes I had to call the doctor. There were innumerable times when Elvis choked on his food. I could not recall how many times I had to put my fingers in his mouth.

'One time I woke up and he wasn't breathing properly. I called the nurse and she called Dr Nick who had him brought to the hospital. Another time in Las Vegas he choked on his food and he was completely out of it. I called the Las Vegas doctor and he came over and gave him some injections to help. He was out for hours.

'Another time, when we were flying back from Vegas to Memphis, he was taken ill on the plane. He couldn't breathe properly and was admitted to hospital as soon as we landed. The story was that he was suffering from exhaustion.'

For more than two years, up to September 1973, few witnessed Elvis's declining health more closely than his valet, 'Hamburger James' Caughley. In his testimony to the DA's investigators, he said: 'I heard about his eccentricities even before I went to work for him. I met someone who had been working with Elvis and had had a blow-out with him and left. Elvis, I heard, was getting difficult to work for because of his temperament and, to a lesser degree, because of the entourage who were with him. Starting off, it wasn't that bad. The best way I could describe it was like a graph: you had to be around him twenty-four hours to notice it and then you'd see the problem mounting slowly, and the problem was drugs.

'Sure, '71 wasn't too bad, in 72 it started to get worse, and the last months I had with Elvis, it was unbelievable. It was still like a graph in as much that there would be highs and lows. Sometimes, when we were back in Memphis, he would stay upstairs twelve days at a time.

'As errand boy, it often fell to me to go get the prescriptions filled; over the time I was with him, I must have brought back hundreds of pills to Graceland. There was Percodan tablets, there'd be codeine, Demerol in pills and in liquid, some amphetamines, occasional Seconal, Valium. There were a lot of throwaway syringes. A lot of times, Elvis would get a lot of stuff from outside Memphis.

'I used to see Dr Nick most days – on the eight different tours I went on, he came with us. I never saw Dr Nick administer anything to Elvis, never once. But they used to disappear into Elvis's private room and you'd notice the change in attitude.

'Most of the time, he'd be taking things himself. One time, on tour, he OD'd badly and I had to send for Nick. It was my personal belief that he had obtained some pills from another doctor. He barely had a pulse. I mean, I was worried. I'd seen him far out before, but never as bad.

'Sometimes he was so far gone that I'd have to sit him up in bed and run a vibrator over his back to get him awake. But this time I couldn't rouse him, so I had to get Nick. Some of the other boys got him into a chair. Nick said he'd see to him, and Joe Esposito closed the door. Nick did seem to care about him and what happened; he used to get mad about the fact that he was getting stuff from other doctors.

'While we were on tour in Vegas, Elvis was quite often careless. He never worried about wealth or possessions. I might pick up a $10,000 ring he'd left lying around, while cleaning up after him, or hanging up his clothes. Whoever was on duty had to watch everything that Elvis did. He just did not care what he did. I used to get mad when I cleaned up the pill bottles and syringes because I'd find bottles with my name on them. He used other people's names to get the drugs in when we were on tour – to protect the name of Elvis Presley.

'Vernon Presley knew what was going on and it worried him. The Colonel knew what was going on only because he had a line from the Guys which kept him informed twenty-four hours a day. On bad days, Elvis would be like a zombie, just sitting in front of the television doing nothing, going nowhere. He was in a sort of twilight stage brought on by these controlled substances. But the twilight times grew longer.'

No one, of course, knew Elvis as well as Joe Esposito. 'I knew him for about eight months before we left the Army,' he told the investigators. 'We got out at the same time and he asked me to go back to Memphis with him and work for him, and I stayed until he died.

'When we got out the job he gave me was a sort of general overseeing of his operation. I would take care of all of Elvis's personal business – looking after the money, paying the bills, make sure everything ran smoothly for him. In order of seniority, it was Elvis, then Vernon and then me. I was the overseer of everything involving Elvis throughout my time with him. I took care of everything that did not fall within the province of Colonel Parker. When I first went there, there was only four of us in the entourage – me, Charlie Hodge who joined us from the Army, Sonny West and Elvis's cousin Gene Smith. Over the years, it became necessary to employ more, but when we got back to Memphis [from the Army], it worked out that Elvis was going straight into the movies.

'The first show we did was in Las Vegas in 1969, two shows a night for a month and then we went out on the road straight afterwards – that was September 1969. They were one-nighters and we got into the routine of playing about 100 towns a year. It was during this period that his health began to deteriorate, although I didn't think much about it at the time. Then he started to have severe problems with his colon in the early Seventies, a twisted colon, and was admitted to hospital for a couple of weeks. He also had blood pressure problems, but it was no big deal.'

Joe was convinced that the loss of Priscilla tipped Elvis into a downward spiral: 'To me, everything started, the erratic behaviour, after his divorce. He could never sit still. He'd be flying around different parts of the country.

'He needed those doctors for his vitamin B12 shots, and medication for his throat. He also needed sleep medication when we were on the road. I don't think Elvis was ever hooked on narcotics, never ever. Yes, he took pills. We all did because of the crazy hours. Otherwise we'd never have got any sleep. But he was never what I would term "hooked". I've seen Elvis go thirty days without taking a pill. I had never seen him overdose.

Sure I'd seen him pass out. He fell asleep while we were talking or whatever.

'It became a problem sometimes to get him to sleep and we had to give him the medication to knock him out. Afterwards, he might have a problem getting up. Before he went on stage, he'd have shots – I can't say definitely what they contained. When he came off, the doctor would give him a tranquillizer to bring him down because Elvis used to get really hyped up on stage.

'I have never seen him overdose,' Esposito continued to insist, 'never in my life. I don't know where that story came from. The three times we went to hospital, it was for medical problems, not overdosing on drugs, definitely not. I agree the drugs were a problem. Some members of the entourage had spoken to me about it as his intake increased, and it got worse, and I'd tell them there was nothing I could do about it. I tried to help him out, we all did. I talked many times to Dr Nick about it. He said it was a problem because he was getting drugs from other people. He said he was trying to control it by giving him placebos.

'Dr Nick asked us to keep watch and try to keep track of what he was taking. I know Dr Nick called other doctors to see what they were giving him. We even went to see his father about it. But Elvis was a very strong guy, you know. When I spoke to him about it, he'd say he wasn't doing anything wrong. In the end, he'd just tell me, if I didn't like it, to get the hell out. I left a couple of times over personal rows, but came back.

'The three times he went into hospital, as far as I was concerned, was not for drugs. The first time was for his colon problem. The second time, when he was brought back from Louisiana, was for exhaustion, and while he was in hospital, they decided to try and get him off some of the drugs. I was never told he had gone in for an overdose; I got the same story as everyone else – that it was exhaustion.

'I knew Elvis had a drug problem, 'specially in the last year of his life. It was a problem, we knew that. I still can't say he was addicted. I've seen addicts and they can't go a day without it.

'I don't like to talk about Elvis. When he died I vowed that I would never talk about him and I never have. I have never talked to anyone about Elvis, never said anything bad about him. It's a personal thing. This is the first time anyone has got anything out of me about Elvis, and no one will again.'

The break-up of the Presleys' marriage had been particularly difficult for Diamond Joe because his wife Joan was a close friend of Priscilla. In Los Angeles, however, the former Mrs Elvis Presley was making up for lost time.

14

PRICILLA'S SECRET LOVER

Love me tender

WHEN THE telephone rang on the table beside Priscilla's bed for the third time that night, her lover slipped from her side and crossed the room. Before he closed the bathroom door behind him, he heard her say yet again: 'No, Elvis, Mike's not here. I told you that before.' She was not lying. Her lover this night was not Mike Stone, the karate instructor for whom she had left Elvis, but the celebrated British photographer Terry O'Neill, in those days a close friend of mine.

Terry, who was later to marry Faye Dunaway, had become used to the calls that interrupted his love-making with Priscilla in her four-poster bed beneath the mirrored ceiling. Elvis felt he had a right to call her at all hours of the day and night. He had, after all, rented for her the comfortable house on Summit Drive in Beverly Hills.

Mike, known to some as 'The Animal', was also desperate for a reconciliation with the ex-wife of the man he had instructed in the martial arts. He had been offered the well-paid job after meeting Elvis and Priscilla in Las Vegas, where he was guarding a prominent record producer. Elvis had learned the basics of karate in the Army, and the idea was that Mike would turn him into a real killer, capable of defending himself against any assailant. In truth, he was never fit enough to train and the whole thing became a charade.

'He just wants to learn the movements to make him look good on stage,' Mike told me. 'I was nothing more to him than a choreographer.'

Mike entered Priscilla's life precisely at a time when she had reached breaking point. 'It had got to the stage with Elvis that I was damned if I left him and damned if I didn't,' she said. 'I wanted badly for people to believe in me. I was always on guard, always dressing to please him, always fighting for territory and fighting for what I believed in. You know – traditions, ideals.

'I wasn't brought up to believe in divorce, and when I married, I thought it would be forever. Everywhere I went, I had women wanting him. Not just wanting him: right in front of me, there were things going on. It was a shock to be confronted with this at such a young age. How to handle it. All the time I was desperate to please. To Elvis, I was like this kid he had raised. He used to refer to himself as "Daddy".'

Just as Elvis demanded that Priscilla dress like a kewpie doll, his own appearance became even more dandified as the marriage went into injury time. At 37, his hair was dyed so black that it turned blue in the light, his fingers jangled with rings and his clothes were covered with jewels. He wore jackets without lapels over scarlet ruffled shirts with high collars. His eyes were shaded behind wire-rimmed glasses with 'ELVIS' engraved on them. He wore a belt with an ornate silver buckle and carried a cane with a silver, diamond-eyed bulldog's head for a handle. Inside was a gun.

However, the thought of losing Priscilla was as unthinkable to Elvis as would have been the idea of Gladys and Vernon splitting up when he was a child. The child bride had become his emotional support system.

'Elvis was at his happiest when he and Priscilla were together,' said Mary Jenkins, the Graceland cook. 'They would go horseback riding or go-kart rallying or go swimming and lay out by the pool. They would go running upstairs, holding hands, playing with each other. Yeah, he was real happy. He was real active then, but after the separation he just laid around a lot. Sometimes he stayed upstairs in his room for two or three weeks.'

In her autobiography, *Elvis and Me,* Priscilla dismissed the switch of men in her life in a single sentence: 'My relationship with Mike had now developed into an affair.' But she admits that the relationship coincided with the discovery of a new confidence in herself: 'Off came my false eyelashes, the jewels and flashy clothes,' she recalled. 'All devices that I'd depended on for security I now shed. I was seeing myself for the first time.'

Everything changed drastically for Priscilla after she left Elvis in 1972 to set up home with Mike, taking 4-year-old Lisa with her. At first, they shared an apartment at Marina Del Rey while Elvis refused to discuss the financial provision of a separation agreement. In June of that year, he played his first concerts in New York, jamming 80,000 fans into

Madison Square Gardens in four nights. Yet just a few weeks later, he signed a penny-pinching, nine-page contract that allowed his wife a miserly $1000 a month plus $500 to support Lisa. Under a much improved deal, he subsequently provided the house on Summit Drive, and Priscilla was allowed to keep the white Mercedes sports car that I saw parked outside on my visits. In those early months, she lived close to the richest people in the world on less money than most of their maids were paid – and it showed.

Priscilla introduced me to Mike Stone, and I took karate instruction from him at her house (an Elvis Presley picture-free zone from what I could see). I paid him $150 a week for six one-hour lessons. He was always pleased to pocket my modest contribution to their coffers, saying that the money gave him a measure of independence. After karate, we would play tennis on the court at the bottom of the garden while Priscilla prepared a light meal, usually devilled eggs and salad. Mike would pick lemons from a tree in the garden and demonstrate his strength by squeezing them with his bare hands to provide the juice for the lemonade we drank with our food.

Invariably, the conversation would turn to Elvis. My 1975 diary is littered with such entries as: 'February 13, 1pm lesson with Mike at the house, then lunch with him and Priscilla. She told me Elvis would be getting out of the hospital tomorrow and must be feeling better since he'd already beaten Rick Stanley [his step-brother] quite badly on a visit.'

One morning, I turned up at Summit Drive, unaware that Mike had gone to Hawaii for a martial arts tournament. Priscilla invited me to stay for lunch.

She was clearly fearful of both men: Mike for his raw strength and Elvis for his almighty power. Both had made it clear to her that they could take care of themselves. It later came out that Elvis had ordered one of his Boys to hire a hit man to blow Stone's head off. Fortunately, wiser counsel prevailed and he had changed his mind. That morning, Priscilla needed to express her concern about Elvis after receiving an anguished phone call from him, even though he had the devoted Linda Thompson on hand to share his troubles.

'It wasn't always like this,' she said. 'Elvis used to be kind, gentle and always attentive. But things changed long before our wedding day. I should have realized I was marrying an entourage and only had a share in its leader. It had to end.

'Graceland was the worst. It wasn't a home, it was a carnival and I was one of the acts. I had to get out and become a woman in my own right. It wasn't because of Mike. He just happened to be there at the right time and be the right man.'

Our conversation was interrupted by the arrival of Lisa, then aged 7. As I tucked into the food Priscilla had prepared, her daughter sat at the table and started to write a letter, pausing from time to time to ask me how to spell certain words. The letter began: 'Dear Daddy, Yesterday I went to a birthday party . . .' and ended: 'I miss you very much and Mummy sends her love.'

Priscilla had mistakenly believed that becoming a father would change Elvis and make him act more responsibly. Above all, she had prayed that his daughter would help him to stop taking the drugs that controlled his personality, and that, she freely admitted, he had persuaded her to try.

Mother and father had joint custody of Lisa, but it was Elvis who indulged her. When she asked to see a film, he rented the cinema; when she wanted a merry-go-round, he hired the amusement park. Elvis bought her a mink coat and a diamond ring, both of which Priscilla made him return. When Lisa told him on the phone that she had never seen snow, he flew from Memphis to Los Angeles in the Convair 880 jet that bore her name (and the call sign 'Hound Dog I'), picked her up and soared on to Utah so that she could play in the snow for twenty minutes. The trip cost around $30,000, but no price was too high if it made Lisa happy.

'He was always up to something, shooting off firecrackers or guns, driving golf carts or snowmobiles,' Lisa remembered, in an interview for *Life* magazine. 'He'd pull me in a sled and scare me to death. In that long steep driveway that goes up to Graceland, he'd be pulling me up and falling at the same time. He called me Buttonhead or Yisa. He'd never call me Lisa unless he was mad at me.

'One night when I was about 5 or 6 we were watching the TV. I looked up at him and said, "Daddy, Daddy, I don't want you to die." And he just looked down at me and said, "OK, I won't. Don't worry about it." I always felt protective of him.'

At the time Terry O'Neill came into Priscilla's life, Mike Stone had moved out. She had fallen for O'Neill the day he stepped into Bis& Beau, the clothes shop she ran with designer Olivia Bis at 9650 Santa

Monica Boulevard. The boutique numbered Cher, Cybill Shepherd and Barbara Eden among its clientele.

'I just walked in there off the street by chance and there she was, looking quite nondescript,' Terry told me, breaking a twenty-year silence about the affair. 'Something had definitely happened between her and Mike Stone, and she and I were instantly attracted to each other.

'She was dressed terribly – I mean, she was wearing the Seventies flower power gear which her shop specialized in. To be honest, she was a bit of a fashion disaster at the time. I hated those big hats she was wearing and the ridiculously flared trousers. Because of the way she dressed I didn't take her to any of the well-known swank restaurants like the Daisy, but to little bars and bistros where nobody recognized her. I told her what I thought: that she was beautiful but that, frankly, she wasn't making the most of herself. No man had ever talked to her like that and it intrigued her.'

But it was a different story at night. Priscilla would spend as much as an hour dressing seductively for bed which, in her case, was a huge mirrored four-poster job. Even in the special low lighting of her bedroom, she looked nothing less than sensational in her black negligée.

It had been a black negligée that, as a teenager, Priscilla had worn on more than one occasion to try to entice Elvis into taking her virginity, an act he restrained himself from performing until their wedding night. 'We have to control our desires so they don't control us,' he would tell her when their heavy petting took them to the edge.

Since leaving Elvis, Priscilla had grown up a great deal. 'She was ultra-feminine, very gentle and terribly romantic,' Terry recalls. 'She was certainly no good-time girl. Before me, there had only been Elvis and Mike Stone, which made her a very chaste woman, particularly by the standards of that town and that era.'

The nights they spent together were always being interrupted by telephone calls from either Elvis or Mike. Although she never told O'Neill what they said – and he certainly wasn't going to ask her. He knew they both wanted her back, particularly Elvis, who she said was heartbroken when she left him. But she returned to the photographers arms each time she put the phone down. 'I didn't see her as Elvis Presley's former wife and I wasn't intimidated by him. I wasn't even frightened of Stone, although I knew his reputation in karate. I can honestly say that I liked Priscilla for herself.

'If she'd gone back to Elvis, she would have been destroyed. Instead, he destroyed himself.'

Recalling the end of their affair just two months after it began, O'Neill said: 'I went back to England, and that was that as far as I was concerned. However, I gather that she was pretty upset because, temporarily at least, I had swept her off her feet. I saw her some-time later at the Troubadour when Elton John was appearing there. I got her moved up to some seats at the front, but I could tell she was not happy with me. She was a lovely, gentle woman and I'm sorry that things had to end the way they did, but I was based in Britain and her life was in California.'

The cameraman also admitted his fling with Priscilla to his old flame Raquel Welch as the three of us dined at San Lorenzo in London in June 1994. Preferring to turn a diplomatic deaf ear to the lothario's admission, Raquel said that she now included an impression of Elvis in her stage act – and then proceeded to give a private performance. Quite what the other diners in Princess Diana's favourite restaurant made of her rendition of 'Hound Dog', complete with choreographed shoulder movements and the Presley curled lip, we will never know.

John and Yoko now decided to try for a child, although Yoko had already miscarried several times. After visiting an acupuncturist called Dr Hong in San Francisco, Yoko became pregnant. There was a collective sigh of relief when she gave birth to the baby on John's 35th birthday, 9 October 1975.

Yoko was so obsessed with numbers that she had insisted on a Caesarean section so that her baby son and John would share the same birthday. John wanted to call the boy 'George Washington United States of America Citizen Lennon', but settled for 'Sean'. 'I feel higher than the Empire State Building,' he said, resolving to forgo his recording career to become a house-husband and look after the infant.

When Elvis and Linda read about John's wild behaviour, they discussed marriage as a way of cementing their own relationship. 'At this time in his life I suppose Elvis was closer to me than anyone,' said Linda. 'At one point we had planned to marry, but not after a while. That was primarily because of his drugs use, but also through his whole lifestyle. There was no way he was going to change.'

As a compromise, Linda suggested that they redecorate Graceland in a style they both liked. Elvis agreed. The blue and white decor, which dated from 1957, was completely replaced. 'The big fifteen-foot-long white sofa, a lot of the lamps and the big coffee table that Elvis used in those rooms from the time he moved in until 1974 – they all went and he brought in the wild red stuff,' said Todd Morgan, the Graceland communications director. 'All through the years, the drapes and carpet had changed colours, but blue and white were pretty standard from the very late Sixties through to the mid-Seventies. It was Hollywoodish elegance.

'The furniture and the drapes from the front rooms – the living-room, music room, dining room and foyer – were put into storage and very faddish new stuff was brought in. It was all very trendy – the whim of somebody who had money to throw around. It was during the same period that Ike and Tina Turner had guitar-shaped coffee tables in their house. This was rock 'n' roll funk: red velvet *faux* French provincial furniture, deep red shag carpet and red velvet drapes. It was kinda wild.'

There was ample time for Bill Eubanks, the decorator Elvis had chosen, to exercise his imagination. His client was on the road for six months during 1974 with only short breaks between trips.

'When we were on tour, Elvis carried a little black bag that contained his medication,' recalls Linda. 'He never went anywhere without it. There were times when he was ready to go on stage and he was still down from sleeping medication, and he would virtually be asleep through his performance. He'd come off hardly knowing he had been on stage and say he was only just waking up. Other times, he was too up on

Dexedrine or whatever so that he was too highly strung, giggling on stage and being silly, sometimes being hostile. It was a big worry.'

Whenever they escaped home to Graceland, Elvis would eagerly check out Eubanks' latest improvements, especially the pool room, the TV room and the 'jungle room' in the basement. He was delighted with the changes. 'Elvis spent, spent, spent and Vernon never got over the fear that tomorrow, it might all be gone,' said Todd. 'When he told him money was running low, Elvis would say, "Oh Daddy, I'll just do a tour or a movie. Don't worry about it."

'So it was a constant problem, but Elvis and his dad were good friends. Certainly he was closer to his mother when he was growing up, but those close to Elvis saw the deepening relationship between him and his father through the years. Vernon was very honest and Elvis trusted him completely. He knew that, as long as his daddy was there running the show at home, every dime would be accounted for because Vernon was known to be tight with a buck.'

Eubanks had swathed the ceiling and walls of the pool room with miles of batik-like fabric, which was gathered and pleated to form an indoor tent fit for a sheikh. Correctly sensing the mood at Graceland, the decorator called it 'Elvis's emotional bomb shelter'.

'In the TV room, Elvis wanted to retain the three TVs he'd put in after hearing that LBJ had three sets sitting side by side so that he could watch all three networks at once,' said Todd.' He was an admirer of Muhammad Ali and watched his fights, and he loved *Monty Python*, Peter Sellers and the *Ed Sullivan Show*.'

The TV room was perfect for entertaining. Under its mirrored ceiling was a yellow-padded Naugahyde bar and soda fountain with matching barstools. A yellow-and-white 'TCB' lightning bolt on one wall reminded guests where they were. There was a stereo system and a jukebox that was wired for sound throughout the house. One hundred 45s could be loaded into the jukebox, and Elvis's collection included offerings by Tom Jones, Bill Black's Combo, Patti Page, Dean Martin, Buddy Holly and Ray Charles.

The 'jungle room' or den adjoining the kitchen was the largest room in the house. Elvis bought the furniture at Donald's Furniture Store because it reminded him of Hawaii. Monkeys and parts of other wild animals were worked into the chairs, and there was a Tiki god and a waterfall cascading down one wall.

'Elvis added the jungle room on to the house and it became the gathering place,' said Todd. 'It was big and roomy and it looked like a typical suburban American family room for a number of years except for the waterfall which, er, was kinda trendy. All this stuff was a short-lived fad around this area. Well, it reminded him of Hawaii and he was just having fun one day. It's just my opinion that it doesn't really represent his taste as much as his sense of humour. He was having a good time.

'Elvis recorded an album-and-a-half in here. RCA brought the portable equipment and moved the furniture out or around, and shag pile carpeting was already on the ceiling. It was a kind of a dish thing, but it helped the acoustics and they hung blankets and quilts on the walls. Musicians and singers would come in and they'd bring in a piano. Elvis would come out of the kitchen and stand on the landing. He used that studio trick of changing the colour of the light bulbs to match the mood of the song they were recording. They would jam all night.

'They recorded the album *From Elvis Presley Boulevard, Memphis, Tennessee* and six songs from the *Moody Blue* album. That was the last album he would ever make and it included his last single *Way Down*, which was in the charts at the time he died.

'Some afternoons, Elvis would eat his breakfast in the jungle room at a coffee table made of polished cypress, while staring at the waterfall. Still stoned, he found that the trickling rainbow colours soothed his mind.

'Elvis was very sensitive about his medication and we talked about it from time to time,' said Linda. 'He said he suffered from insomnia from when he was a child. Then, when he became a star, there was so much going on, so much pressure, that he had taken medication to help him keep going or to sleep.

'I talked to Dr Nick about it and I talked to Joe Esposito. I remember Dr Nick telling me that, frankly, I was not the kind of girl who should be around – I was straight. He advised me to leave. He said no one could ever change Elvis, and he was right – one person cannot change another.

'Over the years I was with him, he had all kinds of different drugs. He was very well versed in their effects and their ingredients and would look them up in the *PDR – The Physician's Desk Reference*.

'Elvis would often complain of being in pain. He'd say he was in pain all over, or he had pulled a hamstring on stage. But I always assumed it was a very convenient pain because he enjoyed the effects of the painkilling medication.

'Elvis was a pillaholic. He also injected a lot; sometimes I had to help him inject. He had a psychological dependence. He thought he could not get up or keep going or go to sleep without medication. It is probably true that sometimes his generosity was drug enhanced. He was generous to a fault anyway, but I think it was possible some people took advantage when they saw what kind of state he was in. I look back now and think, "My God, how did I tolerate all that was going on?" But eventually, of course, I could not and had to leave.'

Reckless generosity was often a means of relieving Elvis's guilt over his bad behaviour. His moods could be vile, sometimes violent, as the Graceland cook Mary Jenkins recalls: 'One day Elvis called downstairs for his dinner, or his breakfast – it was late, but it was still breakfast to him – and the phone didn't ring,' she said. 'We were all sitting there in the kitchen, all the Boys and the kitchen help, but nobody heard the phone ring.

'Suddenly, Elvis was at the top of the stairs shouting, "Hey, where is everybody?" And we all spoke about the same time, "Nobody called down here – the phone hasn't rung." Elvis said, "I been callin' and callin' and it has rung." And we said, "Hey, it didn't ring." And he said, "Well it will ring!" He came downstairs with his pyjamas on and he picked up a chair and took the phone off the wall and beat it into just little pieces.'

Another of those who suffered was Jerry Schilling, who had accompanied Elvis to the White House and on many other escapades. 'I noticed a sustained change [in Elvis] in the last three years of his life,' said Jerry. 'He wasn't having fun anymore, except on stage. I suppose at the root was the medication, but of course, when he started cancelling tours, it sort of focused on the growing health problem. A couple of times in Las Vegas, he was unable to go on and it was attributed to his health. He had an enlarged liver, a twisted colon and high blood pressure. The eye condition glaucoma caused a lot of problems.

'It was like a man who was basically healthy all his life, and in a very short period of time, everything started happening to him. He was either going twenty-four hours a day or he was a recluse. It all started to catch up with him. He took amphetamines to get him up for the show, so he could do what he could do ten years ago, and then to counteract the amphetamines he would take barbiturates afterwards. When he was working night after night on tour, he would build up these immunities and require more and more [drugs]. He would look up the *PDR* and try to discover stronger stuff.'

But as fast as Elvis increased his intake, his addictive illness made him crave even higher doses. In January 1975 around the time of his fortieth birthday, he was smuggled into hospital at four o'clock in the morning. In June, he was back again for two days. In August, he went in after completing only three nights of a two-week booking at the Hilton.

'In the hospital, they actually had to give him medication because he had stayed awake for almost four days,' said Jerry Schilling. 'He really was doing better. He had been in hospital for two weeks. It was a very hard thing for Elvis to let his pride go. He was working with a psychiatrist, and it was a very big statement for him to make.'

263

At least Elvis had the satisfaction of knowing that he had beaten one Beatle record. On that New Year's Eve, he had played to the biggest audience of his life when 60,000 people turned out to see him at Pontiac, Michigan. He had topped the Beatles' multitude at Shea Stadium by a few hundred – but split his pants in the process.

15

SINATRA GETS FRANK WITH ELVIS

Big boss man

NO MATTER who ruled the pop realm, Francis Albert Sinatra was the undisputed emperor of New York, New York. Around midnight on Sunday, 24 August 1975, a merrier-than-usual Tom Jones insisted that we scour Manhattan for Ol' Blue Eyes. Tom had just closed a record-breaking week at a theatre in Westchester and wanted to celebrate with a man he regarded as a mentor.

When we reached Jilly's, Sinatra's regular haunt, we were told that Frank and Jilly were dining at Jimmy Weston's. When we arrived there, a particularly sober Sinatra greeted Tom, Tom's son Mark and me with the words: 'Hey, I just spoke to Elvis in hospital.' As waiters dived in with chairs to accommodate us, Sinatra shook his head sadly. 'He's too young to die,' he said.

Sinatra and Presley had had their differences in the past, but it wasn't in the older man's nature to kick a fellow entertainer when he was down. Frank told us about his phone call.

'When I called the [Baptist Memorial] hospital in Memphis, I asked to be put through to Elvis Presley, the girl on the switchboard said, "Who's calling?" and when I said, "Frank Sinatra." I fully expected her to say, "Oh, yeah, and I'm the Queen of England" or some such dumb line. But she must have recognized my voice because, a few seconds later, Elvis came on the line.

'He didn't sound too good. I thought I'd cheer him up by inviting him to join a stars' syndicate to buy our own hotel in Vegas. I told him that, with the three of us there, they could fire a cannon down the Strip and not hit anyone. But I have to say that Elvis didn't seem to care. I guess he's depressed. I told him he's got to look after himself and quit fooling around. He's too young to die, and I told him so.'

If Frank Sinatra was worried about Elvis, Vernon Presley was doubly so. He resolved to trace Elvis's drug suppliers by hiring private eye John O'Grady, a retired LAPD police sergeant, and Jack Kelly, former regional director of the Federal Bureau of Narcotics.

'Vernon had asked me specifically if I could get into Nichopolous's bag, to see what was there,' O'Grady told the DA's men. 'I never did manage to do that. The only time I spoke to Elvis about getting off medication was in 1975, and the response was, "Absolutely not, you sonovabitch."

'I could see the debilitating activity [while I watched] the show. He had a peculiar walking gait, he would ramble, he would tell stories that didn't make sense. He would call me in the middle of the night many times and I do not regret these calls. He called me one night and said he had just buried Jesse [his stillborn twin] there in Memphis. It was meaningless.

His brain would wander; he would repeat things a thousand times. He would call perhaps at four in the morning and just ramble for forty or fifty minutes. It was a condition brought on by the narcotics.

By 1974, he was in a bad way; it was obvious. From then on to when he died, he was not Elvis Presley. He was a human being under the influence of drugs. 'In 1974, when he was performing in Las Vegas, a hotel employee had found a narcotic needle in Elvis's bed and had turned it in. It was the strangest thing. I was sitting there at the performance, and Elvis got up on the stage in front of everyone and told the entire staff off. They were rotten bastards and should never use narcotics. I watched the show and then went backstage and his aide Lamar Fike said it was ridiculous. Elvis was out there with a 190-degree blood pressure, right now. I couldn't understand why the doctors had let him work. Another thing was his sweating. I've looked at people coming down from drugs and they're covered with perspiration, but I had never seen anyone sweat like that. He would lose seven or eight pounds in a performance. He was such a strong character that he came through it, but I could never understand how any doctor at that point could allow him to work.

'I kept in touch with Joe Esposito to enquire what Elvis's state was because I was mortally afraid that some young narcotics officer would knock Elvis off. Of all the cases I've worked on, hundreds of them, I have never seen so many drugs prescribed for one person ever before, and I have been involved in drugs enforcement for thirty-two years.'

Elvis was too sick to heed Sinatra's well-meaning advice. He reacted to his problems by purging the ranks of the Memphis Mafia. He ordered

Vernon to fire his close friends Red and Sonny West, and another bodyguard, Dave Hebler. The Wests, he decided, were too rough in the strong-arm methods they applied to troublemakers and eager fans, while Hebler was accused of spreading dissent. Elvis recruited Linda's brother, Sam Thompson, as bodyguard and Dick Grob was promoted to security.

'I left the sheriff's department around the middle of June 1976 to go and work for Elvis Presley,' Sam told the DA's investigators. 'He explained my duties would be as a personal bodyguard. Primarily I was concerned with the security of the entourage and Elvis himself while we were on tour. He paid me $350 week and he paid all expenses. Most of the travel was on his private planes.

'Not long after I went to work for him, the relationship between him and my sister became estranged and they separated. Then he began going with this very young girl, Ginger Alden. There seemed to be a strain in keeping up that relationship, which is natural with an older man and a young girl. So I think his personality changes might have been in part due to some emotional stress, plus travelling and working like he did.

'I was with Elvis for twenty months and kept a schedule of all fourteen tours during that period. The tours were headed, for example, "Tour Number Nine under the direction of Colonel Tom Parker". He would go and set up the tours and then hand the schedule to Joe Esposito.

'Usually there were about one hundred people who travelled with Elvis, and there would be other ground staff brought in by Colonel Parker. We had an identification system whereby everyone had a laminated badge with their picture and name, which permitted them entry to, say, backstage areas. There were different coloured passes for each tour, to control the flow of people into the area where Elvis would be.

'When I first went to work for him, it seemed to me – and perhaps I had stars in my eyes – that all the shows were good and he always looked well. But the closer I got to the man, the more time I spent with him, I began to realize that some shows were a lot better than others and some were terrible.

'I saw how much weight he was putting on, and at different times, his mood would be altered drastically in a matter of hours. He would be extremely excitable, hopped-up and erratic, and a few hours later, he would be completely lethargic and almost unable to budge out of the chair or bed. Having been involved in law enforcement, I felt that the man was taking a lot of medication and I didn't feel that it was a stable situation.

'We felt that Elvis was highly irrational. He always carried weapons with him. I'm not going as far as to say we were in fear of our lives, but we did feel that some due caution needed to be taken. I would not have put it down entirely to the drugs. They obviously led to the personality changes, but there were also things about the age of the man.

'We talk about the male menopause when a man reaches 40. Elvis was a superstar, and the fact was that his hair was going grey and he was putting on weight. Image was everything to a man like Elvis. He had no peers. No one in show business had done what he had done. The King of Rock 'n' Roll was going grey, getting a little heavy, a few bags under the eyes. Like most entertainers, his ego was very big.'

One of Elvis's drug suppliers who was frequently named in the DA's enquiry was Dr Max Shapiro, a slight middle-aged man wearing thick glasses and a slippery hairpiece. Shapiro preferred patients to call him 'Dr Max', but his nickname among the Hollywood swingers was 'Dr Feelgood'. When I interviewed him in 1978, he described Elvis as 'a close personal friend for more than twenty years'. It was Shapiro who had taught Elvis about the effects of various drugs and had even given him the copy of *The Physician's Desk Reference*, which had become his medical bible. But there was a touching personal side to the relationship.

'He arranged my wedding to my wife Suzanne,' Shapiro told me. 'He had asked me to go to his home in Palm Springs on 13 January 1977. I asked him if I could take Suzanne along, and he said certainly. He knew we were planning to marry, although she was only 19. In fact, I had taken out a licence that was valid for a year and had it with me on that trip. Elvis talked to me about Suzanne and said she was a wonderful girl and would make a wonderful wife. Then he said, "You know, Max, I've rarely been a best man – can I be yours?" I said we would like that very much. He said, "Well then, let's have the wedding tonight – Ginger would like to be the maid of honour."

'He called in a jeweller to supply a special ring and sent his private plane to Los Angeles to collect a minister. It was two or three in the morning when we were married, and the four of us stayed up until dawn talking about religion. He was deeply religious. He gave us some religious books as wedding presents. He had already given me a Mercedes on a previous occasion, but I had to sell that to pay for my divorce.

'I watched the decline in his health with great sadness. I suppose I first realized Elvis had a heart problem about three years before he died. His hands were badly swollen and there were other symptoms of heart trouble. I warned him and he was very concerned. A few months before he died, I told him I was working on an artificial heart that would have saved him.

'The apparatus is actually a pump powered by the same kind of batteries as a pacemaker, which will step in and either augment a patient's heartbeat or replace the work of the heart if the latter gives out. It is made of silicone and Teflon, and other metals are used in a small electric motor. It will not be rejected because it works on a belt outside the body with tubes going into the groin. I had successfully implanted one in a dog at the University of Wisconsin at Milwaukee and I was convinced that it would work on a human being.

'Elvis asked me to prepare three as quickly as I could – one for himself, one for his father and the third for a member of Ginger Alden's family. I was still working on the first one when he died.

'The stories that I gave him prescriptions for anything he wanted are totally untrue. I only ever prescribed cocaine for him once. He was doing a night-time recording session and was in great pain with toothache. I did surgery on a third molar and gave him cocaine to ease the pain. He went on with the session and made one of his biggest hits of the latter years that night. Elvis was happy; everybody was happy.'

However, the paternal Henri Lewin was far from happy about Elvis's condition. He feared the worst during the final Elvis season at the Hilton. 'I saw him shortly before he died, and he was so loaded up that his eyes were puffed and only half open,' he said. 'I didn't think he was going to die, but he lived a sick type of life. He was just a person who was totally in the world of fantasy. He never had a real life. He was not given the opportunity to have a real relationship with anybody. If he made a mistake, nobody told him.

'When he bought a new car, I remember he said, "I never want to own another red car. I only want black cars," and everybody in the room agreed that black was the best. Somebody bought him a cake and he took a piece and he said, "It tastes like s**t," and everybody said, "It's s**t," and they laughed. He didn't like the way a shirt was ironed, so he sent out for four new ones. How can you go on in life when everybody agrees that everything you say and do is right?'

Seymour Heller recalls enquiring after Elvis's health when he saw the Colonel at the Vegas tables. 'I asked, "How's Elvis?" He replied, "He's in a hospital in Memphis." "How long is he going to be there?" "Up till next week when we go on a tour."

'I was upset about that. I thought, He's your No. 1 client, one of the biggest guns in the world, and you're here gambling for dollars while he's in hospital. I thought, if I were Elvis's manager I'd be standing by his bedside. Elvis Presley was not a regular type commodity. He was a special kid.'

The Colonel undoubtedly agreed with that, but he knew better than anyone else that he had lost his power over Elvis. All he could do was hope that his prayers were answered.

16

GOODBYE ELVIS

So they can bring the curtain down . . .

MARY JENKINS knew something strange was happening the last time she saw Elvis alive. The greatest rock 'n roll star the world has ever known was sitting in the dark and more than anything else on Earth, Elvis feared the dark. In his childhood, his mother Gladys had kept an oil lamp burning throughout the night, as he had never been able to relax without a light of some kind in the room. And that's the reason the TV sets were kept always kept switched on in whichever bedroom he was sleeping, at home or on the road.

Sitting in the kitchen of the modest but comfortable home Elvis had bought for her conveniently close to Graceland, Mary, the woman who had cooked for him since his 28th birthday on 8 January 1963 began to share her story with fellow writer Peter Thompson and me. The sounds from a bubbling stew pot on the stove and the smell of fresh bread wafted from the oven as her eyes glistened briefly behind large gold-rimmed spectacles, but the smile rarely faded from her face as she described the scene that night when she unexpectedly encountered Elvis and Ginger Alden cuddled together in that totally dark room.

A grandmother and devout churchgoer, Mary was wearing the Elvis colours of pink and black, and his picture was boldly imprinted on the back of her black leather jacket. In the fourteen-plus years she had worked for him at Graceland she had become completely relaxed about his curious nocturnal routine. So the summons to go upstairs in the early hours of Tuesday, 16 August 1977 held no surprise for the cook, but what she found there surprised her a great deal.

'Mr P called me on the phone at two o'clock in the morning and asked me to come upstairs and straighten up his room. The maid hadn't got there, so I went up to make his bed. There was no one in the room, so I thought Elvis and Ginger were downstairs on the porch. I was going to fill his water bottles up and the icemaker was in Lisa's room. Lisa was in Memphis, but she was over at the house of her grandfather, Mr Vernon.

'I just pushed the door open and turned the light on and there they were, sitting up in there, and he never sat up in a room without a TV on, yet the TV was off.

'Elvis got up and turned the light off, and I said, "Oh my goodness, y'all in here playing Lovey Joe and I done interrupt everything." He said, "No, May-we, it's nothing like that – all I want to do is rest. I just want to rest."

'I said, "You not going to eat anything for me tonight?" and he said, "No." Well, he hadn't eaten that Sunday night or that Monday, so I said "for me tonight," and he said, "No, I'm not hungry. I just want to rest."

'I said, "OK then, if you not going to eat anything, I am gonna go and I will see you in the morning. Night night." He said, "Night night, May-we" – he always called me May-we. So when I went to go out the door, I said, "I will see y'all in the morning'." And he said, "OK."'

Mary knew that Elvis was due to leave on another exhausting tour at 1.00 am aboard his private plane from Memphis airport the following night, and she could understand his reluctance to eat. At 250 pounds he was well overweight, and his voice was shot from all the medications he was taking. But an 11th hour plea of illness to give him time to recover was out of the question. The Colonel and the advance party were already in place at Portland, Maine, for the sold-out opening concert of the twelve-day tour, and every ticket had been snapped up at Utica (New York), Hartford (Connecticut), Lexington (Kentucky) and several other venues. Most important, the tour was due to end among the home-town faithful at the Mid-South Coliseum in Memphis. He just couldn't back out.

But no matter how much the fans adored him or forgave his ramblings, Elvis knew that his touring days were drawing to a close. The trappings had become more vivid than the performance, and only the American flair for theatre kept the show on the road. His apotheosis into a spiritual icon might be complete, but only his exalted status saved him from being ridiculed as the King of Rock 'n' Roly-Poly.

There was also the additional dread that he would be appearing in public for the first time since the publication, on 1 August, of *Elvis: What Happened?*, the memoirs of the three sacked bodyguards. The shame of Sonny's and Red's allegations about his crazy behaviour was like a dagger in his heart. Yet he couldn't cancel; he needed the money. No-show meant no dough, and Elvis and the Colonel were spending as lavishly as ever.

As Mary Jenkins headed home, she knew from Elvis's solemn demeanour that he and Ginger had been having an argument. It was no secret at Graceland that the 20-year-old Priscilla lookalike had refused to accompany him on the tour. Without a beautiful young woman at his beck and call, Elvis felt old and ugly.

'He liked his girlfriend to go with him,' Mary said. 'Any time Elvis said to Linda, "The Boys are gonna start packing, you start packing," she would go right on and start packing, and when they got ready, she was ready. She went and stayed as long as he stayed, but this child didn't want to go.

'That's what I thought they were arguing about that night. I just thought he was angry. I didn't know he was going to die in a matter of hours.

'I believe if he and Linda had been together, he would be living today because she took care of him. She wouldn't go to sleep, she wouldn't close her eyes, until she knew he was asleep. She really did take care of him. And so did Priscilla: she did the same thing.'

When Sam Thompson was questioned by the DA's men about Elvis's relationship with Ginger, he admitted that there had been friction between them. 'My sister and Elvis had broken up and she was the new girl on the scene,' he said. 'It was a love triangle thing. I know that all the members of the group resented Ginger being in that situation. Nobody felt that she was really taking care of Elvis in terms of his medication.

'In truth, Ginger found Elvis's drug-taking so bewildering that she had no chance of trying to control it. This was one of the reasons that he had chosen her from the other available candidates. She knew nothing about drugs. 'She was so young,' commented Mary Jenkins.

However, the romance had been anything but tranquil since Elvis's old DJ friend George Klein had brought Ginger to Graceland for the first time in November 1976. Elvis had been immediately smitten. Despite her name, Ginger's wavy hair was dyed jet black like Priscilla's. She was tall and shapely with very kissable lips. The only strike against her was that she was a Paul McCartney fan, but Elvis was prepared to overlook that. He called her Gingerbread.

From the outset, Ginger failed to fall in with the King's very explicit demands. She preferred to live at home with her mother in the Alden family's modest wooden ranch-style house rather than move into Graceland. 'Whatever people say, I wasn't just a girlfriend,' she said. 'I didn't live at Graceland, and Elvis respected me for that. He respected me for my religious beliefs, my sincerity, myself.'

According to Ginger, the courtship led to a proposal of marriage on 26 January 1977, in the very bathroom where he was to die. Elvis was an eight according to *Cheiro's Book of Numbers,* and he had checked the date first to make sure it was auspicious. Two plus six equalled eight, so that was all right.

'He loved to surprise me,' said Ginger. 'He called me in, got down on his knees and proposed. I shook and cried and promised him we'd be man and wife. Then he gave me the engagement ring and we just held each other tight and close, but very tenderly. We held hands and prayed.'

Although Ginger wore Elvis's $50,000 gold and diamond ring, their progress towards the altar was decidedly unorthodox. Elvis had several dalliances with other women including Alicia Kirwin, another raven-haired beauty. Born in Memphis, the 20-year-old was a cashier at the United American Bank.

'I knew George Klein since I was about 18, and in April1977, he called me up out of the blue and asked me if I would like to meet Elvis,' said Alicia. 'It was a spur-of-the-moment call. He said Elvis and Ginger Alden had had a fight and Elvis was upset. He said he just wanted me to go up there and talk to him.

'I agreed and I went up to Graceland in my car around 10.00pm and I met Jo Smith, Billy's wife. She was a real good friend of mine. I met Elvis's daughter, Lisa Marie, and we talked. Then Jo took me up to the sitting room, which was full of people. They were talking about a forthcoming tour. Elvis was in the centre. Later on, he and I talked. I had never met him before. We just talked about what I did for a living and so on. It was very relaxed and comfortable. He seemed to be in very good spirits. His physical appearance surprised me. He was very heavy. His voice was slow, but not slurred. I didn't see any kind of medication.

'The room was crowded, the phone was ringing a lot, there were papers everywhere: it was hectic. We talked about Ginger in between times after I'd been there a while. He said he'd had an argument with Ginger and he didn't think he was going to see her any more.

'I left after about two hours. About two days later, I got home from work and my roommate told me someone had called and left a telephone number. It was Elvis and he wanted me to come over. Several hours later, I went over to Graceland.

'I was late, so I was shown into the kitchen, and he kept me waiting for about an hour before I was shown upstairs. In the meantime, I was talking to the maids. Upstairs, I was taken into his daughter's room where Elvis was sitting. Lisa Marie had left that day and he was despondent. He just sat there drinking iced water. He introduced me to Tish Henley, who I learned was his nurse. He had just given her a bracelet and she showed it to me. It was obviously very expensive. She stayed the whole time I was in the bedroom.

'David Stanley also came in, and then one of Ginger's sisters came in. She was obnoxious. She wanted to know what I was doing there. She was very inquisitive. I talked with Elvis for about an hour, and we went for a stroll around the grounds. I left around 11.30 pm. He was calm and natural, no different from the time I met him before. He showed me some of his cars.

'The next day I received another telephone call, and he asked me if I'd come over. I said I already had a date and he was a bit angry about that and he hung up on me. Then about two seconds later, he called back and said, "What about tomorrow?" He asked me if I could get a few days off work. He said he wanted to take me to Las Vegas in his plane.

'So I got permission from my work and I called back. We fixed a date for the following Wednesday and I drove over to Graceland that evening. We took off for the airport with Jo and Billy Smith, Charlie Hodge and Dick Grob. We went to the airport at about 11.00 pm and flew out on one of the smaller planes. We didn't take any luggage except that one of them carried Elvis's little leather bag. I fell asleep on the plane and I didn't wake up until we were there.

'We had a car to the Hilton Hotel, and that night I stayed with Elvis for the first time. There were a few bottles of pills beside his bed. I assumed they were sleeping pills. He told me they were mostly muscle-relaxing pills. He told me if I couldn't sleep, he could solve it. It was the middle of the night by then and I just fell straight to sleep.

'Elvis woke me for breakfast. He was in good spirits. He never went out of the room, just watched television and smoked cigars. We talked quite a bit. I noticed everybody just bowed to his wishes. They laughed when he laughed and got him everything he needed, even a glass of water.

'Then he announced we were leaving and we took off for Palm Springs, where we stayed until Sunday. It was much the same procedure. He stayed in the house and he had one visitor – it could have been a doctor. That was after Elvis got very upset. He had called his father who was angry because we weren't supposed to be there. He hadn't told his father or Tom Parker we were going to Las Vegas. He had said we were going to Nashville. Vernon was real mad. We stayed until Sunday and went back to Memphis.

'I next heard from him while he was on tour. He called me several times, but in June, I told Billy Smith I did not want to see Elvis any more. It was just too much. I couldn't handle it because he was Elvis Presley. I had never been used to this kind of thing, staying up all hours of the night and all. Elvis called me back a few hours later and wanted me to go over, and I went. He said he was very depressed, and he said he wished he could go out on a Saturday night like other people. We just talked and talked, and then I went home at about three in the morning. He didn't want me to leave, but I left anyway. He was ready to go to sleep and wanted to make sure there was someone close by.

'I next heard from him a few weeks later. He called me in the middle of the night; it must have been about 3.00 am. He was terribly depressed and asked me to go up to Graceland. I said I had to go to work the next morning, but he persisted. I stayed for a few hours. He just looked so sad. Then he fell asleep. He had taken some medication, sleeping pills, though I hadn't seen him take a lot. I left for work around 8.00 am and that was the last time I saw him.'

Ginger had waited for this moment for three months. She had once turned up at Graceland while Alicia was there, but Elvis had refused to see her. She telephoned frequently, but Elvis wouldn't take the calls. She was getting the Presley freeze-out. However, as soon as Alicia had left for the last time, her virtue having been in no danger from Elvis, Gingerbread was back.

(Alicia had found the Elvis experience so unsettling that she quit her bank job in Memphis and returned to Las Vegas where she trained as a croupier. She died of a drug overdose a few years later.)

According to Ginger, the thing uppermost in the King's mind as they sat on Lisa's white-furred, hamburger-shaped bed in the dark, early hours of

16 August was their impending marriage. 'He said he was going to introduce me at his concert in Memphis,' she said. 'He told me to look real special. We were going to be married at Christmas.' However, Elvis had other ideas, according to members of the Memphis Mafia and Mary Jenkins.

'It really surprised me,' Mary said. 'He told me that he would not marry anybody unless it was Priscilla. Linda had wanted to get married and have children, but he didn't want that. He told me, "If I ever marry again, it will be to my baby's mother."

'Now Priscilla came to Graceland two years before he died. She had been to New York, had a lay-over here and she came out to the house and stayed there until she was going to get her plane. But she stayed upstairs with him so long that the plane was gone when she got there, and she had to come back. We started laughing. We said, "You wanted that plane to leave," and she laughed. I really believe that they talked about remarrying that day.'

Mary, who was very fond of Priscilla, knew that Elvis's ex-wife had more influence over the King than anyone else. Elvis and Priscilla had spoken on the phone that Monday evening, 15 August, about Lisa's return to Los Angeles. Priscilla was angry with Elvis for delaying their daughter's departure, so it was a tense conversation. But at least they were still on speaking terms. Mary lived in hope that a reunion might curb some of Elvis's wilder excesses. As the Graceland cook, she knew about his self-destructive eating habits better than anyone else.

'He usually started dieting about two weeks before he'd go back on tour,' she said. 'He would stay upstairs, he wouldn't come down for days and he wouldn't call for anything to eat. He would just drink liquids to try and get some of that weight off.'

Tonight the last thing on Elvis's mind was food. By midnight, he had developed a sudden toothache.

Sam Thompson was drinking coffee, playing cards and talking to the maids in the kitchen. 'I was supposed to take Lisa Marie back to her mother in Los Angeles,' he said. Priscilla was very upset because Elvis had been keeping her back until he began the next tour.

'Elvis came downstairs all dressed and ready to go somewhere about midnight. He said he was going to see his dentist, Dr Lester Hofman. Billy Smith, Ginger Alden and Charlie Hodge were with him, and they got into the black Stutz Blackhawk and they left. I was still there playing cards in the kitchen when they came back a couple of hours later.

'They all went upstairs to Elvis's suite, and a few minutes later, Elvis came on the telephone and told me to take Lisa back the following day. I was to take her to Priscilla's house, then I was to fly to Portland, Maine, where the tour began. I telephoned American Airlines and made the reservations. I knew I was going to have a long day, so I went home. I believe that David Stanley was the personal aide on duty.'

After Sam departed, Elvis, Ginger, Billy Smith and his wife Jo went to the racquetball court for some exercise. They didn't play for long. Elvis whacked his leg with his racquet and he retired hurt to the piano, where he played *Unchained Melody* and tested his voice.

Mary Jenkins recalls: 'I was told that, when he came back into the house, Vera Wood the maid said to him, "Mr P, you look like somebody who wants to eat," but he still said, "No, I just wanna rest." And he went on upstairs.

'In the morning about eight o'clock, he calls up his Aunt Delta and tells her to bring him some water. She takes it up, then she says, "Now, hon, you wanna be woke up when Lisa leaves?" But he said, "Aunt Delta, I don't wanna be woke up for nothin'." And she said, "Don't you wanna see ya baby?" He said, "Yeah, you can wake me up for that, but nothin' else." And she said, "I'll wake you up when she's ready to leave. I'll let nobody bother you until then."

'And nobody was going to try and wake him up or anything because Ginger was up there with him. She said that he got up and went in the bathroom to read.'

Five thousand miles away, the roving ambassadors for the Cosmic Kingdom of Nutopia were in the Japanese resort of Karuizawa on a goodwill mission. But John Lennon, the man who had become Elvis Presley's bete noire, could find no peace of mind among Yoko's kith and kin. If anything, he appeared to be closer to his appointed hour with the hereafter than was his great rival. Strung out on drugs, he had been in a trance since the beginning of August. In his own words, he suffered 'a living death' during which he stayed in bed most of the day, either refusing to talk to anyone or unable to do so. He ate no food and became virtually anorexic. The strain of socializing with Yoko's friends and relatives, few of whom spoke any English, had plunged him into a catatonic state.

Each one of his personalities came to visit him like spirits inhabiting an empty temple. The abandoned child gave way to the juvenile bully, the extrovert rock star disappeared in favour of the stoned philosopher. 'I began to see all these different parts of me,' John told a friend when he was able to describe the sensation. 'But I can't be all these people all the time.' The frightening thing was that whatever phase he was in became dominant to the exclusion of all the others. Thus he had no balance, no stability, no sanity.

'I have no device, no magic, to keep an easy flow from one part of my personality to another,' he said. 'I need that because the secret is to change.'

For Elvis, the chance to change was slipping away forever in the loneliness of his plushly carpeted bathroom.

The afternoon of 16 August was sweltering, even in the shade of the spreading Graceland oak trees. Down at the Music Gates, Uncle Vester Presley watched the ninety-degree heat shimmy in waves along the black strip of Elvis Presley Boulevard. Several times that day he had invited groups of sightseers to accompany him up to the house to take pictures of its famous facade. The old boy liked these little guided tours: they broke the monotony of his long stint in the gatehouse. Some of the visitors snapped pictures of the bathroom window above the columned portico and the blackened glass of the room to the right, which, Vester informed them, was his megastar nephew's bedroom. The tourists shouldered their cameras and walked back down the hill to the Music Gates, totally oblivious to the drama that was being enacted upstairs.

At 1.30 pm, Ginger Alden had awoken from a deep sleep in the double king-size bed in that very room, where the temperature never dropped below a bracing sixty-five degrees Fahrenheit. Finding herself alone, she had dressed, applied her make-up and made two phone calls. Then she went looking for Elvis. She tapped on the bathroom door and called: 'Elvis?' There was no reply. '*Elvis?*' It was 2.00 pm. 'Ginger just went into the bathroom and found him lying there,' said Mary Jenkins. Dressed only in gold pyjama pants, Elvis was crouched in the foetal position on the floor. The book he had been reading, *Sex and Psychic Energy*, was nearby.

'I thought at first he might have hit his head because he had fallen out of his black lounging chair and his face was buried in the carpet,' said Ginger. 'I slapped him a few times, and it was like he breathed once when I turned his head. One of his eyes was just blood red and I couldn't move him. I didn't want to think he was dead. God wouldn't want to take him so soon.'

Ginger raced out of the bedroom and shouted for help. 'She called downstairs, and Al [Strada] was the only one there at the time,' said Mary. 'But Joe [Esposito] came in right behind and they sent him straight on upstairs.'

'When Joe turned Elvis's head over, I think he knew he was dead,' said Ginger.' It seemed like hours while we waited for the ambulance.'

The division of the Memphis Fire Department that was stationed one-and-a-half miles away at 2147 Elvis Presley Boulevard received the emergency call at 2.30 pm. Three minutes later, an ambulance with paramedics Charlie Crosby and Ulysses S. Jones Jr on board was screaming towards Graceland. 'As soon as I heard the siren, I opened the gates so they wouldn't have to stop,' said Uncle Vester, who had been alerted by one of the guys at the house. 'They didn't even slow down. 'Leaving some of its paintwork on one of the gates, the ambulance sped up the hill and jerked to a halt between the two stone lions outside the front door. It took five men to carry Elvis downstairs after the medics also failed to get any response. Summoned by a frantic call from Joe Esposito, George Nichopolous arrived in his gold-green Mercedes just in time to jump into the back of the ambulance with Elvis. As the vehicle hurtled in the direction of Baptist Memorial Hospital on Madison Avenue, the physician tried to revive his stricken patient, exhorting him: 'Come on, Presley, breathe. Breathe for me.' At 2.56 pm, Elvis was stretchered into the hospital's emergency room. Staff who witnessed his arrival knew from one glimpse of his blackened, immobile face that he was already beyond human help. At 3.30 pm, Dr Nichopolous officially pronounced Elvis Presley dead, and the hospital announced the news to the world half an hour later. The grief was spontaneous.

'My father came over in Linda's car to take me to Graceland,' said Sam Thompson. 'As I got to the gates, David Stanley came roaring clown the driveway in his Datsun 240Z. He stopped and said, "Have you heard the news – Elvis is dead." He just roared out of the gates and that was the last time I saw David Stanley until the day of the funeral.

'I drove on up and there was a Fire Department ambulance at the front door. I drove round to the back and went in, and I saw Vernon with

Nick beside him. I got there just in time to hear Nick break the news to Vernon, to actually confirm that Elvis had died. Vernon began to moan and cry very loudly. A large group of people were there and it was like a madhouse. The two ambulance attendants were in the dining room, just sitting there. I was told later that they had brought Dr Nick back from the morgue. Then I got a phone call from Dick Grob, who was at the morgue, and he said, "Well, it finally happened."'

Mary Jenkins remembers the precise moment she got the call. 'My niece Barbara Moseley was working at the hospital and she called me at three o'clock in the afternoon and asked me if I had heard the news,' she said. 'I was looking at my soap opera, *Edge of Night,* and it just went off and I got up to put dinner on, and when I passed the telephone, it rang.

'I said, "What news?" I thought she meant just gossip or something, and she said, "Elvis just died." "Girl, hush, Elvis ain't dead – he's not sick or anything," I says, "It's his daddy, 'cos his daddy is sick." She said, "No, Mary, it *is* Elvis Presley who's dead." I said, "I don't believe it – they haven't even called me." And I said, "I know exactly what I am going to do, I am going to get on the phone and call." So I got on the telephone and the yardman, Tommy Henley, answered the phone. He was the husband of Elvis's nurse, Tish Henley. You could hear him hollerin' at the top of his voice, and I said, "Tell me, is it true?" and he said, "Yes, Mary, it's true, it's true."

'I just hung the phone up and roared, and jumped into some clothes and called a cab to go down there. When I got in, I told the driver, "I want to go to Graceland, Elvis has just died," and I was shaking like a leaf on a tree, and he said, "You mean to tell me that Elvis Presley is dead?" and

I said, "He's dead." So we went on and it took us two-and-a-half hours to get just a little better than a block to the gate. Cars were parked all over the streets and they were standing up on cars. It was terrible . . .

'Well, I couldn't get up to the house in the cab so I had to walk up the hill, and when I got there, I went in the back door. I pushed the door in, and Mr Vernon looked at me and he hollered just as loud as he could: "Mary, our Elvis has gone, our Elvis has gone!" All of them were just howling, and his old grandmother just had to lay down. I never went through nothing like this, never have. We were very, very close, Elvis and me.'

Janelle McComb, Elvis's former neighbour, was at her house in Tupelo when the telephone rang. 'The caller said, "Mrs McComb, Elvis is dead." Well, I thought it was a dupe so I hung the phone down. I was always getting crank calls. I went into the living-room and the phone rang again and this time I could hear screaming in the background, and they said, "Mrs McComb, Elvis is really dead . . . Can you hear me?" I don't even remember who it was; I just sat down on the floor. My husband came home from work and I was devastated. I could not believe it. I had to get packed, and it was after dark before I left for Graceland.

'When I got there, it was as if Elvis Presley had merely left the building. His presence, his lust for living, his kindness, his generosity to friends, his infectious smile still remained. These precious memories were in my heart.'

After a post-mortem examination, Elvis's body was brought to Graceland, where Larry Geller made up his face and trimmed his hair for the last time, as a favour to Vernon. The body was placed in an unsealed coffin behind the stained-glass peacock windows of the music room. Thousands came to pay homage.

'The night before the funeral, I walked over and touched his face,' said Janelle. 'I thought of all the things he had sung, going back to that small boy singing "Amazing Grace" in church, and all I could say was, "Farewell, my friend."'

Elvis was buried at the Forest Hill Cemetery just five months short of his 43rd birthday. Memphis sold out of flowers.

George Klein carries a faded piece of paper in his jacket pocket to prove that Elvis died from natural causes. It reads: 25 October 1977. Office of the Shelby County Medical Examiner, Dr Jerry Francisco:

> The cause of death has been ascribed to hypertensive heart disease with coronary artery heart disease as a contributing factor. There is no evidence that medication present in the body of Elvis Presley caused or made any significant contribution to his death. There was an extensive search for illicit drugs and they were not found to be present.

'And that is the legal eagle right there, signed "Jerry Francisco, Shelby County Medical Examiner",' says George, pointing to the seal.

No one who loved Elvis wanted to believe that the prescribed medication had killed him either accidentally or deliberately, but it is beyond doubt that he was a victim of his kamikaze lifestyle. The illness of addiction wanted him dead, and it had succeeded.

Raquel Welch took a realistic Hollywood view. 'When I heard he'd died, I was in a rehearsal room in Los Angeles preparing my own show for Vegas,' she said. 'I remember feeling really sad because he was such a big part of all our lives. Then I remember thinking that I wasn't surprised; it seemed as though a big part of him had already died when we met that last time in Vegas.

'It also seemed as though his public had got what they might have wished – America loves dead heroes and they will be happier with a heart-throb who died at 42 than an old man who became weak and bald and all those things that go with old age.'

John Lennon felt no sadness or remorse. A long-time believer in reincarnation, to him Elvis had simply moved on to a higher state of being. But the death did prompt him to take a close look at his own confused personae. On 24 August, he sat down at a typewriter in his Japanese retreat and began writing himself a letter. In thirteen days, he covered just three single spaced pages. The result – a personal inventory – is like a surreal freefall through time and space. His mind jumps from Yoko to guilt, from loneliness to alienation, from deja vu to the future, from his early inspiration to his lost muse, but it signs off with a cursory farewell to Elvis. 'He died the day he went into the Army' was the punchline of John's epitaph. Secretly, he had longed to write those words since the day he saw GI Blues.

The 'Ballad of John and Elvis' might have finished its run, but for millions of followers, many still unborn on 16 August 1977, Elvis didn't die the day he went into the Army and nor did he die alone in his bathroom at Graceland. In the final analysis, he was too much loved a personality and too important in everyone's lives to be allowed to pass away like any other mere mortal.

The yearning for Elvis to live up to the anagram of his name, 'Lives', has produced a mass of myth-making. Devout followers point to signs and symbols at the time of his death to prove that he was not like other men. On the night he died, the lights in the Meditation Garden suddenly went out, and an angel appeared in the clouds over Graceland. One fan came home to find that her collection of Elvis records had mysteriously melted. That same evening, a couple discovered that the Elvis statue in their den had inexplicably broken apart.

Stacy Horowitz, a 23-year-old Las Vegas cigarette girl, is a typical 'Elvis Lives' believer. 'I was seven years old and watching cartoons on TV at my home in Fort Lauderdale, Florida, when my mother told me Elvis was dead,' she told me. 'My mother is a big fan. She has a pillow with Elvis's face on it and Elvis plates with a gold trim. She was very upset about the news, but I truly believe that he's still alive – he's out there somewhere. I *know* he's out there. He was in too much trouble from doctors and medicine so he covered up his identity and just disappeared.

'But I know Elvis Presley is still out there. I know it for sure . . .'

DIANA'S NIGHTMARE
THE FAMILY

CHRIS HUTCHINS & PETER THOMPSON

EVEN BEFORE Lady Diana Spencer married into the most revered family on earth, she had her suspicions that the kith and kin of Prince Charles were not all they seemed-to-be. No sooner had she become the Princess of Wales and moved into Kensington Palace than her fears were confirmed: the House of Windsor constituted a flawed dynasty. She found herself trapped in a world of scandal, deceit and treachery. *Diana's Nightmare* reveals the previously untold secrets Diana discovered about her royal relatives. This book exposes how intensely Charles and Camilla Parker Bowles contrived to exclude her, it reveals the Queen was angry and bitter at her family's indiscretions, how the Queen Mother's indifference was matched only by Prince Philip's blind range over Diana's determination to find her own path, what really went on between the Duke and Duchess of York and how Prince Edward witnessed Diana's tantrums at Balmoral . . . Diana's own secret life.

And much, much more . . .

HARRY
THE PEOPLE'S PRINCE

CHRIS HUTCHINS

PRINCE HARRY is the most interesting – indeed the most exciting – member of the Royal Family and this no-holds-barred biography tells his story for the first time. Son of the late Princess Diana – the most famous woman on Earth – and Prince Charles, the next king, and brother of William, the king after that, he is determined to live by his mantra: 'I am what I am'. From a childhood overshadowed by his parents' troubled marriage and scarred by the tragic death of his mother, to his brilliant public performances at the Queen's Diamond Jubilee celebrations, the London Olympics and his brother's wedding, this book charts the remarkable journey of a young man with an extraordinary destiny. Following in Diana's footsteps, his charitable works have taken him to far-flung corners of the world including Africa and the South Pole. It also reveals details of his extraordinary love life, telling for the first time what caused his affair with Cressida Bonas to collapse. The author has enjoyed unparalleled access to a wide variety of people whose lives Harry has touched: senior aides, humble members of palace staff, aristocrats, bodyguards, school friends, comrades-in-arms . . . and old flames. They piece together the tale of a young man who admirably has created a life so different from the one set out for him by what he describes as 'an accident of birth'.

FERGIE CONFIDENTIAL

CHRIS HUTCHINS & PETER THOMPSON

IT SEEMS that almost every week Sarah Ferguson – the Duchess of York, known to one and all as Fergie – makes headlines with her efforts to re-brand herself and explain her troubles. There are the weight-loss problems, the ongoing differences with the Royal Family and her financial difficulties. But how did it all start? It seemed like a fairy-tale come true when Sarah married the Queen's favourite son, Prince Andrew, and became one of the best-known women in the world. She was feted wherever she went – and she went everywhere. But the Duchess's world was to come crashing down in spectacular fashion.

We all heard the rumours, now here's a book that sets out the facts about all the scandals. Finally, the explosive truth from two experts – CHRIS HUTCHINS, the writer who broke the palace-rocking story of Fergie's risqué liaison with handsome Texan Steve Wyatt, and PETER THOMPSON, a former editor of London's Daily Mirror, the paper that ran the sexy St. Tropez stories of Fergie and her "financial advisor" Johnny Bryan. The book also details her often-tempestuous relationship with Princess Diana and how both women decided to end their marriages.

ATHINA
THE LAST ONASSIS

CHRIS HUTCHINS & PETER THOMPSON

BY WAY OF LIGHT relief as Greece continues to stand face-to-face with financial meltdown, it is well worth visiting the story of Athina Onassis Roussel, who became the richest little girl in the world when she inherited unimaginable wealth from her heiress mother, Christina Onassis. This compelling book explores the legend of Athina's grandfather, the shipping magnate Aristotle Onassis, and examines the legacy that became Athina's extraordinary birthright as The Last Onassis. No 20th-century saga features more great names than that of the Onassis dynasty; the Kennedys – including JFK and his widow Jacqueline, who became Onassis's second wife – the opera diva Maria Callas who longed to be the third; and Prince Rainier and Princess Grace, with whom he fought a celebrated feud for control of Monte Carlo. The cast list is endless: the Hollywood stars Elizabeth Taylor, Richard Burton, Marilyn Monroe and Greta Garbo, the politicians Sir Winston Churchill and Richard Nixon, the tycoons Stavros Niarchos and Howard Hughes and the FBI chief J. Edgar Hoover

ABRAMOVICH
THE BILLIONAIRE FROM NOWHERE

DOMINIC MIDGLEY AND CHRIS HUTCHINS

'AN INCREDIBLE STORY' – *Mail on Sunday*; 'Well researched and fluently written' – *The Times*; 'Draws a picture of a man of immense ruthlessness, nerve and charm . . . offers a Vanity Fair of Russian oligarchy' – *The Spectator*; A superb insight into the Chelsea boss . . . a must read for both football fans and business tycoons' – *Sunday Business Post*; 'A well-researched investigation into the life and times of Chelsea's owner' – *World Soccer*; 'The first sustained effort to uncover the making of Chelsea's oligarch' – *Guardian*'; 'Authors Dominic Midgley and Chris Hutchins go to commendable lengths to tell the story' – *Sunday Times*; 'Where this book sets itself apart is in its quest to discover Abramovich's true identity. Interviews with his childhood friends, neighbours and teachers in Russia offer an original perspective on the man while access to the informed such as Boris Berezovsky, his one-time mentor, provides a picture of a canny dealmaker and consummate politician' – *The Times*'; 'Most fascinating account . . . should be read by anyone not just with an interest in sport but also in business and in politics' – *Press and Journal.*

GOLDSMITH
MONEY, WOMEN AND POWER

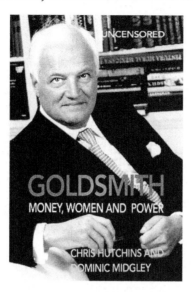

CHRIS HUTCHINS AND DOMINIC MIDGLEY

SIR JAMES GOLDSMITH was one of the most intriguing figures of the twentieth century but as a billionaire with a taste for litigation he successfully ensured that, for much of his life, his background, methods and ambitions escaped far-reaching investigation. This is the first unauthorised biography of Goldsmith and it deals with every aspect of his complex life.

This is a book for anyone interested in how great fortunes are built, the future of Europe, the ongoing controversy over environmental issues and – of course – how a charismatic man can juggle a succession of wives and mistresses.

Has he equipped his children to exploit the fortune he has left to build a vast business empire or has he condemned them to gilded obscurity? GOLDSMITH: Money, Women and Power, tells the incredible story of an extraordinary man and the legacy he has left his family and the world.

THE
BEATLES

Messages from John,
Paul, George and Ringo

by their friend CHRIS HUTCHINS
(Or CRISPY HUTCH as they called him)

CHRIS HUTCHINS

THE POSTCARD on the cover of this book says it all. The card was written by John Lennon and sent to his friend Chris Hutchins. On the card's photograph of the Beatles, John had drawn a fifth member – the founder of the group Stuart Sutcliffe who John went on to describe as the best friend he ever had.

This is the kind of confidence John, Paul George and Ringo shared with writer Hutchins who they befriended in their days as 'unknowns' in Hamburg. He shared their adventures during the heady days of Beatlemania; he was with them during their American tours in the 60s, sharing their euphoria and their sad moments. It was, for example, at Hutchins' Chelsea apartment that Paul met the actress Jane Asher, who he later became engaged to.

And it was Hutchins who arranged a party with Elvis Presley, the man they had always wanted to meet – alas, a meeting which was to cause a cataclysmic feud between Presley and Lennon which the author explains in detail along with how President Nixon and J Edgar Hoover got involved. This is the Beatles story from the inside . . .

MR CONFIDENTIAL

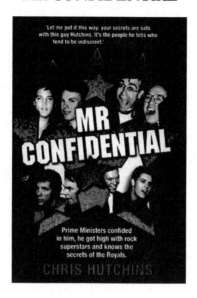

CHRIS HUTCHINS

ELVIS PRESLEY, Princess Diana, Elton John, the Beatles, Tom Jones, Fergie Duchess of York, Richard Branson – they all figure in this extraordinary book of revelations. Previously untold stories of royals, celebrities and the occasional politician are all relayed in this rich and unrivalled mix of anecdotes by the master. For more than a decade his *Confidential* column chronicled the lives of the rich and famous and was featured in three national newspapers as well as being syndicated globally.

At one time he also ran the UK's most successful music PR company, shaping the careers and sharing the lives of Tom Jones, the Bee Gees, Eric Clapton and many other international stars. As a fresh-faced young scribbler on the *New Musical Express* he toured the world with the Beatles and took them to meet Elvis Presley who became his friend. It's been a rocky road for the boy from a Devon housing estate on whom, according to Sir Richard Branson, the future of his Virgin Atlantic airline once briefly depended. He has had encounters along the way which have often been funny, sometimes sad, with such diverse personalities as Sir Elton John, Rupert Murdoch, Lord 'Dickie' Mountbatten, Muhammad Ali, a former British prime minister who got drunk in his house, Rod Steiger, a palace maid and various members of the Royal Family. His is a truly unique look behind the scenes of international celebrity.

Chris Hutchins now more usually writes books about other people's lives. It was fellow journalist and author Ray Connolly who urged him to write one about his own. As the man who has been in on more celebrity secrets than virtually any other writer, Chris Hutchins' own story is the most interesting of them all.

THE WHO BEFORE THE WHO

DOUG SANDOM

DOUG SANDOM'S part in the making of the most exciting rock band in the world can never be underestimated. He joined The Who – then known as The Detours – as their drummer in 1962 after an unexpected meeting with Roger Daltrey on a west London street. It was a time when fires were being lit under the music scene worldwide, everything had to change and The Detours had a long way to go to become revolutionary leaders in their field.

Having finally decided to write his memoirs, Doug Sandom chronicles each stage of the band's transition right up to his, Roger Daltrey's, Pete Townshend's and John Entwistle's emergence from their chrysalis as The Who. It is a punchy tale of gritty determination and ever-burning passion for music. As Pete Townshend writes in his moving Foreword, 'Doug Sandom's work with our band gave me the confidence to drive the band as a writer and creative thinker . . . '

DIANA ON THE EDGE

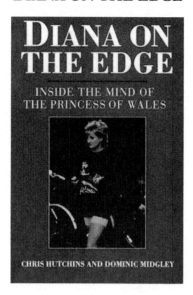

CHRIS HUTCHINS AND DOMINIC MIDGLEY

THIS IS THE BOOK which caused something of a sensation when it was first published since it delved into the mind of the Princess of Wales, one of the most controversial women on earth, during the latter years of her life.

Ostracised by the Royal Family after the breakdown of her marriage to Britain's next monarch, detached from her friends and tainted by stories of her romantic adventures, she was being pushed to the very limits of her endurance. Drawing on high-level sources – some of whom had never spoken before – and a team of distinguished specialists, this book examines her troubled mind. It probes the dark secrets at the root of her bulimia, the childhood traumas that cast a dark shadow over her adult love life, the pressures placed on her by the Palace hierarchy, the obsession with bodily perfection and the angry scenes she seemed unable to avoid. What drove Diana to the brink?

It's all told here.

Printed in Great Britain
by Amazon

18131362R00180